NARRATIVE AND IMAGINATION

Narrative & *Imagination*

PREACHING THE WORLDS THAT SHAPE US

RICHARD L. ESLINGER

FORTRESS PRESS   MINNEAPOLIS

NARRATIVE AND IMAGINATION
Preaching the Worlds That Shape Us

Biblical quotations, unless otherwise noted, are from the Revised Standard Version of the Bible, copyright © 1946, 1952, and 1971 by the Division of Christian Education of the National Council of Churches. Used by permission.

"Divine Appearances and Erecting Altars," on pages 176-86, is reprinted by permission of William C. Turner, Jr. "Follow Me," on pages 193-203, is reprinted by permission of Deneise Deter-Rankin. "Imaginings," on page 65, from *Imagining: A Phenomenological Study* by Edward S. Casey, copyright © 1976 Indiana University Press, Reprinted by permission of Indiana University Press. "Duck/Rabbit," on page 101, from the Macmillan College text *Philosophical Investigations* 3/E by Ludwig Wittgenstein, copyright © 1973 by Macmillan College Publishing Company, Inc. Reprinted by permission of Simon & Schuster, Inc., and Blackwell Publishers. "Lowry Loop," on page 162, from *The Homiletical Plot: The Sermon as Narrative Art Form* by Eugene L. Lowry, copyright © 1980 John Knox Press. Reprinted by permission of Westminster John Knox Press. "Narrative–Imagery Scheme," on page 152, from *Homiletic: Moves and Structures* by David G. Buttrick, copyright © 1987 Fortress Press.

Cover graphic: "Music," by Roland Brenner, by permission of Elizabeth Ohnesorge Powers and Clark G. Ohnesorge
Cover design: Lecy Design
Interior design: Joe Bonyata
Author photo: Elise I. Eslinger

Library of Congress Cataloging-in-Publication Data

Eslinger, Richard L. (Richard Laurence), 1940–
    Narrative and imagination : preaching the worlds that shape us /
Richard L. Eslinger.
        p.   cm.
    Includes bibliographical references and index.
    ISBN 0-8006-2719-9 (alk. paper)
    1. Preaching.   2. Storytelling—Religious aspects—Christianity.
3. Imagination—Religious aspects—Christianity.   I. Title.
BV4211.2.E84   1995
251—dc20   95-2307
                                                                      CIP

The paper used in this publication meets the minimum requirements of American National Standard for Information Sciences—Permanence of Paper for Printed Library Materials, ANSI Z329.48-1984.

Manufactured in the U.S.A.   AF 1-2719

99   98   97   96   95   1   2   3   4   5   6   7   8   9   10

To our children—Crispin, David, and Catherine

Contents

Acknowledgments

The season for writing *Narrative and Imagination* was made possible by my appointment to a sabbatical by Bishop Calvin McConnell of the Seattle Area of the United Methodist Church. The primary setting for this sabbatical was a gift of the generous hospitality of the monks of Saint Meinrad Archabbey and Theological Seminary in Saint Meinrad, Indiana. For the status accorded me as Visiting Scholar at Saint Meinrad, I am deeply indebted to Dean Thomas P. Walters and Associate Dean Barbara C. Schmitz, O.S.B. My research was greatly facilitated by Br. Placid McIver, O.S.B., and Fr. Cajetan White, O.S.B., of the library staff. My meager computer skills called for the frequent expert assistance of Scott Carlisle of the Computer Center staff. Our other home and place of ministry while on sabbatical was provided by Bishop Woodie White of the Indianapolis Area, U.M.C., who appointed me as pastor of the Hatfield and Yankeetown churches in southern Indiana. To the fine members of these two churches for their "Hoosier hospitality" and supportive friendships while we shared ministry, I am also deeply grateful.

The other coordinate of gratitude extends along family lines. First and foremost, to my wife, Elise, for her encouragement and support of this sabbatical venture. *Narrative and Imagination*, moreover, emerged out of an ongoing theological conversation with Elise, my covenant partner. Both of us are profoundly grateful to our families, and especially to Suellen and Elisabeth Eslinger, Rev. Robert and Emily Matheny, and Phillip and Cynthia Brooks.

In my relationship with Fortress Press, I have found in Michael West and Joe Bonyata helpful editors. I am also deeply indebted to those scholars who have been my mentors and who are named in the Narrative Prologue.

Figures

Narrative Prologue

My birth as a homiletician was rapid but painful. It was at a workshop; I was in charge, had invited a representative group of United Methodist clergy, and had secured David Buttrick as the leader of the week-long event. Although a denominational bureaucrat at the time, I, too, had preached the previous day and like the others had come to get my preaching style polished up a bit. Not too long into the first session, it began to feel as though Buttrick knew my recent sermon intimately and had taken that grand homiletic jewel, placed it on the conference table, and smashed it to smithereens with a huge mallet. By noon I was dazed. I thought, *This guy either has to be very wrong or very right in his attack on the old homiletic's approach to Scripture!* By the conclusion of the week, I had decided that he was very right. For several of the following years, I exploited my growing friendship with David to glean every bit of information I could from him on homiletic method (his book *Homiletic*[1] was not yet published). In addition, I now consistently preached Buttrick's "moves and structures." A homiletician, of sorts, had been born.

My homiletic journey split for a while along two related paths. First, with the preaching-as-storytelling movement in the spotlight (this was about a decade ago) I looked with interest at many of the writings extolling preaching and narrative. While I felt a natural attraction to story as a description of Bible and proclamation, I was dissatisfied with this movement's scarce hermeneutic foundations. In meeting Stanley Hauerwas and becoming acquainted with the narrative ethics he represented, I came across an approach to narrative theology which to me more deeply drilled its hermeneutic foundations than had my preaching-as-storytelling colleagues. Also, it soon became clear that as this Notre Dame school of ethicists developed their narrative approach, the issue of vision and therefore of imagery gained central importance. How narratives and images engaged with each other in Scripture, in culture, in psychology, and in preaching became an abiding interest. In the meantime, I was regularly preaching Buttrick's methodology, which insists that each move be imaged out of the lived experience of the congregation. Here was the second path in the journey. On the side of praxis, then, this interest in imagery was taking the form of comparing how static or mobile image systems functioned within a move and exploring all of the aspects of Buttrick's camera model of the homiletic image. (My survey of homiletic method, *A New Hearing*,[2] was written at this stage in my homiletic journey while teaching at Duke University Divinity School.)

With this interest in imagery both at the level of hermeneutics (Hauerwas) and at that of method (Buttrick), I came upon Margaret Miles' work, *Image as Insight*. She introduced me to the "lexicon of imagery," which I then explored in relation to narrative in several articles and in an essay in my next book. Even though I have come to hold quite different positions on the hermeneutics of imagery than Miles, I am deeply indebted to her for her pioneering efforts on behalf of many of us across the church. By this time, I was pastor of a university church in Seattle, Washington, and was still exploring narrative hermeneutics, the role of imagery in preaching, and was still preaching mostly the Buttrick approach. Then several other relationships and new experiences became formative. I met Eugene Lowry and enjoyed both our new friendship and his narrative homiletic model. Soon I was occasionally preaching a "Lowry loop" whenever it felt "meet, right, and salutary." A renewed and deepened friendship with Mary Ann Swenson (now Bishop Swenson of the United Methodist Church) underlined from the homiletics side the "natural" affinity of some women preachers in particular with image-based homiletic plots. I was first introduced to this at times awesome power of image-based preaching by one of my students at Duke, Deneise Deter-Rankin, whose homiletic offerings appeared in *A New Hearing* and now appear in this work. In this regard, I was certain that there was both a hermeneutic program as well as several homiletic options lurking in these powerful sermons. Presenting these previously implicit approaches became one of the primary tasks in writing *Narrative and Imagination.*

While at University Temple United Methodist Church in Seattle, I was invited to teach as a visiting lecturer in preaching at the fine Vancouver School of Theology in British Columbia. During that semester, and in subsequent study week visits to the school, I was able finally to become immersed in a number of different aspects of imagination theory. Chasing rabbits of imagination (not imaginary rabbits!) through VST and various schools of the University of British Columbia became an exciting challenge. Many of the explorations in imagination theory presented in chapter 2, "The House of Imagination," were begun in various libraries on the University of British Columbia and VST campus. By now it was clear that my focus could no longer remain strictly on the image in its hermeneutic implications and homiletic functions. First, focusing on imagery with Miles, then expanding the horizon to the whole perceptual model, the turning to the linguistic, and engaging in imagination as play . . . well, read chapter 2.

Also during my Seattle years, there was a strong settling in on my own narrative home in two senses. On one hand, the postliberal narrative theologies of Hans Frei and George Lindbeck became my own. If anything, one of the gifts of the Pacific Northwest with its dominant liberal ethos in the churches was a sharpening of my own position now firmly in the postliberal camp. On the other hand, I entered an intensely personal journey of therapy related to old and, mainly, childhood issues. With the help of my pastoral counselor, in addition to the liberating experience of moving toward healing of those old wounds, I noticed once again the awesome and formative power of our narratives and their images. And yes, David Buttrick, even the most hidden images, when recovered, come popping back already equipped with often powerful points of view!

One other experience came both to shape my understanding of imagination and impel me to write this volume. For what I now see was most of my life, I have wanted to be a pilot. That particular journey began with a glider demo flight in Arlington, Washington. Upon return to earth in the good hands of a flight instructor, I was essentially one vast grin of joy. I immediately joined Evergreen Soaring Club and later flew my first solo under the club's instructor, Mike Delaney. Among the incredibly rich blessings of this task of learning to fly was the insight that imagination has this pragmatic and proleptic quality known as "imagining-that" and "imagining-how." And Hans-Georg Gadamer, as we shall see, is right about imagination as play, too!

Finally, my family and I decided that I must attempt to put all this together—the narrative hermeneutics and all the parts of imagination theory. Once the decision was made that taking a sabbatical year was the right thing to do, choosing a location was easy. Saint Meinrad Archabbey in southern Indiana had been our spiritual home for a long season. And my first meeting with David Buttrick was when he was on the faculty of the Saint Meinrad School of Theology. My request to come as a visiting scholar was not only granted, but I was welcomed as a teacher and friend. It was in my Saint Meinrad teaching that I realized that the implied readers for *Narrative and Imagination* must include persons in both the Protestant and Catholic traditions. So throughout the book, you will find *sermon* and *homily* used interchangeably (Protestants, please read the former, and, Catholics, the latter). Oddly, the two words operate almost in a mirror image relationship in actual usage within our two churches. That is, for Protestants, a *homily* is the diminutive of *sermon;* for Roman Catholics, the opposite obtains. Additionally, the terms *congregation* and *assembly* speak of the same gathering of the faithful in their Lord's Day worship, with my Catholic sisters and brothers quite appropriately adding that the homily will be preached at the Eucharist.

Finally, to the actual reader, this work must begin twice. Chapter 1 begins with a presentation of narrative theology and hermeneutics. Then chapter 2 begins with imagination theory and traces it through its various manifestations. Stick with that second beginning! It will provide a format for all the explorations of the interplay between narrative and imagination that follow. It is my hope that the journey will be worthwhile for you and will be a modest contribution toward the renewal of Christ's church.

Notes

1. David Buttrick, *Homiletic: Moves and Structures* (Philadelphia: Fortress Press, 1987).
2. *A New Hearing: Living Options in Homiletic Method* (Nashville: Albingdon Press, 1987).
3. Margaret R. Miles, *Image as Insight: Visual Understanding in Western Christianity and Secular Culture* (Boston: Beacon Press, 1985).

Part One

Theory

1

Our Home in the Narrative

To speak of beginnings, for some, is to speak of a story. It may be more accurate to say, however, that to speak of beginnings is to speak *in* stories. Certainly both of these dimensions were expressed when the biblical people spoke of their beginnings, as a people named and called out by a strange desert God. The story begins, "Now the LORD said to Abram, 'Go from your country and your kindred . . .' " (Gen. 12:1). To speak of covenant's inception is impossible without adopting narrative form. That story is told as well in the liturgical rhetoric of the psalms where the narrative sings of the God "who divided the Red Sea in two, . . . and made Israel pass through the midst of it" (Ps. 136:13,14, NRSV). Or the story's beginnings may tell of Abraham and Sarah, childless and barren in their advanced years, and of the mysterious strangers whose advent suddenly thickens the plot. So "in the beginning," for us people of the covenant, the story began with a Word from the Lord, hospitality, and laughter.

Having begun, the descendants of Sarah and Abraham later spoke of the beginning of all things, of the original genesis—but only quite a while after the story of God's dealings with Israel had its beginnings. So now the covenant story is located within a framework of creation, of the God "who by understanding made the heavens . . . who spread out the earth upon the waters" (Ps. 136:5,6). God's people may turn to the beginning, Genesis 1:1ff. and 2:4bff., only since God chose and brought them forth from bondage, only since they discovered that "the precepts of the LORD are right" (Ps. 19:8). Then, as children of promise and custodians of Torah, they spoke of the beginning. And, of course, they told a story, and then another.

We will look at the two creation stories to discern more clearly the elements of story and of the relationship between story and narrative. In the first account, the Priestly text, is discovered a poetic and quite probably liturgical form of narrative.[1] With some of the other aspects of storytelling thereby suppressed, we may notice more clearly several of the underlying structural features of narrative (somewhat like a solar eclipse allows us to study the sun's corona more clearly). These structural features pertain to narrative time, space, and the often overlooked element of a story's rhetoric, its distinctive "voice." Notice first, then, that a temporal dimension is introduced—created, really—as creation is begun. In fact, that temporal element becomes structured into "days," thereby both beginning story time and ordering it along with all that unruly chaos. Notice, too, that with creation the spatiality of narrative is created as well, quite amorphous at first, but by the third day, earth becomes the story's place. With regard to this story's rhetoric, within its poetic expression, the only speech is that of God, Word going out and creating. Only after humankind is created, though, is there divine speech *with* any part of creation.[2] That conversation begins with the words "Be fruitful and multiply . . ." (1:28). However, what may be missed here is another aspect of the narrative's rhetoric—the discourse, the voice of the narrator. Here, probably spoken to a people in exile, perhaps in the context of lament-filled liturgy: this is when God's people first hear that distinctive voice.

When we turn to the second (though earlier) creation account, the "Yahwist" tradition, there is no subduing of the rich elements of biblical narrative. Now we bump into the additional narrative elements of character, plot, setting, and this story's own distinctive tone,[3] as God forms Adam from the dust of the earth and breathes life into that hand-formed *humus*. Still, those same underlying elements (the temporal, spatial, and rhetorical) noted in the Priestly account persist, though it may be a greater effort to spot them when the narrator speaks of God "walking in the garden at the time of the evening breeze" (3:8, NRSV). However, they remain, and will as long as narrative endures. We shall therefore speak of "narrative" by way of speaking of all of these elements that together create the narrative form, and we shall speak of "story" when these elements come together in the distinctiveness of a particular story.[4]

Now if to speak of beginnings is to speak *of* story as well as *in* story, this awareness may be of no little importance for those called to preach. The remainder of this book's explorations may be best understood, then, as one response to the question, "When we preach, where and how do we begin?" We will shift somewhat in "voice" as those explorations now begin. But we already may have concluded at least this, that to speak of homiletic beginnings within the context of biblical faith will have a narrative form into which the *ruach* of God will need to breathe life.

Beginning Again: Narrativity

In his seminal paper "The Narrative Quality of Experience," Stephen Crites elevates narrativity as the essential mode of human life qua human life. "I want to argue," he begins, "that the formal quality of experience through time is inherently narrative."[5] A "person" is disclosed to the world and to one's own self through actions that are performed with a distinctive style. These actions, however, do not connect in such a way as to provide for the unity of human consciousness, being too discrete and occasional. Happily, though, there is within our consciousness a form that provides for coherence through time; this "epoxy glue" of human experience is the sense of temporal flow. Consciousness "grasps its objects" and notes its actions in a temporally based form, and Crites adds, "that temporality is retained in the unity of its experience as a whole" (298).

Once the temporal form of consciousness is spotted, Crites then proceeds to argue that the only way to secure the unity of the self experienced in the present, with its tensed modalities of past (memory) and future (anticipation), is through narrative. "Narrative alone can contain the full temporality of experience in a unity of form" (303). Narrative, however, gains expression both as mundane and as sacred stories. The former, mundane stories, serve to function by clarifying a person's sense of "world," that particular social and personal place of habitation. As such, mundane stories are set within a world that shapes and, in turn, allows us to express our "experience-within-world." Sacred stories, on the other hand, serve more to create consciousness in the first place; "they form consciousness rather than being among the objects of which it is directly aware" (295). Crites labels these narratives as "sacred" not because they are explicitly religious but by virtue of their power to create the sense of meaning, of self and world, that evokes our consciousness. Sacred stories do not enter consciousness as objects of this world; rather, they render consciousness and its world in the first place. Hence, "every sacred story is creation story: not merely that one may name creation of world and self as its 'theme' but also that the story itself creates a world of consciousness and the self that is oriented to it" (296).

The end result of this approach is to assume narrative as a universal condition of human consciousness. Persons have the kind of experiences they have, as David Kelsey reports of this position, because of the distinctive form of consciousness that is best described as temporal and as narrative.[6] Recall, however, that Crites posits the narrative subspecie of "sacred story" as the originating agent of consciousness, not as another variant of story grasped by consciousness. By virtue of this prevenience of sacred story, consciousness gains its distinctive form and quality. Story (in this "creation story" sense) is for Crites the necessary condition for human consciousness to emerge and persist. Engaging in self-reflection, consciousness finds itself temporally ordered in a way best described as narrative experience.

The significance of Crites' approach for theology and proclamation is that biblical narrative is interpreted as resting upon the foundation of a ubiquitous form of human consciousness—narrativity. This narrative form, consequently, lends a distinctive shape and quality to the objects that come into consciousness; we humans inevitably locate our experiences in a temporal and narrative manner. So as the narratives of Christian faith come into consciousness, they are grasped as one possible set of sacred and mundane stories through which the present is rendered coherent and connected with the past and future. Therefore, this set of stories called Christian faith becomes "one valid instance among many of human consciousness' inescapable religiosity."[7]

Preaching as Storytelling

Within such a framework, some of those looking for fresh insights into their vocation as preachers have seized on this claim regarding a narrative quality of experience. Indeed, one whole movement within recent homiletics has celebrated preaching as storytelling, a movement that has found warm congeniality with Stephen Crites' position. Most preachers, in fact, by now have grown accustomed to the description of their task as that of connecting "our stories with The Story." (Notice in passing, however, that it is a misreading of Crites to equate the former with "mundane stories" and the latter with "sacred stories.") Still, a significant collection of preachers and homileticians have been drawn to Crites' message concerning a narrative quality of human experience as a way out of the old discursive homiletics (usually characterized as "three points and a poem"). Typically, storytelling homiletics and its homilies employ an identifiable logic based on a "narrative quality" foundation. This logic involves a set of assumptions:

1. If there is narrative quality of experience, then, as Crites maintains, this quality is evidenced primarily in the temporal form of consciousness. "Past" and "future" are "tensed modalities of the present itself,"[8] hence the unity achieved within the temporality of consciousness. Homileticians such as Eugene Lowry and Charles Rice have employed this analysis both to critique the discursive preaching tradition and to undergird an alternative narrative or story homiletics. Lowry, for example, argues that "a sermon is an ordered form of moving time."[9] Ideas, propositions, thematics—all of these have a spatial quality; we were conditioned to speak of "building the sermon" through outlines, points, and theme sentences. But if, however, human experience is inherently temporal, a homily will be designed to shape experience rather than to assemble thoughts. Temporality in human experience invokes mobility in preaching, an ordering of time and experience.[10]

2. Given this foundational assessment that all human experience "is at least in some rudimentary sense narrative,"[11] the preaching-as-storytelling advocates have naturally assumed for

story this formal claim of universality. All people, of whatever
time or culture, tend to organize experience in a narrative form
and therefore find stories most congenial to their experience. Just
at this point, the matter shifts from phenomenological analysis
(our experience is inherently temporal and durational) to theological claim (narrative is the primal form of consciousness, and
becoming fully human involves the fullest achievement of this
narrative form). The opposite side of the coin here is the judgment
that impoverished stories result in a people less than fully human.
So, for example, as Terrence Tilley considers the context within
which a story theology has emerged, he focuses on the narrative
quality of experience at length.[12] Follow the sequence from analytic insight to theological claim:

> If our experience is basically durational, how can we talk of
> it? The answer fits perfectly: in narratives. Stories do tell of
> a "body impacted in a world." They portray experience
> through time. . . . When we lose our stories, our critical
> abilities run rampant and become vicious, as Crites has
> noted. . . . The implication of this view is that without a story
> that is both faithful to our on-going experience and actions,
> and examined critically for its truthfulness, we cannot be
> fully human.[13]

Based on a "story theology," then, the preaching-as-storytelling
movement turns to a dual hermeneutic—exegeting both Scripture
and personal and communal experience today as story. The
storytelling preacher thereby is presented with the challenge of
ferrying back and forth between The Story and our stories.[14] Observe how this dual hermeneutic operates with Charles Rice. First,
for Rice, "the openness and ability to hear a story, to really enter
in and follow a story is essential to understanding the Bible."[15]
Second, "we need to learn to hear and tell our own stories we
share—not just our individual stories, but the stories we share
with a given community and humankind—as much as we need
to enter in and follow the Bible's unfolding story of God's ways
with us."[16] What has occurred in the midst of this argument, as
we now can nicely spot, is a movement from Crites' analysis of
the narrative quality of experience to a shift in focus to the stories
that become the objects within consciousness. Implicit in this

methodological shift, moreover, is an assignment of the designation of "sacred story" to the biblical tradition.
    3. Consciousness as the model for the interpretation of self,
text, and world is similarly shared by Stephen Crites and a number
of homileticians. While David Buttrick adopts a phenomenological approach depending on a notion of consciousness for his entire
project, the more clearly story-based homileticians draw only in
a selective fashion on Crites' portrayal of consciousness. One
particular aspect of the model that has proven attractive is the
somewhat circular analysis Crites provides for the relationship
between consciousness and narrative. On one hand, consciousness
offers the field within which stories are experienced and gain
meaning. On the other hand, there are certain qualities of narrative
whose very purpose is to create human consciousness. In
one form or another, story and narrative theology has consistently
argued for the priority of story in relation to the emergence of the
self. Eugene Lowry, for example, celebrates Crites' suggestion
that "consciousness is created by story, and not story by
consciousness."[17]
    If story theology and a homiletics of storytelling do rest upon
these three aspects of Crites' analysis, then it is appropriate to
inquire as to the adequacy of these foundations and the consis-
tency with which they are applied. Taking these characteristics
in reverse order, we are initially presented with this fascinating
notion of consciousness as the model for interpretation and for
proclamation. Notice how significantly a preacher's sense of the
"implied hearer" shifts when a modern, rationalist anthropology
is supplanted by a postmodern focus on consciousness. As the
chief homiletic spokesperson for this phenomenological position,
David Buttrick repeatedly urges preachers to forgo homilies addressed to rationalist selves. How preaching occurs, he insists,
has everything to do with assumptions concerning our audience.
Addressing the assembly within the framework of communal consciousness, our preaching will assemble plots and perform intentions aligned with the biblical text.[18] Conversely, our homilies
will not trade in propositions addressed to rationalist minds.
    A second issue related to the employment of a notion of con-
sciousness within hermeneutic method is precisely the adequacy

of this phenomenological foundation. Does such an approach "appeal to extratextual criteria" for scriptural interpretation,[19] or does the method's bracketing of ontological questions along with its "fusion of horizons" (a fusion of the text and the reader's consciousness) actually aid and abet faithful biblical preaching? Another way of posing the question is to ask whether a phenomenological hermeneutic inevitably involves some sort of allegorization in its use of Scripture. For Mark Ellingsen, the answer is an unambiguous yes. To use phenomenology in biblical interpretation is to "reject the possibility of discerning a text's descriptive, normative meaning."[20] He adds that this occurs because of an insistence "that a text's meaning is partially determined by the impact the text's structures has [sic] on an interpreter."[21] Without any apology whatsoever, David Buttrick would likely respond that no interpreter of Scripture nor any community gathered to hear it read can remain immune to the impact of a text's movement and structure. Moreover, since any number of biblical literary critics have located the meaning within the text as conveyed through its plotted intention, it is difficult to see how such structure can fail to impact the hearer/interpreter. In his discussion of this perceived problem, Ellingsen groups together within one allegorizing gaggle, both phenomenologists and storytelling homileticians. As will be seen, however, these birds are of quite a different methodological sort who generally do not flock together.

Beyond the issues related to the notion of consciousness as hermeneutic context, a far more extensive use of Crites by storytelling preachers involves other critical hermeneutic concerns. By now, the preaching-as-storytelling minstrels have sung the virtues of "God's Story–our stories" in every village, hamlet, and seminary. Yet when the underlying assumptions are unpacked, some observers have detected a critical flaw in the position. Central is the problem that the stories on each side of the hyphen keep splitting off from each other. The preacher may be encouraged to ferry back and forth between the Bible story and our modern stories, but the metaphor breaks down (or sinks, perhaps). The problem seems to be inherent in storytelling's methodology. First, the story homileticians run with Crites' assessment as to the ubiquity of a narrative quality of experience. In turn, this narrative quality is rendered as the ubiquity of stories within human experience. Finally, this quality of human life and the stories that are objects within consciousness are aligned with the story of God's choosing and dealing with the people of the Bible, especially through Jesus. Notice just where the ferry founders: On one hand, narrative is celebrated as a perennial quality of human life—human beings experience their lives as narratively ordered and in addition discover stories to be the content of that experience. On the other hand, there is an appeal to an authoritative tradition delivered within a normative community. That is, the faithful tell stories of the people within The Story, stories of Israel's God and of Jesus Christ and the church. The system is inherently unstable since, as Gregory Jones points out, there is "a formal claim that . . . is not specific to any traditions" while a claim is also made "that epistemology is tradition-specific."[22] Simply put, one cannot at once proclaim story as a ubiquitous human experience and announce one Story as normative. Either the first assertion is taken seriously (narrative quality as transcendent human experience), in which case no tradition may make a normative claim, or the normative claim is staked, in which case "narrative quality" becomes a projection of a particular Christian anthropology onto the vast and varied sweep of human experience. Encouragements to ferry between the Bible's story and our modern stories founder on a fundamental flaw in hermeneutic method.

It is not surprising, therefore, that this lack of "fit" between a general hermeneutic based on the narrative quality of experience and a specific commitment to a normative storied tradition shows up repeatedly in storytelling sermons. Given "the stories of our lives" and "the Story of our faith," the former tend to shape the content and ideological perspective of the latter. "The Story" most typically becomes reduced to a series of texts, a "homiletical canon," most compatible to the interpretive context of "the stories of our lives." Moreover, the methodological flow is evident in most every storytelling homiletic and story sermon. Those preaching or writing about story "still tend to begin with our stories and then fit the biblical narratives into the world of our experience."[23]

The project does not hold together at the level of praxis nor with regard to its hermeneutics.

Finally, Crites' initial claim itself must be scrutinized; that is, that there is a narrative quality to human experience. At first glance, the assertion seems self-evident, indeed axiomatic. Upon further reflection, however, it may well be the case that this presumably self-evident claim may not be universalized to encompass all human experience. So Gregory Jones argues that "it is not clear that [one] can *know* in principle that human life *qua* human life is narrative in form."[24] In order to assert the ubiquity of a narrative quality to human experience, it would be necessary to establish that diverse cultures and religious communities all read the "story" of individual birth to death with some broadly shared narrative structure. However, it is not difficult to find religious traditions where, for example, a belief in reincarnation strongly qualifies the sense of ending of the individual self. At least within the Christian tradition, physical birth is qualified both by the witness to the prior and on-going life of the *communio sanctorum* as well as by the sacrament of baptism. Jones aptly concludes, then, that any "claim about the narrative quality of human life is dependent upon a specific description of a teleologically-oriented historicity which is [believed to be] fundamental to an adequate understanding of human life [i.e., he is presupposing a normative tradition]."[25] It may well be that, with Jones and others, the most that can be achieved through Crites' phenomenological scrutiny of human experience is a notion of consciousness temporally formed but not narratively ordered.[26]

Toward a Postliberal Hermeneutic

The Cognitive Model

If the attempt to ground the particularity of the Christian tradition within a notion of narrative as a transcendent quality of experience has foundered, the interpretive question emerges afresh. Where shall the preacher turn in her or his need for a framework for interpreting text, self, and world? According to George Lindbeck, two dominant alternatives have offered themselves, a "cognitive model" and an "experiential-expressive" one. In the former, having its ideological roots solidly in the Enlightenment, there is a stress on "the ways in which church doctrines function as informative propositions or truth claims about objective reality."[27] The homiletic expression of this familiar model needs little elaboration for those who preach. Given the formation received in seminary and church practice for over a century now, the cognitive model has been simply assumed. Take most any gathering of preachers, show a portion of biblical narrative, and ask, "How shall we begin our analysis here?" The answer will come quickly and easily in the form of extracted main ideas and "proto-sermon title" thematics. Applied to interpretation, the cognitive model approaches biblical texts, including those of a narrative literary form, by way of a "hermeneutic of distillation."[28] Armed with this model, preachers bring to the hermeneutic quest an assumption that a discursive "point" of some sort is the payoff to nearly every narrative in the Bible.

It is in the arena of parable interpretation that this reductionistic approach to biblical narrative came to its fullest expression and then experienced its most devastating critique. In a tradition begun almost a century ago by Adolf Jülicher,[29] most parable exegetes shared the belief that one, and only one, main idea was the retrievable meaning of each parable. Jülicher's intent and achievement was "to attack and destroy the allegorical interpretation of parable which had reigned until his time."[30] With multiple external references blocked by his interpretive strategy of the single point, allegorical interpretation was successfully stymied. However, the prevailing alternative locked into place a rationalist hermeneutic in relation to parables in particular and came to widen to include any biblical narrative within its field. The parable was to have one and only one main idea as its meaning! Of course, liberal interpreters came to find moralistic liberal main ideas while pietists found single points nicely fitting within their own faith tradition. For the first half of this century, though, there was little notice of the contradiction at the heart of this rationalist model. If there was only one main idea latent in every parable, then a diversity of interpreters should all be coming up with that same main idea. Such was not the case, of course, but only with the naming of parable as narrative metaphor by Amos Wilder[31] and Robert Funk[32] was the main-idea approach successfully challenged. Nevertheless, this single-point assumption regarding parable interpretation dies hard; the centennial of Jülicher's monumental work will find many preachers still approaching biblical narrative in general and the parables in particular looking for a single point thematic. There is perhaps no clearer example of the cognitive model of doctrine and interpretation than this tradition of the main idea.

The Experiential-Expressive Model

The alternative to the cognitive model of interpretation and doctrine for George Lindbeck focuses on humanity's "noninformative and nondiscursive symbols of inner feelings, attitudes, and existential orientations."[33] This "expressive-experiential model" has its ideological roots in Romanticism's reaction to the "Age of Reason," and, in particular, in the theological program of Friedrich Schleiermacher. As with the cognitive model, the meaning of Scripture is sought external to the text but now within some nonpropositional context that "authorizes" the continued use of the text. Central to the hermeneutics of this model is the conviction that there exists some kind of "shared interior experience" that is normative, unique, and irreducible.[34] Given such a definition, we can now see that the whole "narrative quality of experience" argument is one vast attempt at an expressive-experiential model of interpretation. For any portion of Scripture to be "true" or "authoritative" is for it to be discovered as an instance of this prior experience.

Whether encountered in the preaching of the day, in ministry to higher education apologetics, or in the rhetoric of ecclesiastical bureaucracy, the experiential-expressive model has for some time now become the "conventional wisdom" of the interpretation of Christian faith. Especially given the individualism and narcissism of American culture, the liberal inclination has been to ground most any aspect of Scripture and faith in some external construct of universal experience. From a closer analytic perspective, several dominant expressions of this interpretive model become evident:

The foundationist approach. For the advocates of this method of doing theology and proclamation, the Christian narratives are exemplary of some prior construct from which they have evolved. In other words, some sort of pre-Christian system or experience precedes the church's claims; consequently, the latter are derivative from the former. In this regard, the precedent has the authoritative high ground, and Christian faith becomes a regional instance of a more "real" original. So, for example, a currently popular movement in the churches seeks to locate Christian stories and its second order theology within a general category of myth. In the widely popular work of Joseph Campbell,[35] the authority of the mythic types and experiences is clear in relation to Christian faith. The former, the mythic, is the foundation, being ubiquitous to human experience, while the latter, the Christian narrative, is meaningful as an example of (or as *distortion* of) the more primordial myth world.[36]

This foundationist approach appears in contemporary preaching most often in one of two ways. On one hand, homilists move easily across cultural and religious traditions in celebration of analogies of Christian experience. Jesus' time in the wilderness is equated with a Native American vision quest, while the birth of Christ is couched in terms of Celtic ritual and beliefs surrounding the winter solstice. On the other hand, sermons will be found containing rationales for Christian faith based on the prior and more authoritative claims of the religion of the American state. This American civil religion, first documented by Robert Bellah,[37] derives many of its central tenets from a secularized version of the biblical theology of covenant coupled with a doctrine of sacrifice introduced and later embodied by Abraham Lincoln. Interestingly, although the civil religion has its ideological roots in the accounts of covenant and sacrifice in the Bible, it has for decades functioned as an autonomous religious system complete with its own symbols, narratives, and "liturgical year."[38] So foundational has the civil religion become that any preaching that attempts to deal with Scripture's witness to freedom, justice, or sacrifice, for example, will quite reflexively be framed within a civil religion context. Given the pervasiveness of this form of the expressive-experiential model, David Buttrick's recent work on the person and death of Christ must devote considerable attention to a ground-clearing operation vis-à-vis the various cultural expressions of the civil religion.[39] Clearly, that effort is some prominent testimony to the pervasiveness of a foundational belief system in American civil religion held by Christians in the United States.

Once preachers become aware of the magnitude of the problems for proclamation inherent in these and a host of other foundationist approaches, it becomes evident that a "hermeneutics of suspicion" will need to become an essential point of view. Ironically, the American church, across a wide span of ideological thinking, is deeply immersed in this variety of the experiential-expressive model. The liberal wing in the churches goes off after other more authoritative religious and cultural experiences in the name of "pluralism." The conservative wing in the churches—in many cases unaware—marches under the banner of the red, white, and blue!

The illustrative approach. Our "spirit of the age" is marked by an increasingly rapid turnover in cultural and intellectual interests, religious movements, and fads.[40] For those of us who are called to preach, this ever-shifting map of social consciousness can encourage those called to preach to be alert to new images and stories that can be useful in proclamation. Given this spirit of the age, however, the temptation is always nearby to authorize or interpret the biblical witness with regard to whatever is now in fashion. As George Lindbeck notes, "It is much easier in our day for religious interests to take the experiential-expressive form of individual quests for personal meaning."[41] It is not surprising, then, that sermons are heard that locate the significance and value of Christian faith "in terms of" such constructs as Jungian psychology or a liberation theology grounded in Marxist thought.[42] With these or numerous other examples of the illustrative approach, the tendency is "to make the story of Jesus only pedagogically necessary and ultimately dispensable."[43] Biblical narratives, we find, are viewed as illustrations of some ideology or social movement external to the world of the text. The question gets raised with precision in a discussion with regard to process theology (not one of the more pervasive examples of this approach): "Is process theology," asks Charles Pinches, "essentially or incidentally Christian?"[44] He then queries, "Does the Christian story . . . nicely *illustrate* the truths of process theology—truths which could be and have been differently illustrated without crucial loss—or are the Christian story and these truths absolutely inseparable?"[45] To the extent that any approach illustrates its own *primary* truths by employing *secondary* Christian references, the experiential-expressive model is at play. Real authority and real truth claims are located within the external symbol system or ideology that may then illustrate that authority and truth by turning to the Christian texts. The litmus test is nicely raised by Pinches as to whether the external system could be illustrated by narratives other than biblical ones "without crucial loss."

The approach of succession. If we have a dispensable gospel in principle with the illustrative approach, another manifestation of the experiential-expressive model is designed to show how, in fact, Christian faith is surpassed, left behind. More radical forms of the approach offer "another gospel," such as *The Book of Mormon* or *The Divine Principle* of the Unification Church. Christian faith is portrayed as a partial, historically superseded phenomenon in light of a new and complete revelation. A variation of the approach by succession is seen in Elisabeth Schüssler Fiorenza's feminist construct, which assigns the biblical narrative the status of "prototype." The contrast is with an archetype that is "a normative pattern, any deviation from which is an error; . . . [However], a prototype is a first attempt, from which one may learn both positively and negatively, and which may and probably should be surpassed."[46] By assigning the designation of "prototype" to biblical faith, Schüssler Fiorenza sets up an approach of succession by which elements of the prototype may be selected or deselected according to the dictates of her own position.

More conventionally, the approach of succession in a liberal context assumes a stance that tends to relativize most all religious truth claims in the name of pluralism. The logic here seems to be that "the various religions are diverse symbolizations of one and the same core experience of the Ultimate, and that therefore they must respect each other, learn from each other, and reciprocally enrich each other."[47] A more highly imaged rendition of this point of view was recently provided by a church consultant:

> Imagine we are fish swimming up a stream. After a while, we become aware that we are not alone, there are other fish,

much like ourselves, also swimming upstream. We travel
along together and may even call ourselves "Christian fish."
But we may come to realize in time that there are other
streams, with other fish swimming up those streams. And
finally, if we can see the big picture, we can see that we are
all swimming up the same mountain toward the same final
goal.

Having relativized the particular truth claims of any religious
tradition, a perennial liberal tendency is to project a future point
of convergence at which distinctiveness and particularity are
erased.

Lindbeck, in his analysis of the cognitive and expressive-
experiential models of doctrine, makes two assumptions regarding
the relative influence of the models in shaping theology and praxis.
First, by virtue of devoting the bulk of attention to the
experiential-expressive model, a judgment is being made concerning this model's congeniality in a world characterized by "individualism, rapid change, and pluralism."[48] Second, Lindbeck develops the two models more as alternative methodological
options. After all, the cognitive model derives from the Enlightenment while the experiential-expressive model emanates from
Schleiermacher and Romanticism! But with regard to modern
preaching, both of Lindbeck's assumptions need to be qualified.
For many within the guild of preachers, the weekly search persists
for the points, propositions, or main ideas of a biblical text. An
ideational redaction of the text is pursued in the assurance that
each piece of Scripture must yield some thematic, given appropriate exegesis. Moreover, most of the same homilists who are
wedded to the cognitive model also invoke the second model both
as a means of getting to the message behind the text (involving
the use of "historical imagination") and as a source for introducing
subjectivity into the homiletical landscape (mostly in the form
of story illustrations). Modern preaching has for the course of its
ascendancy, then, proceeded with one foot in the cognitive model
and the other very much in the experiential-expressive. Or as
David Buttrick observed, "The result is that we now have a romantic concept of 'inspiration' coupled with rational method, a
mix found in most homiletic texts today."[49] Given the considerable evidence of the breakdown in this homiletic synthesis, the

time may be ripe for the emergence of a new and postliberal model for interpreting and proclaiming biblical narrative.

A Cultural-Linguistic Model

The modern era in scriptural interpretation and preaching can be designated with considerable accuracy as that period of time following the Enlightenment when biblical narrative lost its pre-eminence. Following a cognitive model, the meaning of the narrative was sought in the ideas to which it referred. When the preacher extracted the point from the Bible story, its narrative shape was of no further consequence—the preacher grabbed for subpoints and illustrations to fill out the sermonic outline. Yet the experiential-expressive model also functioned to suppress the biblical narrative. Viewing the text as a deposit of truths or as an instance of contemporary human experience meant "treating the biblical narratives as examples or lessons or illustrations of general principles, whose meaning does not lie in their narrative structure."[50] Modernity for preachers and the church has been, as Hans Frei carefully has established, the time of the eclipse of biblical narrative.[51]

The recovery of biblical narrative, as noted, is not simply a matter of telling stories from the pulpit. Rather, it is crucial that those who are called to preach grapple with a profound shift in the hermeneutic task that has come to be labeled as "postliberal theology." As George Lindbeck moves from his critique, mainly of the experiential-expressive model, his constructive work begins by defining doctrine as "communally authoritative rules of discourse, attitude and action."[52] Viewing a religious community as analogous to a culture or language, it "shapes the subjectivities of individuals rather than being primarily a manifestation of those subjectivities."[53] Put directly, our community of faith forms us by giving us birth within a tradition of story, ritual, and actions such that our religious experience is inevitably "Christian experience." There is simply no such thing as a prelinguistic experience, no normative and shared inner human experience not shaped and mediated by our faith (or that of others), its grammar, and its distinctive culture (hence, the "cultural-linguistic model"). As

Placher observes, "Language *creates* the possibility of religious experience, indeed of any fully human experience. . . . Therefore different religions do not represent different expressions of the same experience."[54]

Now the grammar of Christian faith and its cultural expressions come to expression most centrally within the context of worship, as the biblical witness is read, sung, and proclaimed, and as that story is "experienced anew" through the sacraments. In the recovery of the Easter vigil across the church, for example, there is a profound sign that the eclipse of biblical narrative is passing its umbral, or darkest, stage. On that night of nights, the community in Christ gathers in darkness, lights the new fire, and immediately attends to its narrative. Through a succession of readings, the vast sweep of the biblical narrative is traced. The story of creation and the flood, of Abraham's faith, and of the Israelites' deliverance from bondage in Egypt and crossing of the sea is recited. Once more the prophetic promises are heard of Zion renewed, the covenant restored, and of dry bones made alive. Then the community is reminded of its baptismal story, of dying and rising with Christ. In the fullness of time, the Easter gospel is heard—empty tomb, risen Lord. At the center of the linguistic/cultural world of Christian life is this night with its mystery of the passover of Christ from death to new life.

The radical assertion implied in the cultural-linguistic model of doctrine and interpretation is that any and all so-called inner experiences are shaped by the formative environment of culture and of language. For the church, that culture and language come to fullest expression as the biblical narrative shapes its worship, guides its preaching, and is lived again in its sacramental life— ultimately at the heart of the matter in the Easter vigil. However, this insistence on the preeminence of biblical narrative in its cultural-linguistic setting vis-à-vis our experience of faith involves several central assumptions that must in turn be addressed. The first is the judgment that narrative is the most appropriate mode for the interpretation of the biblical witness. Then I will argue "the primacy of the world created by the biblical narratives over the world of our experience for a Christian reading of the Bible."[55] Finally, I will claim that the necessary context for an appropriate interpretation of Scripture necessarily is from within the community of faith.

The primacy of the narrative mode of interpreting Scripture. The preaching-as-storytelling homileticians frequently celebrated the remarkable plentitude of stories within biblical literature. While such a finding is to be celebrated, it is not yet a hermeneutic claim that Scripture is best construed within the category of narrative. One remarkable fruit of this retrieval of biblical narrative has been the abundance of literary critical studies in biblical narrative.[56] A next step is taken by those who celebrate the abundance of stories in the Bible and add the judgment "that narrative is central to the Bible's own interests in communicating its message."[57] Here, the conclusion would follow that a narrative form of homiletics is integral to Scripture's own interests in communication. To adopt some other homiletic strategy would, therefore, be to work at cross-purpose with the intention of the text. A final step is made, however, when the primacy of the narrative mode of interpreting Scripture is claimed. Here, in addition to a narrative literary "core," the scope of our interpretation enlarges to include that nonnarrative literature, which, for Mark Ellingsen, "seems to be concerned with questions about how the narratives should be interpreted or with elaboration on the narratives through praise."[58] Examples of the former most obviously include the Pauline corpus and the covenant law portions of Deuteronomy. Samples of doxological elaboration include many of the psalms and other liturgical material, especially the canticles, which are thick with narrative reference. At issue still is the question as to whether one may now speak of the narrative unity of Scripture.

Those who take issue with this assignment of narrative as the dominant mode of biblical interpretation do so most frequently by appealing to the wisdom literature and to apocalyptic as remaining unsusceptible to a narrative reading.[59] The renaissance in wisdom literature studies in recent years uncovers a literary form that was extant prior to and independent of the context of Israel's covenant with God.[60] Obviously this collection of sayings, proverbs, and psalms gets caught up in the covenantal net by being included in the canon. Even so, it is mostly nonnarrative in form and remains in an ambiguous relation to "the biblical story." (Proverbs can be found, interestingly, that may either undergird or undermine specific biblical narratives.) Still, given the distinctiveness of this wisdom tradition, it is not only the canonical process that relates it to narrative. Some wisdom psalms (e.g., Psalms 1, 14, 37) are incipient narratives themselves with stock characters—the wise (and righteous), the wicked (or evildoers), and the foolish—with characteristic plot trajectories. When these trajectories are accomplished, a followable world is reinforced. When those plots are confounded, the biblical writers turn to narrative to address the question as to why the evil prosper while the good suffer, as in the Book of Job. More generally, however, William Beardslee has contributed a keen insight to the discussion of the relationship between proverbs and narrative in Scripture. Reacting against Bultmann's construal of proverbs as expressing a general truth, Beardslee asserts that

> it is somewhat misleading to speak of the proverb as a statement of general truth. It is a statement about a particular kind of occurrence or situation, an orderly tract of experience which can be repeated. In this sense, though it is not a narrative, the proverb implies a story, something that happens, that moves through as sequence in a way which can be known.[61]

In Jesus' proverbial speech, however, there is frequently an intensification—chiefly through hyperbole and paradox—of the form of discourse such that it can no longer be said that proverbs are the genre of the status quo. There is a "jolt" to these intensified proverbs that puts pressure on their previously assumed function of signaling and maintaining equilibrium, "of making a continuous whole out of one's existence."[62] In fact, Beardslee documents a recurring dynamic in Synoptic proverbial usage whereby a turn toward eschatology is clearly at work. The "story" that the proverb implies, in Jesus' usage, will no longer remain that of the continuity of human existence. In the advent of the kingdom of God, the old story is called into question, broken apart. A new narrative of God's people is begun. Simply put, the Bible itself will not let the wisdom literature remain independent of its story!

With regard to apocalyptic—the other biblical literature indicated as resisting a narrative contextualization—the issue is more immediate to our concerns. To the extent that a hermeneutic is being proposed in these pages that seeks to integrate within a single field both narrative and imagery, apocalyptic becomes a significant expression of this intersection. The Book of Revelation, for example, consists of a story, the story of a vision. Yet that story is rendered as a plotted sequence only in the most formal sense—we may speak of it more as a "scenario," projected forward and therefore a "thin" form of narrative. The sweep of movement within the vision confronts the viewer (is it not better to say "viewer" than "hearer" in apocalyptic?) with a succession of bold and striking images. If those images, then, derive from Scripture's own narratives as well as the world's stories, we may have in apocalyptic a uniquely presented fusion of narrative and imagery. It is also the case with apocalytic as with the proverbs that in Jesus' speech an "internal subversion" is at work.[63] The apocalyptic form "is simultaneously employed, transgressed, and upset by its new usage."[64] Only the narrative context of the Gospels is capable of locating this reworking of apocalytic with reference to Jesus and the nearness of the mystery of God's reign.

Having noted the possible issues of wisdom literature and apocalyptic, it now becomes possible to propose with Ronald Thiemann that "narrative highlights both a predominant literary category within the Bible and an appropriate theological category for interpreting the canon as a whole."[65] To argue that proposal, though, is to adopt one or both of the following lines of reasoning. First, in the tradition of Auerbach and others,[66] the narratives of the Pentateuch and the Gospels may be likened to the literary genre of realistic novel. As realistic narrative novel, these texts present a history-like world, "preoccupied with chronology and with mundane, often conflicting events, as is realistic and historical literature."[67] Ellingsen chronicles the other distinguishing elements of realistic narrative as follows: "The action is narrated from an internal perspective, not from an omniscient one. The identities of characters in these texts are unsubstitutable; they are unique individuals. And the texts posit an irreducible identity of character and action."[68] Such a description of biblical narrative achieves a number of significant advances in hermeneutics, primary among them being the bypassing of the old liberal-conservative debate concerning historical reference. Both sides for over a century now have mistaken the "history-likeness" of realistic narrative for historical facticity. Liberals, on one hand, sought to detach the texts from their presumed historical referent in favor of some extratextual religious meaning (the expressive-experiential model). Conservatives, on the other hand, fought to maintain the identity of the biblical narrative with the historical truth of the text; both sides joined in tacit agreement "that reading the texts literally is the same thing as taking them to be historically accurate reports."[69] Treating these texts as realistic narrative provides a way into a more general construal of Scripture as narrative.

The singular caution at this point was raised by Hans Frei, who earlier, in *The Eclipse of Biblical Narrative*, employed Auerbach's analysis with reference to a precritical "literal sense" of reading Scripture.[70] More recently, however, Frei has raised a caution flag with regard to the category of realistic narrative, specifically with regard to its potential for once again rendering the biblical witness into an example or instance of some externally grounded authorization. So to ground the Gospels and their witness to Jesus Christ in a literary world of the late-nineteenth century would be for Frei "to put the cart before the horse—and then cut the reins and claim the vehicle is self-propelled."[71] If there is to be a narrative mode of biblical interpretation, it will need to be on the basis of a paradigm derived *from* the canon and not brought to it. Frei concludes, "The reason why the intratextual universe of this Christian symbol system is a narrative one is that a specific set of texts, which happen to be narrative, has become primary, even within scripture, and has been assigned a literal reading as their primary or 'plain' sense."[72] We will not, then, with Ellingsen, base a narrative construal of Scripture on the *hard version* that the Bible "as a single book, . . . like any good piece of literature, . . . must hang together."[73] Rather, we will risk a journey with a *soft version* of the Bible's narrative character, disclosed in the skein of its internal and conventional relationships, best grasped as narrative.

The primacy of the biblical narrative world. It is one thing to argue for a narrative mode of biblical interpretation, yet it is quite another to claim for that biblical world a primacy with regard to all other social and cultural worlds. That is, to assert the primacy of the scriptural narrative is also to assign the designation of "fiction" or even "lie" to the stories offered up by the secular and religious worlds! Given that such an assertion sounds wildly radical to our churchly ears accustomed to enthusiastic speech about "pluralism" and "inclusiveness," still this insistence on Christian faith's particularity and truth is at the heart of our tradition. For the reformers, and their descendants, Thiemann observes, "scripture depicts a real world, temporally structured, which encompasses both the times and stories of the text and those of the reader." He then adds that "since the world depicted by the Bible is the only real world, the reader must fit his or her own experience into scripture's cumulative narrative, thus becoming a 'figure' of the text."[74]

As this (for many) radical and postliberal assertion of the primacy of the biblical narrative world is elaborated, its argument is seen to have several facets. One of these facets highlights the way in which the Bible invites the hearer to become a part of the story. Worldly stories become external and relativized for the Christian community that has been graced with internal, storied relations with Scripture, "the sort of relations that are depicted in narratives."[75] Another facet of this assertion deals with the capability of the biblical world to interpret each and every world external to itself. A patterned framework exists for the Christian interpretation of the world's stories, such that persons within the community of faith are formed to experience all of reality, including themselves, according to this pattern. Nothing, on earth or in heaven, remains outside the interpretive field of the biblical paradigm. For Christians, no place exists external to our storied relations to the biblical narrative toward which we can move into a relaxed neutrality. So, for example, the world may depict itself as including a Jesus who was not raised from the dead. Such a world may be interesting to explore; however, it is no longer the world of the Gospels' story of Jesus.[76] Finally, another related facet springs into brilliance here. If the biblical world interprets all of our extrabiblical worlds, along with the "world" of our storied self, there is a sense in which it is "able to absorb the universe. It supplies the interpretive framework within which believers seek to live their lives and understand reality."[77]

The primacy of the ecclesial context for narrative interpretation. We have maintained that there are no "neutral sites" from which to interpret the biblical narrative (not even the comparative religion departments of state universities!). Rather, the relationship of a reader to the Bible on one hand may be discovered to be an illustrative one in which Scripture points to truth (cognitive model) or experiences (experiential-expressive model) grounded elsewhere within the self or the world. On the other hand, one may have a storied relationship with the text in which "the Christian story and the life and world of the reader do not exist in isolation, but constitute one world and one story."[78] What prevents this from careening off into the orbit of "the narrative quality of human experience," however, is the insistence on the primacy of a church location for the interpretation of Scripture. When interrogated, this essential hermeneutic location yields two distinctive components.

First, the somewhat self-evident observation will be made that the Bible's coming into being is covenantal and reflects a community's "vested interests" (Brueggemann's nice phrasing).[79] Conversely, the Bible itself has a vested interest in the formation and mission of a community of faith that extends itself subsequent to the canon. This latter vested interest of Scripture—toward the formation of a community of faith external to but in continuity with itself—provides a necessary elaboration of Lindbeck's notion of intratextuality.[80] Within this more expansive notion of intratextuality, the biblical story "is not self-referential but rather creates a people capable of being the continuation of the narrative by witnessing to the world that all creation is ordered to God's good end. The church is the necessary context for the testing of that narrative."[81] Other religious or worldly communities may well like to peer over into the biblical story for all sorts of reasons. The claim here is that the community that is the "vested interest" of Scripture—the church of Jesus Christ—has an intended primacy as the hermeneutic context for the interpretation of Scripture's texts.

Narrative: Disclosing a "World" and God

Characteristic of biblical narrative is having as its "self-interest" the ongoing life of a people of faith. The trajectory of Scripture's focus on the people of covenant extends beyond the canon to embrace contemporary Christian communities that are then connected back to their biblical roots by a story-formed tradition and by life in communion with all the saints and their stories. They are also connected forward to a future in which all creation will be restored (and therefore "re-storied," i.e., will achieve an integration of humanity with itself and all creation in Christ). Such biblical images as Isaiah's "peaceable kingdom" in which God promises to create "new heavens and a new earth" (Isa. 65:17-25) or the Book of Revelation's vision of a new heaven and a new earth (Rev. 21:1-4) point to this "incorporation" of all humanity and all creation within the scope of Scripture's sweeping narrative. The vested interest of the biblical narrative is not satisfied with even the ongoing life of the church within the world. Ultimately, as Frei has noted, the world of Scripture absorbs the world!

Also characteristic of biblical narrative is disclosing to the assembly of the faithful a "world" in which to dwell. Indeed, any narrative functions to disclose some kind of world, whether of romantic escape or horror (two of our culture's most popular "worlds" just now) or of some other sort. Again, it must be asserted against the assumptions of liberalism that no "world" can claim for itself the leverage of clear objectivity and self-evidential authority. All persons and communties dwell within story-formed worlds. In this regard, Christians are those who dwell within one distinctive world as disclosed within its biblical narrative and its storied tradition. The distinctiveness of that biblical narrative, the church confesses, is in the character of the world it discloses— a world in which outcasts are sought and restored to community, sinners are forgiven, healing is found, and hospitality is extended and received. This world is both *intratextual*—that is, the world of the internal relationship of the Bible's texts—and *ecclesial*— incorporating the church's life here and now. So, Hauerwas celebrates Frei's insistence that the church is both subject as well as agent of biblical narrative, since "narrative does not refer but that rather people do."[82] Hauerwas adds that "to isolate biblical narratives in and of themselves would be equivalent to considering the truth or falsity of sentences apart from their utterance."[83] Both sides of the coin obtain; it is in Scripture's self-interest that the church persist in faithfulness and witness. The world that evokes that faith and shapes that witness is disclosed by Scripture.

Closely related to biblical narrative's function in disclosing a world is its power to render the character of God. Within the stories of the Bible, God's character and agency are disclosed "not by telling what God is in and of himself, but by accounts of the interaction of his deeds and purposes, with those of creatures in their everchanging circumstances."[84] Noticeable throughout these narratives, however, is the way God remains mysterious and hidden, even as God's agency is acknowledged as present in, or behind, the story. Related to this often hidden quality of God's deeds or purposes is the fact that the "omniscient" biblical narrator "is presumed to know, quite literally, what God knows."[85]

One stereotyped convention of narrators in the Old Testament is to conclude a sequence, for example, with a pronouncement as to God's pleasure or displeasure with one of the characters. Interesting in this regard is the manner in which the narrative itself can unfold at length without specifically referencing or alluding to God as a character. In the Gospels, however, the narrators do not declare God's perspective on a person; "God enters the story and says so (Matt. 3:17; 17:5; Mark 1:11; Luke 3:22)."[86] Notice, though, how infrequently God is presented as a character within the Gospel narratives. Thiemann is on solid ground, therefore, when he observes that "Scripture's 'main character' is God and yet his direct actions are only rarely described."[87] Even in the Fourth Gospel, with its emphasis on God's glory revealed in Jesus, the Johannine signs offer only hiddenness and mystery at the epicenter of divine intervention. (John tells of "the water that had become wine" [2:9] and of the man born blind who washed and "came back able to see" [9:7].) There is a "narrative modesty" to the signs, especially to the ultimate sign of God's power revealed in the resurrection of Jesus from the dead. "The narrative rather focuses on the consequences of that power in the vivid stories of the empty tomb and the post-resurrection appearances."[88] This strange hiddenness of the character of God in biblical narrative is of epistemological significance regarding the nature of that "world" within which we "live, move, and have our being." The "increasing convergence between the activity of Jesus and that of the hidden God of Israel"[89] in the New Testament patterns our perception of God's agency in our own personal and communal narratives. God remains hidden, absent even, yet we recognize the Christ of God in the patterns of events within the liturgy and its preaching or in the world. From this perspective preachers may overstep either by excessively denoting how God is at work in this personal experience or that political cause or by remaining vague about God's agency altogether! There is a "narrative modesty" appropriate to preaching that more effectively renders the character of God in ways congruent with the biblical narration itself.

Narrative: Formation and Proclamation

Christians first speak to each other of the biblical narrative to disclose a world and to disclose the identity of God in Christ. Scripture's self-interest in the birth and sustaining of a people of faith, though, is also fulfilled in this retelling of the biblical story. For in naming God, we find ourselves named; in recounting the stories of the Bible, we discover ourselves in storied relation to them. Gregory Jones sums it up: "It is only when the story of God is told that Christians are able to have their identity disclosed to them."[90]

This curious dynamic seems to invert conventional notions of God and church. After all, do people not "join a church," become active in its programs, and assume some information about God as an eventual payoff? Perhaps. But observe, too, that at its best the church in welcoming the return of one of its many "baptized secularists" begins immediately the task of immersing that catechumen in the narratives of the biblical witness. Two assumptions relate to this interplay of discipleship and the biblical narrative. First, the church seeks to live out the intention of the Bible, namely that God's people continue the biblical story in the here and now. So as Kathryn Tanner states, the narrative character

of the Bible "leaves open—better, forces open—the material spec-
ifications of a distinctively Christian way of life."[91] Second, we
come to realize that a Christian hearing of Scripture is conditioned
by the character of the community within which the stories are
told. The issue of Tanner's "distinctively Christian way of life"
is of hermeneutic as well as ethical importance. That is, the Bible
intends a community equipped with virtues rendering it capable
of hearing the biblical Word and doing it. There is, then, a double
movement of the Christian community with regard to its biblical
narrative—on one hand, a calling in the stories inviting Christians
to become who they are; and on the other, a formative intending
so that those Christian people may truly hear the Word.

It is inevitable, then, that a narrative theology of the sort articulated by Hans Frei and others would push the hermeneutic
question in the direction of the character of the assembly and its
members. Yet again, a double movement is implied. Scripture's
self-interest is in the vitality of a distinctive community, the
church. In order for that community to embody Christian faith,
it will need to be formed by the stories of the Bible so that it can
rightly hear the biblical story. In other words, once we respond
to the cognitive and experiential-expressive models of doctrine
and interpretation with an approach claiming distinct primacy for
biblical narrative, the question of character necessarily is raised.
It is raised not only because human beings inevitably will be
formed by the narrativity of whatever community to which they
grant themselves, but also because the stories of the Bible point
to a particular community equipped with distinctive virtues—as
the appropriate context for a true hearing of its Word.

So within a hermeneutic shaped by the narrative considerations
of biblical faith, character and story go together. And the question
now confronts us directly: "How do stories play their role in the
formation of character in community?"[92] Richard Bondi answers
this question:

> Central to this formation is the impact of powerful stories
> with their accompanying symbols and visions of the good life.
> These touch our hearts in a way that provides an interpretive
> lens to view reasons for intentional actions to focus the af-
> fections and order the passions, to present virtues embodied

in lives, and to give a new angle of vision on our subjection to the accidents of history.[93]

Given this formative power of stories to render communal and personal virtues, the double movement of narrative interpretation points the question in another direction: What are those virtues needful for a faithful hearing of our stories? Although one's "short list" of these virtues or "capacities"[94] varies according to the pastoral situation (as is reflected in Paul's various listings in the epistles), four come to mind with respect to our special interests in proclamation:

Hospitality. The version of hospitality offered by late twentieth-century liberalism is argued on the basis of the need for inclusiveness in an age of pluralism. Yet as Diana L. Eck and Susan A. M. Shumaker have detected,[95] the notion of "pluralism" is not without its assumptions—assumptions typically found in the experiential-expressive model. Speaking of our cultural situation as one of "plurality," they contend that pluralism is one possible response by religious communities. The liberal argument, therefore, is really not *from* pluralism but to it, with most of that argument remaining unarticulated.

Looking into the life and mission of early Christianity, we find quite a different expression of hospitality in the face of a similarly diverse and pluralistic age. Connected to the biblical tradition through liturgy, sacraments, preaching, and catechesis, those Christians embodied the virtue of hospitality precisely as they proclaimed their particularity as God's new Israel. Their biblical narrative told of a God who named Israel as God's own and also who insisted that this covenant people extend hospitality to strangers, widows, and the poor. The early church was remarkably diverse in its expressions of piety, encouraged in that diversity by the multiple stories of Jesus contained in the Gospels. However, Christians in the early church also linked their hospitality to a discipline based upon the character of their story-formed community. So "inclusiveness" stopped short of baptizing officers in the military (who took an oath to Caesar as lord), participants or officials in the gladiatorial games, and most obviously "a heathen priest or anyone who tend[ed] idols."[96] Hippolytus added that sculptors and painters might be welcomed to the catechumenate only if they desisted from the making of idols.[97] The limits of hospitality involved issues of idolatry and split allegiance to authorities claiming ultimacy (Christ and Caesar). Given our present church situation, with our culture's suspicions of any claims of religious particularity, however, the main thrust of a recovered virtue of hospitality may well be that of welcoming once more the biblical story itself in all its richness and diversity into our life together.

Freedom. Given the spirit of the present age, "freedom of choice" would seem to be as ubiquitous to the human condition as a narrative quality. In fact, one of pluralism's central tenets is that persons come equipped with this capacity and may therefore freely select from among the religious values offered by this multicultural world. Biblical faith is much more subtle in its assessment of freedom, insisting that it is as much God's gift as is covenant itself. In fact, the two go together; individualism in whatever guise winds up as slavery. Freedom, in this view, "is not the starting point of the moral life, never its transcendental assumption," offers Richard Bondi.[98] And if freedom is found within Israel and the faithful gathered as Christ's body, then there will need to be an ongoing attending to the stories constitutive of covenant community.

Forgiveness. Discovering this narrative-based life in Christ as communal, with hospitality and freedom being central virtues, we should not be surprised to find our capacity for forgiveness being stretched once again. In an American church increasingly polarized along a "great fracture" between liberals and evangelicals, forgiveness has become a diminished virtue. Could it be, however, that such schismatic tendencies really derive from the loss of biblical narrative across the ecclesiastical scene? And if so, notice how we go about blending cultural notions of inclusiveness in the absence of particularity with an exclusiveness toward those claiming particularity. Ironically, the biblical virtues undercut any such *hubris.*

An insistence on the centrality of the virtue of forgiveness, moreover, offers a crucial perspective on the "grammar" of the entire "virtues-system." It is not the case, liberal attitudes to the contrary, that virtues float about in culture and religion as atomistic units, discreet in their meaning and their implications for praxis. Rather, in the words of Robert Roberts, "each virtue gets its character from the surrounding geography of concepts and practice—what I have called the virtues-system—to which it belongs."[99] Only one "amendment by addition" is needed with regard to Robert's definition: The concepts and practices of each virtues-system are located within a narrative-based tradition shared by some community or other. Therefore, it follows from this now expanded definition that a virtue will "mean" and be enacted differently as its geographic environs change.

The virtue of forgiveness becomes a choice test case of this claim. Roberts compares in some detail the commonalities and differences of the "therapeutic" notion of forgiveness and a "Christian" perspective on that virtue. Although forgiveness shares a number of points of overlap between the two virtues-systems, their *difference* is highlighted when the issue of motive is addressed. For the therapeutic model, "the characteristic motive for forgiving is the forgiver's desire to heal himself or herself of hatred."[100] A Christian construal of forgiveness, on the other hand, is grounded in what is "fitting," given the biblical narrative, the person and work of Jesus Christ, the nature of the church, and its eschatological vision. We are called to forgive because we have first received divine mercy through the cross of Christ, Paul would say. The grammar of the virtue of forgiveness, then, is not interchangeable in principle between various virtues-systems. Like other core virtues, its meaning and practice are disclosed within a particular systematic context.

The capacity of the heart. Character is intimately related to our capacity for memory. Our stories, and most centrally those of Scripture, both form us as persons and as a people and connect us to the character of our God. To speak of the capacity of the heart is, with Bondi, to locate through this biblical image that place within us that remembers, hopes, intends, and imagines. Without a robust capacity of the heart, we are cut off from our storied tradition and from a future we imagine as its fulfillment. Lacking "heart," the community must adopt alien means to bind itself together, such as ideology or simply the banal appeal to institutional loyalty.

More critically, without "heart" and its capacity for memory, the sense of the character of God grows vague since God's presence in Christ is to be found in the stories and their signs (a prototype meaning of "sacrament"). The loss of heart for Christians becomes experienced as a loss of God. To announce the death of God, then, is most bluntly to speak of the church's loss of its biblical narrative, its storied tradition; in short, it is to talk about its grave sickness of heart. After all, "narrative," Stanley Hauerwas reminds us, "is but a reminder that the church is a community that lives by memory."[101]

The response to such a condition is clear. Since "stories beckon the heart," our task becomes that of exercising personal and communal memory through those means commended by the tradition as central to character formation. We are invited once again into our narrative home when the assembly attends to its liturgical and sacramental life as the Scriptures are read and proclaimed.

From this perspective, the worship of the church is the vital "aerobics class" for the Christian virtues. Much in the way God's miracles always surprise, the Second Vatican Council gave much of the Western church a three-year lectionary that recovers a wonderfully enlarged portion of the biblical narrative. (Who would have predicted that Rome would speak the prophetic word to all of us that the Scriptures must be opened more lavishly to the people?)[102] And now, with many of our communities of faith blessed with reformed liturgies and the vigorously aerobic ecumenical lectionary, the challenge for those of us called to preach is the biblical narrative that the capacity of heart is rekindled and once more burns brightly. "The preached Word's power," Hauerwas notes, "is its capacity to create a people receptive to being formed by that Word."

To maintain that preaching the biblical narrative in the midst of the congregation has formative power is to invoke the capability of stories to beckon the heart. Moreover, the forthcoming explorations of the role of imagination in relation to story and communal and personal formation significantly will enhance this sense of beckoning. Still, biblical narrative's power to evoke the character of Christian faith is not, again, self-referential. (We are formed by the narrative; we must be formed in order to rightly hear the Bible's stories.) Just as "it is not the preacher who makes the sermon efficacious,"[103] so it is not merely a retelling of the stories of Scripture that *ex opere operato* form us as church. When Ellingsen proposes that "questions of truth, relevance, and modern meaning will take care of themselves because these (biblical) stories have a way of transforming the lives of those who hear them,"[104] he articulates one half of the equation. Narrative hermeneutics inevitably involves a lively doctrine of the Holy Spirit—the other half of the equation. A dual epiclesis resides at the heart of narrative interpretation and homiletics. The work of the Spirit, with Calvin, renders Scripture as God's Word to us, while the same Spirit "must make us a body of people capable of hearing that Word rightly."[105] A narrative construal of the Bible that claims primacy for that story's world necessarily elevates the work of the Holy Spirit in the church's work of interpretation, its sacramental life, its preaching, its community-in-Spirit, and its mission in the world.

"These Things" Are True

The "*tauta*" referred to at the conclusion of John's story of Jesus (21:24), as Barrett notes, "may refer to the last paragraph (vv. 15-23), to ch. 21, or more probably to the entire gospel."[106] "These things," then, will include all the narratives, signs, and discourses comprising the Gospel. In a broader scope, I have argued that the *tauta* refer to all of Scripture, the biblical narrative in all its diverse wholeness. To speak of these things being true, however, is now being raised afresh, because the modern notion of truth as delimited to historical reference is of diminishing "purchase" in a postliberal age. Preachers and congregations increasingly will not be searching behind the text for some "world" within which original meaning may be found. Even more so, homilists and assemblies will not be "solving" the problem of the truth of Scripture by reinterpreting the text on behalf of some external and universal human experience, mythos, or ideology. Therefore, if we rightly resist framing the question of narrative truth within either a cognitive or experiential-expressive model, what are the options within one that is "cultural-linguistic?" From the perspective of narrative theology, how are "these things" true? Or as Garrett Green puts the question, "Granted that storytelling is basic to religion generally, and more specifically that biblical narrative is crucial to Christian faith, are the stories true?"[107] Several alternative responses present themselves:

1. Narratives may be "meaningful" but never "true," since the world they offer is ultimately unfollowable.

2. Biblical stories are nonfictional realistic narratives that have the capacity to overwhelm the hearer with their truth.

3. The truth of Scripture is to be evaluated with reference to the character of the community it projects into the here and now.

4. Truth of these meaningful biblical stories is configurational/intratextual. The question becomes the usefulness of the entire Christian paradigm for interpreting self, God, and world.[108]

The first position is championed most forcefully by Frank Kermode in *The Genesis of Secrecy*.[109] Presenting his argument chiefly through an analysis of Mark's Gospel, Kermode centers on the "insider-outsider" landscape of Mark 4:10-12. Then, as Amos Wilder observes, this motif, with its recurring sense of the enigmatic, is extended "first in the parables and later more generally in Mark as a whole, with special attention to its baffling conclusion at 16:8."[110] Finally, even the insiders, the disciples, disclose their stance within the enigmatic "outside." They fail to grasp the "spiritual sense" of the narrative, abandon Jesus, and flee in panic and confusion. In so doing, these ostensible insiders become signs "that all narratives are essentially dark."[111] Ultimately we are never *inside* any narrative and "from the outside may never experience anything more than some radiant intimation of the source of all these senses."[112]

In the second option, the focus is not on some "radiant intimation" of truth, but on the followable world of biblical narrative. Within such a literary genre as "realistic narrative," to frame the question of truth as historical reference is either of secondary concern only (Ellingsen) or is dismissed as methodologically fallacious (Peterson).[113] The uniqueness and particularity of the narrative of the Bible, though, is based on its capacity to disclose a world and render the character of God. Questions of truth, as Ellingsen insists, "take care of themselves" as this "true," non-fictional world is preached.[114]

The third alternative—offered most forcefully by Stanley Hauerwas—shares with the previous position an interpretation of Scripture as realistic narrative. In fact, the fundamental logic of a character-based Christian ethics is that the truthful stories of the Bible inevitably evoke a community which then interprets the world according to that truth and is, moreover, shaped by that narrative. The payoff is once more expressed within a hermeneutic interplay between text and community—the formative power of Scripture is manifest in its capability of sustaining a community of faith and truthfulness. Conversely, the question of what distinctive virtues the community in Christ needs to embody relates directly to such a people's ability rightly to welcome, understand, and enact the biblical witness. Either way, the truth-value of Scripture expresses itself within the Christian community: "What is crucial," Hauerwas insists, "is not that Christians know the truth, but that they be the truth."[115] The truth they are to be *is* the truth of the Bible's narrative!

The fourth approach to scriptural truth agrees with Hans Frei that Scripture constitutes a world that depicts the character of God, locating the issue of narrative truth, however, more within the patterns of reality Christians are formed to envision. Truth is a paradigmatic issue, in which the question of contextualization is critical. Christians can, and do, with Lindbeck, speak of the truth of Scripture within a cultural-linguistic world shaped by the faithful retelling of those texts. However, we are not left here with a narrow circularity. As William Placher observes, narrative truth cannot be restricted to the grammatical rules of conversation by the church with "other communities, other rules—and no ontological claims, one way or the other."[116] Rather, the community of faith insists on truth claims of various sorts for its biblical world. Placher summarizes these as:

> (1) Christians believe that no subsequent experience will refute the essential pattern we as Christians see in things.
> (2) We believe that the patterns of which Christians now catch a glimpse will ultimately be perspicacious to all.

(3) Mysterious as all talk of God is, we believe that our
actions in faith respond to prior acts of God, and therefore
talk of God cannot be interpreted without remainder as a way
of talking about human thoughts or practices.[117]

Given the latter approach, with its insight into the "patterned
world" within which believers live, the decisive role of biblical
narrative is retained with Frei and Ellingsen. And while Placher
is cautious about rendering the truthfulness of biblical narrative
within the context of the truth-telling of Christian community,
still, the virtues Hauerwas elevates do seem essential to a right
reading of Scripture.[118] Also, this "configurational" approach to
narrative truth allows for Kermode's categories of "insider" and
"outsider." Insiders, though, having been formed by the biblical
Word, are graced with the capacity to interpret God, self, and world
within the context of a vision formed by that Word. In so doing,
we must agree with Thiemann and argue against Kermode that
"biblical narratives do illumine a followable world for the readers of scriptural texts."[119] However, I hasten to add with
Thiemann that

> in so responding, the faithful reader becomes a disciple who
> acknowledges that the chief character in the stories (and the
> one who issues the invitation to faith and discipleship) is
> God. Such acceptance may appear to be a futile act based
> upon an implausible claim, particularly since God is rarely
> depicted in the stories and almost never engages the reader
> in direct address. I want to argue instead that the claim is
> ironic but true. Precisely in upsetting our expectations about
> how a god ought to be revealed, the stories introduce readers
> to Yahweh, God of promise who has raised Jesus from the
> dead.[120]

It is as disciples that we are given the ability to follow this
narrative world of Scripture. Moreover, we are beginning to
appreciate that this narrative world is a highly imaginative
construct. In this regard, our journey through the followable
world of the biblical story finds us eventually at the threshold
of the house of the image and an exploration of the theories of
imagination.

Notes

1. Walter Brueggemann, *Genesis, Interpretation: A Bible Commentary for Teaching and Preaching* (Atlanta: John Knox Press, 1982), 22.
2. Ibid., 24.
3. See Wesley A. Kort, *Narrative Elements and Religious Meaning* (Philadelphia: Fortress Press, 1975).
4. This distinction is taken with gratitude from Eugene L. Lowry, *How to Preach a Parable: Designs for Narrative Sermons* (Nashville: Abingdon Press, 1989), 25.
5. Stephen Crites, "The Narrative Quality of Experience," *Journal of the American Academy of Religion* 39 (September 1971): 291. Hereafter cited in the text.
6. David Kelsey, "Biblical Narrative and Theological Anthropology," in *Scriptural Authority and Narrative Interpretation*, ed. Garrett Green (Philadelphia: Fortress Press, 1987), 122. See 122–23 and 131–33 for a careful analysis of Crites' "foundationist" type of narrative anthropology.
7. Ibid., 123.
8. Crites, "Experience," 303.
9. Eugene Lowry, *Doing Time in the Pulpit: The Relationship between Narrative and Preaching* (Nashville: Abingdon Press, 1985), 8.
10. See ibid., 11–28, for a detailed analysis of the homiletic alternatives of building ideas or shaping experience in preaching.
11. Crites, "Experience," 297.
12. Terrence W. Tilley, *Story Theology* (Wilmington, Del.: Michael Glazier, 1985), 23–26.
13. Ibid., 25–26.
14. Charles Rice's image in "Shaping Sermons by the Interplay of Text and Metaphor," in *Creating Sermons in the Shape of Scripture*, ed. Don M. Wardlaw (Philadelphia: Westminster Press, 1983), 104–105. Of course, to "ferry across" is the root meaning of "metaphor."
15. Charles Rice, "Just Church Bells? One Man's View of Preaching Today," *The Drew Gateway* 49 (Spring 1979): 25.
16. Ibid., 25.
17. Lowry, *Doing Time*, 39.
18. David Buttrick, *Homiletic: Moves and Structures* (Philadelphia: Fortress Press, 1987). See especially 285–303 on plots and intentionality.
19. Mark Ellingsen, *The Integrity of Biblical Narrative: Story in Theology and Proclamation* (Minneapolis: Fortress Press, 1990), 56.
20. Ibid.
21. Ibid. Ellingsen argues that what holds the biblical stories and secular stories together for a number of scholars including Buttrick "can only be a common flow in the action they narrate, common structures."
22. L. Gregory Jones, "Alasdair MacIntyre on Narrative, Community, and the Moral Life," *Modern Theology* 4 (October 1987): 58. Jones directs

this critique at MacIntrye, but it is equally applicable to the story homileticians and preachers to the extent that both parties share Crites'
"narrative quality" foundational claim while asserting the particularity
of Christian truth claims.

23. Ibid.

24. Ibid., 59.

25. Ibid., 55.

26. Argued from a different perspective, rather than focusing on the
narrative quality of experience, process thinkers argue the adequacy of
stressing this "temporal structure of human experience." Leslie A. Muray,
"Confessional Postmodernism and the Process-Relational Vision," *Process Studies* 18 (Summer 1989). Muray is arguing against the position of
Stanley Hauerwas, which he reads (erroneously, I believe) as based on
Crites' "narrative quality" foundation. See Charles Pinches, "Hauerwas
Represented: A Response to Muray," *Process Studies* 18, (Summer
1989): 95–101.

27. George A. Lindbeck, *The Nature of Doctrine in a Postliberal Age*
(Philadelphia: Westminster Press, 1984), 16.

28. David Buttrick's term. See my *"Homiletic:* A Hermeneutic Review" in *Reformed Liturgy and Worship* 22 (Winter 1988): 45–47. Buttrick characterizes this approach to biblical texts as assuming "(1) that
content can be separated from words, (2) that content can be translated
from one time-language to another without alteration, and (3) that such
content can be grasped as an objective truth apart from particular datable
words" (*Homiletic,* 265).

29. Adolf Jülicher, *Die Gleichnisreden Jesu,* 2 vols. (Darmstadt: Wis-
senschaftliche Buchgesellschaft, 1899).

30. Bernard Brandon Scott, *Hear Then the Parable: A Commentary
on the Parables of Jesus* (Minneapolis: Fortress Press, 1989), 42–43. See
my "Preaching the Parables and the Main Idea," *Perkins Theological
School Journal* 36 (Fall 1983): 22–32; and David G. Buttrick, "On Preaching the Parables: The Problem of Homiletic Method," *Reformed Liturgy
and Music* 17 (Winter 1983): 16–22.

31. Amos Wilder, *The Language of the Gospel: Early Christian Rhetoric* (Cambridge, Mass.: Harvard Univ. Press, 1971).

32. Robert W. Funk, *Language, Hermeneutics, and the Word of God*
(New York: Harper & Row, 1966).

33. Lindbeck, *Doctrine,* 16.

34. Hans Frei, " 'Literal Reading' of Biblical Narrative in Christian
Tradition," in *The Bible and the Narrative Tradition,* ed. Frank Mc-
Connell (New York: Oxford Univ. Press, 1986), 61.

35. See Joseph Campbell, *The Hero with a Thousand Faces* (Princeton,
N.J.: Princeton Univ. Press, 1968); *idem, The Masks of God: Creative
Mythology* (New York: Viking Press, 1968); *idem* with Bill Moyers, *The
Power of Myth* (New York: Doubleday, 1988).

36. Quite appropriately, then, Robert A. Segal detects how myth functions as a "collective Bible for all humanity" for Campbell. Segal adds, "Dreams, ritual, art, literature, ideology and science become *varieties* of myth rather than *alternatives* to it" (in "The Romanticism of Joseph Campbell," *The Christian Century* 107 [April 4, 1990]: 333). Also see Segal's "Joseph Campbell's Antithesis: Myth Versus Religion," in *The Joseph Campbell Phenomenon: Implications for the Contemporary Church*, ed. Lawrence Madden (Washington, D.C.: The Pastoral Press, 1992), 41–55.

37. Robert Bellah, "Civil Religion in America," *Daedalus* 96 (Winter 1967): 1–21. See also Bellah's *The Broken Covenant: American Civil Religion in Time of Trial* (Chicago: Univ. of Chicago Press, 1992).

38. See my "Civil Religion and the Year of Grace," *Worship* 58 (July 1984): 372–83.

39. David Buttrick, *The Mystery and the Passion: A Homiletic Reading of the Gospel Traditions* (Minneapolis: Fortress Press, 1992). See, e.g., Buttrick's analysis "The Dangers of Preaching the Gospel," 50–52.

40. One excellent survey of "the spiritual and religious dimensions of contemporary American culture" is William D. Dinges, "Joseph Campbell and the Contemporary American Spiritual Milieu," in *The Joseph Campbell Phenomenon*, 9–40.

41. Lindbeck, *Doctrine*, 22.

42. See, e.g., Fred Herzog, *God-Walk: Liberation Shaping Dogmatics* (Maryknoll, N.Y.: Orbis Books, 1988). Herzog assigns to Marxism the "grace" to articulate class struggle as the driving force in history (211ff.).

43. Michael Root, "The Narrative Structure of Soteriology," *Modern Theology* 2 (January 1986): 147.

44. Pinches, "A Response," 98.

45. Ibid., 98.

46. Charles M. Wood, "Hermeneutics and the Authority of Scripture," in *Scriptural Authority and Narrative Interpretation*, ed. Garrett Green (Philadelphia: Fortress Press, 1987), 7. See Elisabeth Schüssler Fiorenza, *Bread Not Stone: The Challenge of Feminist Biblical Interpretation* (Boston: Beacon Press, 1984), 61ff.

47. Lindbeck, *Doctrine*, 23.

48. Stanley Hauerwas and L. Gregory Jones, "Seeking a Clear Alternative to Liberalism," review of George A. Lindbeck, *The Nature of Doctrine: Religion and Theology in a Postliberal Age*, in *Books and Religion* 13 (January/February 1985): 7.

49. David Buttrick, "Interpretation and Preaching," *Interpretation: A Journal of Bible and Theology* 35 (January 1981): 47.

50. William C. Placher, "Paul Ricoeur and Postliberal Theology: A Conflict of Interpretations?" *Modern Theology* 4 (October 1987): 37.

51. Hans Frei, *The Eclipse of Biblical Narrative: A Study in Eighteenth and Nineteenth Century Hermeneutics* (New Haven: Yale Univ. Press, 1974).

52. Lindbeck, *Doctrine*, 18.

53. Ibid., 33.

54. Placher, "Ricoeur," 37.

55. Ibid., 38. Placher lists as the three theses of a Frei-Lindbeck position the first two presented here along with that of the primacy of language as creating the possibility of human experience. Since that assertion has been developed here in some detail, my third thesis becomes the insistence by Hauerwas and others on the ecclesial context as primary for an appropriate interpretation of Scripture.

56. See, e.g., Robert Alter, *The Art of Biblical Narrative* (New York: Basic Books, 1981), and Meir Sternberg, *The Poetics of Biblical Narrative: Ideological Literature and the Drama of Reading* (Bloomington, Ind.: Indiana Univ. Press, 1987), for two excellent studies of narrative in the Hebrew Scripture. For a comprehensive list of such studies, see the bibliography in Mark Allan Powell, *What Is Narrative Criticism?* (Minneapolis: Fortress Press, 1990), 124–25.

57. John C. Holbert, *Preaching the Old Testament: Proclamation and Narrative in the Hebrew Bible* (Nashville: Abingdon Press, 1991), 21.

58. Ellingsen, *Integrity*, 22.

59. Interestingly, proverbs and apocalyptic would seem to occupy a polar relationship to each other regarding the intention of their respective rhetorical strategies. The former, the proverbs, "are the product of a culture in equilibrium, while the latter along with prophecy "are the literary genres of crisis" (Thomas G. Long, *Preaching and the Literary Forms of the Bible* [Philadelphia: Fortress Press, 1989], 58).

60. So Roland Murphy writes that "the wisdom heritage is international. While Israel gives it an Israelite home and expression, she keeps it separate from the historical traditions" (*Wisdom Literature and Psalms* [Nashville: Abingdon Press, 1983], 26).

61. William Beardslee, "Uses of the Proverb in the Synoptic Gospels, *Interpretation* 24 (January 1970): 65. I am indebted to Alyce McKenzie for her helpfulness in locating Beardslee's insights on the implications of the proverbs for a narrative construal of Scripture.

62. Beardslee, "Uses," 67.

63. Ricoeur, *Biblical Hermeneutics*, 112.

64. Ibid., 110.

65. Thiemann, *Revelation*, 83.

66. See Erich Auerbach's magisterial *Mimesis: The Representation of Reality in Western Literature* (Princeton: Princeton Univ. Press, 1953).

67. Ellingsen, *Integrity*, 20.

68. Ibid., 20–21.

Our Home in the Narrative 43

69. Garrett Green, "Fictional Narrative and Scriptural Truth," in *Scriptural Authority and Narrative Interpretation*, ed. Garrett Green (Philadelphia: Fortress Press, 1987), 80. See also Norman R. Peterson, *Literary Criticism for New Testament Critics* (Philadelphia: Fortress Press, 1978), 39–40, for a discussion of this "referential fallacy."

70. Frei, *Eclipse*, 2–16.

71. Hans Frei, " 'Literal Reading' of Biblical Narrative in Christian Tradition," in *The Bible and the Narrative Tradition*, ed. Frank McConnell (New York: Oxford Univ. Press, 1986), 66.

72. Frei, " 'Literal Reading,' " 72.

73. Ellingsen, *Integrity*, 21.

74. Thiemann, *Revelation*, 84–85.

75. Root, "Soteriology," 147.

76. Ellingsen, *Integrity*, 37.

77. Lindbeck, *Doctrine*, p. 117. William C. Placher notes that the patterning of this Christian interpretive perspective tends to play out in one of two ways corresponding to "the traditional theological ideas of typology and the history of salvation" (*Unapologetic Theology: A Christian Voice in a Pluralistic Conversation* [Louisville, Ky.: Westminster/John Knox Press, 1989], 126–27).

78. Root, "Soteriology," 147.

79. Walter Brueggemann, "The Social Nature of the Biblical Text for Preaching," in *Preaching as a Social Act: Theology and Practice*, ed. Art Van Seters (Nashville: Abingdon Press, 1988), 130. Brueggemann observes that "there is no textual activity that is not linked with a vested interest. . . . We know, for example, that the early community around Moses authorized certain texts that served the interest of liberation" (130).

80. Lindbeck states that "intratextual theology redescribes reality within the scriptural framework rather than translating Scripture into extrascriptural categories. It is the text, so to speak, which absorbs the world rather than the world the text." (*Doctrine*, 118).

81. Stanley Hauerwas, "The Church as God's New Language," in *Scriptural Authority and Narrative Interpretation*, ed. Garrett Green (Philadelphia: Fortress Press, 1987), 193.

82. Hauerwas, "God's New Language," 192. John S. McClure interprets the narrative theologians as offering an intratextual world "limited to a way of recalling and the world-in-consciousness that it intends." He concludes that "the language of recall cannot get beyond itself" (*The Four Codes of Preaching: Rhetorical Strategies* [Minneapolis: Fortress Press, 1991], 33–34). While this critique may apply to Ellingsen, the notion of the church as subject within the context of narrative interpretation—with Frei and Hauerwas—serves to liberate the narrative world of Scripture from a self-referential circularity.

83. Hauerwas, "God's New Language," 192.

84. Lindbeck, *Doctrine*, 121.

85. Alter, *Biblical Narrative*, 157.

86. Powell, *What Is Narrative Criticism?* 26.

87. Thiemann, *Revelation*, 88. See Thiemann, 88–91, for a fine analysis of biblical narrative's strategies for rendering the character of God, albeit with both presence and hiddenness.

88. Ibid., 89.

89. Ibid.

90. Jones, "MacIntyre," 60.

91. Kathryn Tanner, "Theology and the Plain Sense," in *Scriptural Authority and Narrative Interpretation*, ed. Garrett Green (Philadelphia: Fortress Press, 1987), 74.

92. Richard Bondi, "The Elements of Character," *The Journal of Religious Ethics* 12 (Fall 1984): 201.

93. Bondi, "Elements," 212.

94. Bondi selects the term "capacity" as "the powers and abilities which are common to all human beings, but which are realized only in their exercise" ("Elements," 205).

95. Diana L. Eck and Susan A. M. Shumaker, "The Pluralism Project: A Preliminary Report," *Bulletin of the Council of Societies for the Study of Religion* 21 (April 1992): 35.

96. *The Apostolic Tradition of Hippolytus*, trans. Burton Scott Easton (Cambridge, England: Cambridge Univ. Press, 1934), 42.

97. Ibid.

98. Bondi, "Elements," 212.

99. See Robert C. Roberts, "The Grammar of Virtue," in *The Grammar of the Heart: New Essays in Moral Philosophy and Theology*, ed. Richard H. Bell, (San Francisco: Harper & Row, 1988), 149–70.

100. Ibid., 155.

101. Hauerwas, "God's New Language," 190.

102. "Constitution on the Sacred Liturgy," in *Vatican Council II: The Conciliar and Post Conciliar Documents*, ed. Austin Flannery, O.P., new rev. ed. (Collegeville, Minn.: The Liturgical Press, 1988), 3.A.24 and 3.C.35 (1), 10 and 12.

103. Hauerwas, "God's New Language," 192.

104. Ellingsen, *Integrity*, 28.

105. Hauerwas, "God's New Language," 193. Mark Allen Powell adds that "since revelation is considered to be an event that happens now, through an interaction of the reader and the text, an active role for the Spirit is crucial to the process of interpretation" (*Narrative Criticism?* 88).

106. C. K. Barrett, *The Gospel according to St. John: An Introduction with Commentary and Notes on the Greek Text* (London: S.P.C.K., 1962), 489.

107. Green, "Fictional Narrative and Scriptural Truth," 79.

108. Dissatisfied with the alternatives presented by Crites and Hauerwas, Julian Hartt argues for the "fact-assertive (assertoric)" dimension of narrative truth. By its assertorical character, Hartt means first that certain biblical narratives claim a historical truth and second, that the faith presented through those narratives is ontologically true ("Theological Investments in Story: Some Comments on Recent Developments and Some Proposals," *Why Narrative? Readings in Narrative Theology*, 283). See 279–319 for this conversation on narrative truth between Hartt, Crites, and Hauerwas.

109. Frank Kermode, *The Genesis of Secrecy: On the Interpretation of Narrative* (Cambridge, Mass.: Harvard Univ. Press, 1979).

110. Amos Wilder, "The Gospels as Narrative," review of *The Genesis of Secrecy* in *Interpretation: A Journal of Bible and Theology* 35 (July 1980): 297.

111. Kermode, *Secrecy*, 45.

112. Ibid. Amos Wilder questions whether Kermode can generalize from the enigmatic character of such motifs as Mark 4:10–12 "to confirm the opaqueness of the Gospel as a whole." Wilder concludes that such texts "should not be made a paradigm for the Gospel as a whole" ("Gospels as Narrative," 298).

113. See Norman R. Peterson, *Literary Criticism*, 38–40, for a discussion of Umberto Eco's notion of the "referential fallacy" within the context of Roman Jakobson's communications model.

114. Ellingsen, *Integrity*, 28. See 40–41 for his argument for the truth of the claims of the gospel within a narrative model of interpretation.

115. Stanley Hauerwas, *A Community of Character: Toward a Constructive Christian Social Ethic* (Notre Dame, Ind.: Univ. of Notre Dame Press, 1981), 150. William Placher queries whether "a people's willingness to bear the burden of the story with joy somehow makes the story itself true, as well as making this particular telling of the story morally appropriate. That seems to me to confuse completely different issues" (*Unapologetic Theology*, 172).

116. Placher, *Unapologetic Theology*, 165–66.

117. Ibid., 166.

118. Perhaps Hauerwas's clearest exposition of his notion of the relationship between narrative truth and the character of communities formed by such truth-telling (or untruth-telling) is located within his treatment of Richard Adam's narrative, *Watership Down*. Here, the author's depiction of the various rabbit communities "suggests that they are to be judged primarily by their ability to sustain the narratives that define the very nature of man, or in this case rabbits" (*Character*, 12).

119. Ronald F. Thiemann, "Radiance and Obscurity in Biblical Narrative," in *Scriptural Authority and Narrative Interpretation*, ed. Garrett Green (Philadelphia: Fortress Press, 1987), 25.

120. Ibid., 31.

2

The House of Imagination

Images have become ubiquitous in American culture. The observation may seem so self-evident as to be superfluous in a culture overwhelmed by the visual media, especially in their advertising modes. People are swamped by imagery these days, long since gone into "sensory overload" in households defined by television commercials, CNN and MTV,[1] and video games. No wonder preachers have been muttering lately about the inadequacy of their craft, limited so thoroughly to words, in the face of this culture's addiction to images.

Now with all of the above in mind, we turn to the academy and discover within a multitude of disciplines a growing interest in imagery, its function, and its interpretive foundations. (We also discover that these disciplines are not yet much engaged in a "cross-cultural" conversation with each other.) Liturgical scholars for some time now have been exploring the images attendant to liturgical texts and actions, reaping an early harvest of important insights. For example, a number of liturgical theologians have critiqued the architectural settings for the assembly's worship, and in the way of reform suggested that the focal images of liturgical space need to be derived from what the assembly does. Therefore, these focal images become font, Table, pulpit or ambo, and in catholic practice, the chair for the presider. Moreover, imagery located within the context of communal prayer and praise is being explored for its biblical, pastoral, and liturgical implications. Images, Gordon Lathrop observes, have a yes-no-yes dynamic about them.[2] They emerge within the life of the biblical people and come to gain normative status. Then historical events overtake the image and act to contradict it; in the experience of the exile there is a profound no to Israel's image of God as a rock, to select an obvious example. Then, for the New Testament church, that image is reappropriated with an Easter yes. "The stone which the builders rejected has become the cornerstone. Alleluia!" rings the Easter antiphon. There is similar interest in such explorations of imagery within other, related theological disciplines such as pastoral counseling and spiritual formation. We are also struck by the findings and controversies concerning imagery in fields outside the arena of theological studies.

The Image as Mental Image

The history of the image within the field of psychology manifests its own kind of yes-no-yes dynamic. Early psychologists began their explorations into the working of the mind with a considerable intellectual heritage regarding the status and function of mental imagery. In the philosophical movements most influential to the beginnings of modern psychology, David Hume and Immanuel Kant had vested in the image a crucial role in the achievements of human knowledge and memory. Here

> we saw a developing account of imagination as that which functions both in the presence of an object of perception in the world, and in its absence, when we turn to it in our thoughts. Imagination both presents and represents things to us. Its power is the power of forming images, which may be used as the means of interpreting what is before our eyes and ears in the perceptual world, or as *constituting* our interpreted world, when we are separated from the actual objects of which our images *are* the images.[3]

Linked to perception, images-in-mind are the product of imagination and provide the capacity of recognition—that *this* dog is a dog—and of imagining any dog in the absence of that object of perception.

Closely related to the suggestions of Hume and Kant are the explorations of image and imagination by Coleridge and Wordsworth, both in their poetry and in their commentaries on aesthetics and poetic creativity. Along with their philosophic colleagues, Coleridge and Wordsworth assign to imagination as its primary role the creation of images. And with Hume and Kant, the Romantics locate this image-making function as essential to recognition, memory, and recall. Poetic imagination represents a more intense expression of precisely the same capabilities that are exercised in other, more mundane aspects of human existence. Moreover, in the evoking of images often a powerful surge of feeling is released; there is an affective side to imagination's work. So Coleridge describes the poet as gifted with a livelier sensibility than other persons. The poet possesses

> a disposition to be affected more than other men by absent things as if they were present; an ability of conjuring up in himself passions which . . . do more nearly resemble the passions produced by real events than anything which, from the motions of their own mind merely, other men are accustomed to feel in themselves.[4]

If gifted poets are capable of evoking these sensibilities and passions, it is chiefly because others still retain less brilliant memories of their experiences. This perspective on imagination, construing images as a kind of faded perception, therefore, has come to dominate much of what constitutes the "conventional wisdom" concerning the imagination throughout the modern era.

Another aspect of imagination's work celebrated by Wordsworth and Coleridge also becomes deeply intrenched in modern imagination theory, particularly in the development of the notion of homiletic imagination. This is the view that images that have not had their origin in an act of perception are grasped by a lively imagination. These sublime images are grasped by the vivid imagination of the poet "whether these are now perceived or have been perceived in the past."[5] In other words, there is a subjective achievement of imagination to bring to mind things and feelings not previously brought to mind by perception. In fact, much will be made of the imagination's ability to evoke situations that transcend our normal perceptual experience. Imagination for the Romantics, then, has an objective and a subjective component. The former relates to imagination's power to "bring near" objects of perception in the way of memory or recall. The latter, subjective component has the distinctive capability of presenting to mind those sublime things and feelings that mundane perception can never present to us alone.[6] Here images that perception itself is incapable of rendering present or bringing near are brought to mind through poetics (or preaching).

A vigorous no to any notion of mental imagery, however, was chorused from two camps early in this century. On one hand, phenomenologists after Brentano opposed models of perception in which presuppositions regarding any kind of "pure" phenomena can be conceived (such as sublime mental images). Instead, Husserl, Merleau-Ponty, and others insisted that perceptions be considered as they occur, and in so doing they found no need for any objective-subjective dichotomy. With the collapse of the Cartesian dualism in epistemology, the need for any mental imagery mediating the two was also rendered null and void. Imagery's supposed role of mediation between an objective out-there world and a mental in-here world becomes superfluous within a phenomenological model of perceiving and knowing. Images are no longer needed conceptually to grasp the perceived object, nor are they necessary to mediate to consciousness any object in its absence. Speaking for the entire movement, Gilbert Ryle simply rejects any need for the notion of mental imagery. Rather, Ryle likens images to "stage murders," which wind up having neither murders nor victims, adding that "seeing things in one's mind's eye does not involve either the existence of things seen, or the occurrence of acts of seeing them."[7] So while we may continue to insist that images do in fact pop into consciousness, whether intentionally recalled, fantasized, or dreamed, the phenomenologists may or may not dispute the validity of our claims (Ryle would). What is emphatically denied, however, is any epistemological significance to what it is we may or may not be "seeing."

The other camp of modern "naysayers" to the notion of the mental image came to include most all of those engaged in experimental psychology. An initial stage of psychology in the late nineteenth century looked with interest on the experience of mental imagery, especially in the pioneering work of Wilhelm Wundt (1832–1920). Adapting a method of introspection, "followers of Wundt probed their own internal imagery and painstakingly analyzed self-reports by their trained subjects."[8] But as Gardner adds,

in a little over twenty-five years after these investigations, the
fortunes of mental imagery plummeted to the depths. Now,

> the more ephemeral and less reliable aspects of imagery were
> underlined. Not everyone had images, it turned out, and those
> who did introspected about them in different ways. There
> was no reliable way to define imagery in an experimental
> situation, no agreement about what should count as an im-
> agistic or imaginary experience. . . . For such reasons, the
> ghostly image was exorcised for half a century from respect-
> able academic psychology.[9]

It is only within the last two decades that a resurgence of
interest in mental imagery has occurred within experimental psychology. Impelled by Stephen Kosslyn's[10] carefully detailed work
of investigating mental processing of shapes and forms, the conclusion was drawn that persons do indeed have something like
"pictures in their heads" when asked to analyze problems in spatially based mapping and shifts in perspective of geometric models.
Kosslyn discovered that the time subjects needed to "travel" along
routes on a mental map varied directly in proportion to the "distances" involved in that mapping. Also, a direct correlation was
discovered between the degrees of tilt of geometric forms and the
time subjects needed to identify them with reference to a pre-
established model.[11] The conclusion became inescapable for these
researchers; there must exist some kind of a " 'quasi-pictorial'
form of mental representation called 'imagery.' "[12] This new yes
to mental imagery has turned up some fascinating insights into
the way the brain functions as images come to mind. Apparently
two distinctive cortical networks are involved in the work of
mental imaging, a spatial network plus one serving to provide
such visual information as color, texture, and shading. Contrary
to conventional wisdom here, these cortical networks are largely
found in the *left* brain![13]

Image as Insight

The question of imagery for theology and interpretation cannot
be limited to the various findings on mental imagery by research

psychologists. Rather, our investigations—keeping the former debates in mind—will need to reach most fully into the social and communal world within which images are encountered. Moreover, this interest in imagery will relate as well to its formative power in the "construction" of such social worlds. Christian proclamation addresses the gospel to these worlds and therefore must learn of imagery's formative function in a social and communal context; we will therefore attend as well to their function in the sermon. Already identified is the way in which life in Christian community abounds in imagery evoked by the narratives of the faith. Consequently, preachers will need to attend to the formative power of the image within a community of faith, its tradition, and its view of God, self, and world. Fortunately, a useful pathway into this personal and social world of imagery is available in the form of Margaret Miles' volume, *Image as Insight*.[14] In this book and in the conversations it has evoked, we have a *cursillo* on imagery.[15] It is to this "short course," now, that we must attend.

Miles initiates her exploration of the image by observing that our access to historical communities and individuals has largely been through an analysis of textual evidence alone. What has been missing is a balanced usage of both "verbal and visual texts," a balance needed so that they may serve "to illuminate, to correct, and to supplement the impressions we get from each."[16] Attending only to verbal texts (literary documents) biases historical investigation in several critical ways. First, it gives precedence to the views and analyses of "language users," an observation which at first glance appears to be a tautology. Then Miles shifts her readers' attention to the vast majority of historical persons who were "nonlanguage users." Related to this distinction is the gender issue. It is the case that in Western Christianity, the vast majority of language users have been men while women comprise the bulk of the nonlanguage users. On the contrary, Miles adds, the by far largest group "whose history can be approached by using visual images in addition to verbal texts is women" (10). She considers, therefore, that "the use of visual images as historical evidence promises to provide a range and depth of material for women's history that is simply unavailable in verbal texts, the great majority of which were neither written by nor read by historical women" (10).

Miles' analysis of the historical situation in the Western church yields several dichotomies aligned along two trajectories. Males historically have been language users, writing and reading texts, and therefore maintaining themselves in a privileged position both in their particular social and ecclesial situations as well as in historical scholarship. Women historically are to be found mostly among nonlanguage users who nevertheless have a distinctive capability to relate to "visual texts" and, in fact, are found depicted in abundance within the visual texts of each era. The fact—acknowledged by Miles—that such visual texts were for the most part sponsored by and created by men within the tradition does not void the programmatic duality of her project. There exists inevitably a distinction between the message given in text or image and the message received. "We will 'read' images," Miles insists, "for a specifically theological life-informing content, that is, for messages *received* rather than messages *given* by the commissioners and creators of the images" (28).

When we turn to Miles' exegesis of visual texts, this focus on message received entails an appreciation of the central functions of imagery within historical contexts. How images function is elaborated through three primary attributes—their ability to move and shape the will, their ability to yield multiple meanings to persons and communities (multivalence), and their ability to evoke affective response as a significant aspect of their meaning. Miles elaborates each of these functions as follows below.

Shaping the Will

From the earliest Christian tradition, images were recognized as having the capability of generating and concentrating emotion and of "directing human desire and longing to an infinite object" (144). What images have always done best, Miles insists, is to orient the will by virtue of their attractive power within perceptions. Images attract and thereby form the will through their power to shape a person's self-image, values, and longings (147). Therefore, "if the image attracts me, it speaks to me in a 'significant and definite way' . . . that I can come to understand by being attentive to the complex of memories, associations, and longings gathered in me, over time, by the image" (145). On the other hand, language provides for the analysis and anticipation of events for the self and its world as well as the communication of factual information. And at its worst, language becomes coercive, "as a standard, in alliance with social, political, or ecclesiastical institutions that require universal assent to particular formulae" (145). So while language may serve therapeutic or coercive purposes, what it cannot do, however, is "to engage and train the will" (see 146ff.)—to shape the will by attraction; only imagery offers the possibility for such motive power.

Multiple Meanings

If language leans toward the denotive side of human understanding, the image, for the most part, resists rationalistic or discursive interpretation. In fact, one aspect of Miles' celebration of imagery is precisely that "detachable conclusions" by language users are impossible to secure. The images always present the viewer with multiple meanings (they are inherently multivalent), meanings that are not susceptible to precisely articulated propositions (178).

On the constructive side of her notion of multivalency, Miles explores the role of images along two vectors. First, the multivalence of images has to do with their character as objects of perception. Visual images possess in inherent ambiguity a "floating chain of signifieds" (35) within some sort of "spectrum of meanings" (34). Anyone seeking to interpret imagery, then, is presented with the challenge of locating the width of its meaning spectrum along with *possible* denotations within that spectrum. The interpreter must realize all the while, Miles might caution, that any given meaning of an image is never exhaustive or authoritative over other possible meanings.

If the first aspect of imagery's multivalence has to do with an irreducible perceived ambiguity, the second takes into account the always varied context of the interpreter. Images in their presentational capacity "can offer formulation and expression simultaneously to a wide variety of persons with different perspectives" (37–38). The power of images lies in their ability to focus the will of nonlanguage users as well as language users, women as well as men, communities along with individuals. Here, Miles spots an affinity between the multivalence of imagery and "the discontinuity featured in women's physical existence" (38). Male physical existence is more normatively marked by continuity, lending a subtle but powerful bias toward texts and their historical development. Given the discontinuities of women's physical existence—birth, menstruation, first intercourse, and so on—the multiple meanings of the image resonate more readily and immediately as compared to a textual history of ideas or doctrine. The conclusion drawn from such analyses is that "the visual 'language' of images, although specific and precise to each viewer, is singularly adaptable to a variety of interpretations—whether or not articulated—by a diversity of individuals" (144).

Embodied Existence

Closely related to this analysis of male and female existence as related to text and imagery is the latter's capabilities to move persons at the level of affect. "Life in the body" is the stuff of images—what they most often depict, our bodily existence. Consequently, the subject, the person or community, engaging with the image often finds its impact not only "in the mind," but "in the body" as well. Such engagement, for Miles, is never dispassionate, but unleashes the image's power to "generate and concentrate emotion" (144).[17] The orientation of imagery toward a depiction of human life "in the body" inevitably leads to the affective dimensions of "the great, lonely, yet universal preverbal experiences of birth, growth, maturation, pain, illness, ecstasy, weakness, age, sex, death" (36).

One of Miles' most significant insights about imagery relates to the essentially communal context of the experience and interpretation. Historical persons did not encounter images from a solitary perspective and an emotive distance. Rather, the images that were most available to persons were those encountered in personal devotion and public worship. Here "the individual viewer confronted the image as a member of an interpreting community, and the image itself was also part of the architectural and liturgical presentation of an ordered cosmos of being, reality and value" (8).

Within such liturgical and communal contexts—even personal contemplation, Miles notes, is an act performed within a community of interpretation—images function to move the will, focus perception, and orient the person and her or his memories within an "enriched present." Especially within the context of worship, the lexicon of imagery is discovered in its most expansive manifestation.

Since the community at worship was and is comprised of a wide diversity of language users as well as nonlanguage users (aligned chiefly along gender lines for Miles), the ample presence of imagery in the liturgy invited the people's fullest possible participation. On one hand, then, this communal/liturgical context for the experiencing of images adds a new depth to the sense of their multivalence. Not only is there an inherent ambiguity with the image, such that it cannot be reduced to a single meaning; it is also the case that the very character of the community contributes to the richness of possible interpretation. Women and men, young and old, language and nonlanguage user—all of these constitutive members of the communal life, and more, contribute to imagery's surplus of meaning, "their spectrum of messages" (17). On the other hand, one may readily conclude that liturgical and homiletical enactments that present an impoverished diet of images will inevitably exclude portions of the community. Overdependence on words alone in worship tends "to exclude people who cannot subscribe to a precisely defined concept" (133). We can conclude, therefore, that worship and preaching that leans toward the discursive and textual lacks the capability of relating to every member of the community. Imagery is essential to the diversity of any religious community, especially to its array of affective expression and longing.

Image as Insight Reviewed

Image as Insight has been the subject of numerous reviews and the source of frequent citations across a wide spectrum of scholarship. As is the case in homiletics, Miles understands her work as interdisciplinary and innovative, and as such has evoked an

ongoing conversation that now finds its way into these hermeneutic investigations. With other reviewers, most all of us who
are about the homiletic vocation would celebrate the attention
Professor Miles has generated with regard to imagery. The insistence on the communal and liturgical context for exegeting images
as well as texts is an insight that stands reiteration in the contemporary church situation. Worship and preaching impoverished
of ample imagery has been the heritage of many in North American Christianity, and Miles rightly discloses the political implications of such poverty.[18]

For the purposes of this exploration of imagination theory and
an interest in narrative hermeneutics, the dichotomy developed
by Miles between text and image demands attention. (The ar-
guments concerning the interpretation of various paintings and
architecture will be left to other commentators!) Unfortunately,
Miles tends to overdraw the schism between text and image, along
with a companion dichotomy between language users (mostly
male) and nonlanguage users (mainly female). The actual situation
in the contemporary conversations concerning texts and imagery
is far more complex and subtle in its analysis than Miles admits,
and in its complexity and subtlety perhaps mitigates against the
book's feminist assertions. First, it is appropriate to recall the
state of interpretation, as found within recent literary criticism,
regarding the diversity of forms of literary expression as well as
their "spectrum of meanings." Mostly, "text" in *Image as Insight*
refers explicitly to discursive and implicitly to creedal or confessional documents. Absent is an appreciation of the "second order"
nature of these texts and an awareness of their dependence on
"first order" narratives. Even within the genre of narrative, the
wide gamut from denotation to evocation found, for example, in
Crossan's analysis is not acknowledged even as Miles argues for
an analogous sweep of meanings for imagery.[19] If images "for-
mulate by attraction," so, too, do the language-based metaphor
and narrative. Indeed, much of what is celebrated as imagery's
unique character can be, and has been, applied with equal facility
to parable as narrative metaphor.[20]

If Miles' construal of the text is biased toward discursive and
denotative literary documents, other difficulties are encountered

with regard to the notion of imagery. Here, the problems cluster around two central assumptions regarding images and their functions (Miles' "lexicon of images"). On one hand, with the possible exception of several references to architectural forms, images are construed as visual phenomena within the perceptual field. That images also present themselves as verbal in character seems precluded more by Miles' assignment of such occurrences to male language users than by her hermeneutic method.[21] This formal exclusion of verbal imagery short circuits a potentially useful conversation with those engaged in a phenomenology of language and rhetoric. And such a delimitation is particularly ironic in light of the interdisciplinary commitments of the project.

On the other hand, a collection of problems cluster around an inattention to the nature of the imagination while imagery is subjected to scrutiny. Attempting to explore images without attention to imagination is like analyzing the structural and aesthetic aspects of wings without relating them to flight. Indeed, the most radically drawn dichotomies portrayed in *Image as Insight* appear capable of being maintained only if a conversation with those investigating human imagination is not undertaken. Similarly, within the field of homiletics, readers may find all sorts of gestures toward the significance of imagery for preaching without the homiletic imagination being considered in the least. For contemporary preaching, an intimate engagement with visual imagery is of keen and abiding importance. However, such explorations will need to be located within the context of the broader issue of the imagination. Interested in images, the preacher will also attend to the flight of imagination.[22]

The Perceptual Model: "Seeing as"

To speak of images is to speak of perception, and increasingly perception is being interpreted as an imaginative act. That is, our perceiving and its role in our knowing is viewed more and more as creative in its functioning, constructive and not merely receptive. Still, as Mary Warnock observes, "the production of images is the work, *par excellence*, of imagination."[23] The issue, following upon Miles, is now to locate imagery within the context of a perceptual model of imagination. Following these considerations, other models of imagination will also be explored, keeping in mind the proviso of almost everyone reflecting on human imagination that a sense of "fault" (Ricoeur) or ambiguity (Murray) attends all of our dealings with this mysterious dimension of ourselves. W. J. T. Mitchell bluntly states, "There is no consensus and nothing approaching a general theory of the image."[24]

Whatever its limitations or faults, the perceptual model remains the starting point for investigations into human imagination. Put another way, "We cannot isolate the question of images and try to answer it by itself. . . . In order to understand the image, we need to understand the diverse but related functions of imagination."[25] This then leads to an "excellent provisional definition of the imagination," which is Mary Warnock's notion of "seeing-as."[26] The capability of recognizing and interpreting the perceived world depends on the imagination's ability to elicit and retain the image or shape of our perceived world's objects. However, these images in themselves "are not separate from our interpretations of the world; they are our way of thinking of the objects in the world."[27] This is not to say, however, that mental imagery must be brought to consciousness before recognition of the object is possible. Rather, what Warnock insists is that (1) there is the ability to bring the object "to mind" if desired, and that (2) images and their form are a necessary mediation between perception and recognition. Regarding both functions, then, images "do not take the place of objects of perception, of a world transcending our subjectivity, but mediate between the world and the self in a way that opens the self to the world."[28]

Of particular note to a homiletical interest is the variety of ways in which this imaginative seeing-as comes into play. Warnock identifies several functions of the ocular model of imagination, differing ways in which we see as. Bryant summarizes them as follows: through imagination we see everyday objects as everyday, we are able to focus on a particular aspect of what we see, and we are able through the imagination to have presented to us new views on everyday realities "by focusing on their hitherto hidden or largely ignored features."[29] Taking Bryant's example, we recognize a tree by virtue of the imaginative act of associating it with familiar images—which, again, we may or may not "call to mind." However, related to the second aspect of the imagination's work, our images are never photograph-like imitations of the perceived object. Images are comprised of some forms or features of the object of our perception and memory sufficient to allow us to identify that object for ourselves. With Wittgenstein, we may label this function of imagination as "aspect seeing."[30] Warnock comments, however, that this function introduces some sloppiness, since our representations of the object may be too incomplete or biased to the extent that we misname (misinterpret) the object.[31] Nevertheless, human understanding proceeds on the basis of this admittedly untidy function of the imagination.

If the first two functions of imaginative seeing-as serve to present us with a recognizable world, the third enables the important dynamic of defamiliarization. What sparks such shocks of recognition is imagination's capacity to focus on the "hitherto hidden or largely ignored features" of our perceived world.[32] While the first function permits the recognition of a tree and the second to image it with reference, say, to its seasonal variations in foliage, the third breaks new ground. What if, Bryant asks, a lumberjack comes to see the tree as a birdwatcher?[33]—or vice versa, we might add. Clearly the point of view of lumberjack and birdwatcher is not merely a question of spatial reference, of aspect seeing, although their respective "locations" in relation to the tree do differ. Rather, we are instructed once more of Warnock's insight into the inherently interpretive character of perception. Here the shift from one perspective to another involves "seeing" the tree with new insight as to its value and utility. Such a new seeing likely will involve a new seeing of the self as well.

Considering our lumberjack and birdwatcher, Margaret Miles' insistence on the affective dimension of seeing-as leaps back into the conversation. One does not have to be committed to Romanticism to admit with Wordsworth and Coleridge that images bring with them attendant feeling states when brought to mind. There is, with Miles, a sense in which "life in the body" becomes a significant aspect in our lexicon of imagery; images come to mind and with their advent we feel the significance of what we experience. Then it also obtains that "the ability to feel the significance of something we experience depends on the ability to reproduce an image of it, to see it as something with a certain significance for us and therefore as something that carries a certain affective impact."[34]

"Imagining-That," "Imagining-How"

The capacity to form images, however, while of great importance, does not exhaust the awesome repertoire of the imagination. Two other capacities of the imagination, imagining that and imagining-how, mark the movement beyond a focus on imagery and its attendant affective states. Images characteristically "appear" within consciousness as distinct objects and events having sensuous forms. This phenomenon is most readily experienced as visual in nature, and this sense of seeing-as consequently tends to hide from ourselves the fact that images may also relate to other than a visual modality. In addition to visual imaging, Edward Casey reminds us, there must be listed "audializing, smelling in the mind's nose, feeling in the mind's muscles, tasting in the mind's tongue, and so on."[35] However, there also exists the capacity to imagine that a state of affairs exists and to imagine how some state of affairs may be evoked or achieved. The two are related but distinct in their functions.

Imagining-That

By indicating that the imagination may deal with a "state of affairs," several imaginative achievements are attributed beyond that of imaging. A state of affairs, according to Edward Casey, posits the objects or events of imagination "in a number of possible relations—e.g., temporal precedence, spatial contiguity, causal connection, and modifications of various kinds."[36] There is "a nexus of relations" that are foremost to any state of affairs, and it is this complex character that initially distinguishes such mental achievements from imagery. Casey adds that this complexity results from the presence within imagining-that of both a nominative and a verbal component. In other words, we may imagine that—to use Casey's illustration—"the Washington monument is walking,"[37] or that the Bill of Rights is amended. These examples also convey a collateral insight: "What we imagine as constituting a state of affairs does not have to assume a sensuous guise."[38] As these two states of affairs are imagined, we find the former to possess more immediately a visual character, while the latter can be construed in a completely nonsensuous way.

By identifying the function of imagining-that, we find a significant movement beyond an exclusive focus on imaging as an imaginative act. In addition to the complexity of its relational matrix, another component may be identified—its intentional character. While images may either be brought to mind ("imagine your mother with green hair") or be more or less spontaneous (as in dreaming about your mother and her green hair), imagining a state of affairs is an overtly intentional activity. It is quite easy to sense the imaginative act involved in pondering a walking Washington Monument. Nevertheless, one of the major contributions of recent phenomenologists to the concept of imagination is their insistence that irrespective of the degree of spontaneity or controlledness, all imagining is intentional. Even the most apparently spontaneous act of imagination is a presentation of consciousness (or subconsciousness) and is therefore inherently intentional. "Hence intentionality pervades imagination as a whole (Casey insists): it makes no sense to say that imagining is partly intentional, partly nonintentional. It is intentional altogether or not at all."[39]

Imagining-How

All appearances between imagining that and imagining how bear a similarity. Both take as their frame of reference some state of affairs or other, that dynamic complex of relationships involving things along with their interaction. But imagining-how involves *"what it would be like if such-and-such a state of affairs were to obtain."*[40] Here the issue has moved beyond imagining that some state of affairs is of a certain set of conditions. Rather, as Margaret Kelleher observes, one is participating in the imagined state of affairs."[41] To the extent that imagining-how tends more explicitly toward personal agency—which is also present though "muted" (Casey's nice designation) in imagining-that—the former often utilizes "time-binding" as a necessary interim stage. That is, before arriving at next Sunday's homiletic state of affairs (preaching within the liturgy), a considerable amount of time and imaginative effort will be devoted to imagining-how. In some expressions, this involves projecting a homiletic plot related to the state of affairs in the biblical text. It will also, of necessity, involve an imagining-how with regard to the parish and its members as well as the larger community and the world. Here, imagining-how takes an emphatic expression; the preacher may have to imagine how to suffer or celebrate in distinctive contexts.[42] Imagining-how, therefore, does gain expression as a rehearsing activity involving both enactment of a role as well as the utilization of specific skills (such as attending to the preparation and delivery of a homily). But imagining-how in its empathic mode is more than mental rehearsal of anticipated or fantasized enactments. To imagine-how is also to refine skills in the creative relocation of self into settings from which fresh insight into the human and divine condition may be learned.

In addition to imagining-how in its functions as mental rehearsal of agency, a more self-reflective mode has been articulated. Here the issue is the "how" of imaginative creativity, its process and its typical stages of development. In other words, we now shift to a consideration of how imagination proceeds in its sequence of creative moves. The guide for such exploration is Philip Wheelwright, who in his seminal work, *The Burning Fountain*,[43] outlined the stages of imaginative creativity with regard to poetics. These four successive activities include the confrontative, stylistic, compositive, and archetypal imagination. Each calls for some elaboration.

Confrontative imagination. Engaging in an act of poetic creativity, Wheelwright speaks of an initiating immediacy. By "confrontative," he means to suggest that this process begins with an imaginative stance "which acts upon its object by particularizing and intensifying it" (33). Poetic language speaks with directness, and particularity, and "experiential precision" (35). Wheelwright adds that "a lively recognition of the particular and unique in experience is an imaginative achievement, and that when keyed to the highest pitch it may become an imaginative achievement of a very high order" (35–36). This immediate engagement with the poetic object, however, is not to be confused with either a conceptual object or with those in "the objective world." Poetically sensitive consciousness "largely makes and articulates its own phenomenological object" (38).

The poem may contain or evoke concepts and may or may not intend any kind of historical reference. What the poet imagines in this confrontative mode is the language and tenor of the work along with its phenomenological objects. By virtue of this engagement with the particularities of experience, moreover, Wheelwright notices a tendency toward personification in the creation of the poetic object. He comments: "An object as directly confronted tends to be not merely described but also addressed. Confrontative immediacy contains the seed of the *I-you* relationship, even though the grammatical form of expression may remain in the third person" (40).

Imaginative distancing. Once the object of experience has been confronted with immediacy and particularity, there is then the need for an imaginative distance. The latter is necessitated first in order that the focus on the phenomenal object does not become simply everyday and commonplace. New perspectives on the objects of our experience will only come with an aesthetic distancing that allows other points of view. However, there are boundaries to this necessary stepping back. An "overdistancing" will lead to an inappropriate idealizing, seen most clearly in some religious and ideological art. Here the object has been removed from "profaner objects in the environment" and through "a symbolic removal from its ordinary context of occurrence" (42). Also, this overdistancing may be seen in some contemporary art where the result is an alienation of art from our human experience. How could anyone ever fall in love with a Picasso female "whose eyes, mouth and breasts have been transposed to suit the painter's ruthlessly neo-geometrising spirit"? inquires Wheelwright (42).

Composite imagination. The first two stages, confrontative imagination and distancing, have resulted in a new collection of "disparate elements" that stand in need of some sort of blending.

Poetic creativity, typically, achieves this blending in one of two ways: the poet may approach the diverse aesthetic objects with a prior commitment of "interpretation," that is, with the belief that *"there is a bit of everything in everything else"* (48). The second option is a creative synthesis of these disparate phenomena, resulting in *"radical novelty through synthesis of heterogeneous elements"* (48). In the former instance, the common attributes of the diverse objects are brought together on the basis of some hitherto unnoticed commonality of theme, description, point of view, or other aspect. In the latter case, an incipient stage on the way to metaphor may be detected. However, Wheelwright cautions at this point that not just any elements may succeed in a composite synthesis. Some "degree of unified sensibility" must obtain as well (49). He concludes:

> All meaning has as its subjective condition a certain mental responsiveness—a readiness to make connections and to associate this with that, a readiness to see this and that in a single perspective, as forming a single individuality, a single semantic object, an *ousia*, a Something Meant (49–50).

Archetypal imagining. The reader and the critic readily agree with Wheelwright that certain poets, certain poems, and certain portions of a poem convey more of a sense of depth than do others. And the agreement would also extend to a recognition that this sense of depth conveys with it distinctive and often powerful feeling states. What has been encountered in such cases is the achievement of the archetypal imagination, whereby some universal is evoked in the particularity of the poetic image. What is *not* suggested, though, is that the thing evoked is "a gray abstract idea" (53). Rather, by denoting the universal as an archetype, Wheelwright means to link it inherently to the poetic particular. With Jung, he sees these findings of the archetypal imagination as closer to "natural human vision than the products of brain ingenuity" (55). Such archetypes, then, are never simply subjective to the individual, but in some way or other have a life of their own and are available to persons through the medium of poetic discourse.

As with imagining-that, it should be noted that an imagining-how may either take a perceptual expression or occur devoid of sensory images. As various strategies for preaching on a particular text are pondered, for example, imagining-how may involve mental imagery of a scribbled charting of a homiletical plot or an aural image of how the homily would proceed through a given sequence. On the other hand, as preachers bind time and play at various illustrative systems, imagining-how may occur in a totally nonsensory mode. What is discovered, then, is a taxonomy of sensory and nonsensory possibilities for imagination construed as imaging, imagining-that, and imagining-how. Edward Casey depicts the relationship between these imaginative achievements and their respective degrees of sensuous expression through the schema in figure 2.1.

Fig. 2.1 Types of Imagination

Type of Content \ Sensory Status	Sensory	Nonsensory
Single Object or Event	Imaging	
State of Affairs	Imagining-that (sensuously)	Imagining-that (nonsensuously)
State of Affairs Involving the Imaginer (or Surrogate) as Agent	Imagining–how (sensuously)	Imagining–how (nonsensuously)

The three forms of imagining are related, following each other with ease and having numerous possibilities of interaction and overlap. They form a natural and easy sequence. Casey offers an example:

> I might begin by imagining, say, the god Jupiter in isolation from all other contexts, as clothed in a certain way, and as standing in a certain fixed pose. But I can also imagine the same Jupiter as speaking, thereby adding an audialized dimension to my visual presentation, or again as moving, which adds a kinetic element to the same presentation. (46)

Here Casey restricts himself to imaging, although each successive step becomes more complex. However, the shift to an imagining that is relatively simple to imagine:

> Suppose that I imagine Jupiter lounging around in an elegant Olympian pool. In this case, I am *imaging-that* a certain state of affairs obtains, namely "that-Jupiter-and-other-gods-lounge-around-an-Olympian-pool." (46)

The step, then, to imagining how is equally simple to make:

> I can imagine-how it would be to act like one of these gods, . . . e.g., "how-it-is-to-walk-as-a-god," "how-it-is-to-envy-other-gods." (47)

The three modes of imagining follow easily upon each other, and it is entertaining (perhaps) to protract this sequence in an increasingly complex imaginative achievement. The schema, then, offers a sort of road map for such imaginative performances. While the schema does portray the structural alignment of these three types of imagining, however, Casey adds a pointed qualification. In the midst of all of the interactions and overlappings involved, "only one possibility is excluded: the simultaneous occurrence of two or more forms of imagining" (47). We may image an object, imagine-that or imagine-how in relationship to it, but each performance is singular. We may not imagine more than one performance at a time.[44]

Imagination and Metaphor

We have noted the predominance of the ocular model of imagination that typically treated imagining as a kind of faded perception, especially of a visual sort. Certainly the conventional suite of imagination talk reveals this perceptual and vision-based construal of imagination. "Seeing with the mind's eye" has become a kind of shorthand definition of the act of imagining, with subsequent distinctions—seeing as things really are or as illusory, for example—remaining firmly within the ocular world. Two unfortunate fruits of this perceptual and visual rendering of imagination, though, have plagued its long history. First, a series of dichotomies refused to be alleviated—between the objective and subjective worlds and between text and image—to list only two more obvious examples. Second, the seeing-as approach lent itself to an overemphasis on subjectivity (since, as we all know, people tend to "see" things differently). The new day in imagination theory came with the shift from this ocular model to a semantic/linguistic one as a new interpretation of the significance of metaphor was articulated by Paul Ricoeur and others.

In classic thought, metaphor was defined as a literary device whereby a word having a realistic and literal meaning was intentionally associated with a more figurative term. The fundamental relationship involved their similarity although the latter, "embellishing word was substituted for the more proper one, to serve some esthetic or artistic purpose."[45] While the aesthetic achievement may indeed color or decorate language, nothing of substance was achieved. (In fact, through metaphors, the imagination was most likely to lure persons away from what was of substance, the real or formal world!)

The new approach to metaphor as an imaginative act drastically reverses all of the assumptions of the classical theory that had been held since Aristotle. Particularly as articulated by Paul Ricoeur in his developing sense of the "hermeneutical imagination,"[46] metaphor now is characterized as the "birthing room" of meaning. Instead of an emphasis on the similarity between ground and figure, the innovative power of metaphor lies in its conjunction of dissimilarities, a strategy of absurdities.[47] This "semantic impertinence"[48] involves ostensibly contradictory meanings—now no longer involving simply words (expressing imagery), or nominative and verbal elements (imagining that and how), but discourse, sentences—and in this act of collision, an eruption of new meaning occurs. The resultant "similarity" is on one level absurd; metaphor works much like Ryle's category mistake. So, as Bryant summarizes,

> Ricoeur sees metaphor's duality in terms of a figurative meaning that arises from the ruins of a literally contradicted meaning. That is to say, when metaphor is located at the level of discourse rather than words, one's concern is primarily with the meanings connected with the statement as a whole instead of with meanings of individual words. In the case of

metaphor, the meaning of the statement, when literally interpreted, is logically absurd. . . . The meaning of the metaphor, therefore, can emerge only when one allows its literal
meaning to self-destruct.[49]

No longer regarded as an ornamental trope, for Ricoeur metaphor
is now positioned at the heart of his hermeneutics—all language
originates as metaphor. At this semantic level, then, we notice a
necessary extension of imaginative discourse to the scope of a
sentence. The sentence is the generative context for metaphoric
creativity. Hence, Ricoeur states:

Metaphor depends on the semantics of the sentence before it
concerns a semantics of the word. Metaphor is only meaningful in a statement; it is a phenomenon of prediction . . .
we must not speak of words used metaphorically, but of the
metaphorical *statement. Metaphor proceeds from the fusion
between all the terms in a metaphorical statement.*[50]

Once born, though, such metaphors typically follow the life cycle
of solar objects—they may burst on the scene, remain alive for
some considerable time, and die out. Yet, like the cooling hulk
of an old star, dead metaphors remain. Most language, Ricoeur
observes, consists of these burned-out dormant metaphors.

Given this primacy of semantic/linguistic imagination, the
issue now becomes that of the image and its place in such a
postmodern hermeneutic. As Ricoeur poses the question, it concerns "the status of a sensible, thus non-verbal, factor inside a
semantic theory."[51] Taking as a test case the highly "visual" imagery of poetic texts, Ricoeur notes that their meaning is not
"free," but "tied." "This is imagery involved in language itself."[52]
Images offered by the text are never meaningful in and of themselves. Only as they gain location within some discourse or other,
some semantic environment, can images become signs of some
semantic expression of meaning. Ricoeur then rephrases the question as to the relation between imagery and language:

Are we not ready to recognise in the power of imagination,
no longer the faculty of deriving "images" from our sensory
experience, but the capacity for letting new worlds shape our

understanding of ourselves? This power would not be conveyed by images, but by the emergent meanings in our language. Imagination would thus be treated as a dimension of
language.[53]

Here is presented the mirror image of Miles' view of the relation
between language and imagery. Human imagination is first a matter of language users and their metaphoric spawning of meaning.
Perceptual images are derivative in meaning from, and actually
serve to abstract significance from, the activity of semantic
innovation!

At the heart of the imaginative event of metaphoric discourse
is a new "surplus of meaning," a redescription of reality.[54] Living
metaphors are precisely fields of new meaning, opening up our
world in a way that reorganizes prior understanding. It is not
surprising, given this world-reorganizing function of metaphor
that Ricoeur suggests, that there is an affective dimension to its
power. The force of its double meaning—its conflict of interpretation—extends from the conceptual to the affective as well.[55]
Since the two contrasting meanings disclose a way of being in
the world, Bryant observes, "feelings are a central element in this
way of being."[56] What Bryant notes about affect in relation to the
power of metaphor, however, is that the modern notions of "objective" and "subjective" no longer obtain for Ricoeur. Rather,
feelings come into being along with the other aspects of metaphoric meaning and may be sensed as being *in* the things out there
or as representing affective states within the self. There is a "lack
of distinction between interior and exterior," Ricoeur insists, a
"reciprocity of the inner and the outer."[57]

The Play of Imagination

If for Paul Ricoeur, metaphor involves that semantic imaginative
act that results in a surplus of meaning including some significant
affective dimension, Hans Gadamer has extended imagination's
role once again in his notion of play. To play, Gadamer observes,
is to engage in activity that has its own world with its own rules
and roles, "which only count as such within the closed world of
play."[58] On one hand, to enter the activity of play means to lay

aside inhibitions, prejudices, and self-consciousness. A person cannot truly play and yet retain a self-awareness of playing— hence the disruptive force of a novice actor's giggle or the grand-standing of the athlete who breaks out of the game to "play" to the crowd. On the other hand, Gadamer insists that when we most fully play, or enter into the play world, it is more accurate to say that *we* are played; the game plays us as we become a presentation of the game. Therefore, with Bryant, "the players are not the subjects of the game, though the game cannot become actual without them."[59]

Gadamer's foundational notion of play, then, involves the in-sight that the full meaning and expression of the game is located only within its playing. A rule book is not the game, yet the players play by the rules. Its field, whether the play space of a child's nursery or the painted lines defining a basketball court, is not the game, though play of necessity implies limit to some play field. Thus, "to play is to sacrifice freedom and accept limits. . . . Being limited, being played, is a condition of playing at all."[60] At the same time, novelty is a constant companion of limit as we play. No two games are ever the same; the freedom given in playing the game is a liberation from self-consciousness as the player is played by the game in this or that unique presentation.

The possible correlate to this activity of the player's "self-presentation" in the game[61] is that other persons may also be spectators to it. Here, once more, paradoxical quality attends our playing and our watching of the play. If in playing there is a self-conscious playing to the audience, the character of the activity as play is lost. At the same time, precisely by attending to the play as spectators, closed off from playing, there happens a "being caught up" in the game. Ultimately, "the play itself is the whole consisting of players and spectators."[62]

Now the implications of Gadamer's root metaphor of play for imagination lie first in the metaphor's ability to encompass within its meaning all of the prior components of imaginative theory. So play catches up within its nets the perceptual-oriental aspects of imagination as a seeing-as. (Players report an intensified sensory experience as they play the game and as it plays them.) Essential to the performance of a game, moreover, is the whole imaginative process of imagining how, both in its sense of "mental rehearsal" and in its empathic role. Moreover, play takes up within itself the metaphor, since the game itself is only possible as it is performed as meaningful activity in contradiction to all definitions of meaningful activity by a world that does not know how to play! David Bryant concludes by observing that

> when one plays, one is not merely engaged in viewing things in a certain way. Rather, one's whole self is engaged in the movement of play, so that not only one's sight but also all of one's senses, as well as one's pattern of action are taken into the structure of play and are shaped by it.[63]

We are invited into the game, asked to yield self-consciousness and accept limit and restriction, yet find ourselves being played by the game. Playing and being played we find freedom and meaning in the give-and-take, back-and-forth structure of the game. Imagination, then, in its most profound expression, involves the full giving of self in play "by which we are initially taken into a structure of meanings, (and) is the presupposition for all conscious imaginative activity of the subject."[64] In the activity of play is the hermeneutic clue to human experience, not in spite of its closed context of self-presentation, but precisely because of that delimited arena of the play. Here, then, is the clue to human being: "Play itself is a transformation of such a kind that the identity of the player does not continue to exist for anybody. . . . The players (or playwright) no longer exist, only what they are playing."[65] This world wrought by the imagination has become our world.

Notes

1. Notice that with the advent of MTV, music for the youth culture began to be expressed primarily as a visual rather than an acoustic experience. The visual impact of the video performance initially provides the impetus for sales of tapes and compact discs and then continues to function as the imaginative context within which the music is subsequently heard.

2. Gordon Lathrop, "A Rebirth of Images," *Worship* 58 (July 1984): 291–304.

3. Mary Warnock, *Imagination* (Berkeley and Los Angeles: Univ. of California Press, 1976), 102. See part 1:13–34, for a detailed analysis of the notions of image and imagination in Hume and Kant. For a more

extensive treatment of the modern history of imagination, see Eva T. H. Braun, *The World of the Imagination* (Savage, Md.: Rowman & Littlefield, 1991), 69–117, which surveys thinkers from Descartes to Bergson.

4. Samuel Taylor Coleridge, preface to *Lyrical Ballads*, quoted in Warnock, *Imagination*, 112.

5. Warnock, *Imagination*, 129. Ricoeur labels these two modes of imaging as "objective" and "subjective." The former involves a bringing near in mind of objects now distant in some manner (temporally or spatially). The latter functions to bring into immediacy images and thoughts that are incapable of being grasped by conventional human perception. These two poles become the standard means of expressing imagination's role in preaching through over a century of modern homiletic's lore and practice. See Appendix.

6. For a discussion of objective and subjective imagination, see Richard Kearney's treatment of Ricoeur's analysis in Kearney's *Poetics of Imagining: From Husserl to Lyotard* (London: HarperCollinsAcademic, 1991), 138–39.

7. Gilbert Ryle, *The Concept of Mind* (New York: Barnes & Noble, 1949), 245. The reader is also referred to Ryles' eighth chapter, which Mary Warnock describes as "the locus classicus of the twentieth century attack on the image" (*Imagination*, 152).

8. See Howard Gardner, *The Mind's New Science: A History of the Cognitive Revolution* (New York: Basic Books, 1987), 98ff., for an account of the early development of psychology in the nineteenth century, and 102–5 for a description of Wundt's innovative project.

9. Gardner, *New Science*, 324.

10. See ibid., 326–39, for a treatment of Kosslyn's model and the continuing debate in psychology and philosophy regarding mental imagery.

11. For a comprehensive analysis of recent research on mental imagery, see John R. Anderson, *Cognitive Psychology and Its Implications* (New York: W. H. Freeman, 1990), 91–111.

12. Gardner, *New Science*, 327.

13. I am indebted to David Shoemaker for these insights.

14. Margaret Miles, *Image as Insight: Visual Understanding in Western Christianity and Secular Culture* (Boston: Beacon Press, 1985).

15. For a sampling of this conversation, see reviews by Denise Lardner Carmody in *Horizons: The Journal of the College Theology Society* 14 (Spring 1987): 201–2; Michael Graves in *The Quarterly Journal of Speech* 74 (August 1988): 377–79; and Thomas H. Troeger, in *Homiletic: A Review of Publications in Religious Communication* 11 (December 1986): 29–32.

16. Miles, *Insight*, 10. Hereafter cited in the text.

17. This connection of the image to memory and therefore to emotional states has been noticed as far back as Aristotle. See Eva T. H. Braun,

Imagination, 44–46, for a concise summary of Aristotle's depiction of the relationship between imagination, memory, and the passions.

18. See Robin Green's comments on "symbolic sterility" in worship in *Intimate Mystery: Our Need to Worship* (Cambridge, Mass.: Cowley Publications, 1988), 67–68.

19. See John Dominic Crossan, *The Dark Interval: Towards a Theology of Story* (Allen, Tex.: Argus Communications, 1975), 47ff., for an analysis of the "spectrum of story" (59).

20. Michael Graves therefore concludes that in *Image as Insight*, little attention is devoted to "the spectrum of aesthetic and creative language use" (review in *The Quarterly Journal of Speech*, 378).

21. See Alla Bozarth-Campbell, *The Word's Body: An Incarnational Aesthetic of Interpretation* (Tuscaloosa, Ala.: Univ. of Alabama Press, 1979). Her brilliant work on aesthetics consistently stands in opposition to Miles' overdrawn dichotomies. Regarding aural images, Bozarth-Campbell states that "the function of the *logos* (word) is to let something be seen (image)" (39).

22. Notice the nuances of the "flight of imagination" on one hand and "flights of imagination" on the other. Commenting on the respective meanings of the terms *imaginative* and *imaginary*, Paul Pruyser comments that "these words sum up the wisdom of the ages that distinguished respectable products from disreputable figments of the imagination." "The latter," he adds, "are held to be mere fabrications, contrived to suit a personal whimsy or welling up from an unsound mind" (Paul Pruyser, *The Play of Imagination: Toward a Psychoanalysis of Culture* [New York: International Univ. Press, 1983], 9).

23. Warnock, *Imagination*, 182. See 131–95 for a survey of the recent history of imagery and imagination from Hume to the phenomenologists.

24. W. J. T. Mitchell, ed., *The Language of Images* (Chicago: Univ. of Chicago Press, 1980), 7.

25. Warnock, *Imagination*, 172–73.

26. David J. Bryant, *Faith and the Play of Imagination: On the Role of Imagination in Religion* (Macon, Ga.: Mercer Univ. Press, 1989), 85.

27. Warnock, *Imagination*, 172–73.

28. Ibid., 194.

29. Bryant, *Play*, 91.

30. Ludwig Wittgenstein, *Philosophical Investigations*, trans. G. E. M. Anscombe (Oxford, England: Basil Blackwell, 1968), 193ff. Wittgenstein labels the "aspect seeing" role in object recognition as "half visual experience half thought" (197). Someone who does not immediately recognize a familiar object by reason of lighting, shift in point of view, and so on has a different experience from someone who knows the object at once.

31. Warnock comments that to the extent that we always see only an aspect of any object, the imaginative act of interpretation is intrinsic to

perception. She concludes, "We cannot separate the interpretive function of the imagination from its image-forming function. . . . The images themselves are not separate from our interpretations of the objects in the world; they are our way of thinking of the objects in the world" (*Imagination*, 194).

32. Bryant, *Play*, 91.

33. Ibid.

34. Ibid. It may well be important to note that this characteristic interplay between imagery and affect may be thwarted in the case of severe personal psychopathology or communal trauma. Acute depression, for example, will typically have as its shrunken affective palette psychic pain. Moreover, as Paul Pruyser observes, "the stuff of compensatory daydreams, which usually abound in vivid images, is not available for a flight into pleasantry, a moment's respite." Hence, "there is hardly any imagery left when the depth of depressive regression is hit" (Pruyser, *Play of Imagination*, 22).

35. Edward S. Casey, *Imagining: A Phenomenological Study* (Bloomington, Ind.: Indiana Univ. Press, 1976), 41.

36. Casey, *Imagining*, 42. Writing to a more ecclesial audience, Casey might have invited his readers to imagine that "the mountains skipped like rams, the hills like lambs" (Ps. 114:4, NRSV).

37. Casey, *Imagining*, 42. Casey comments that "the state of affairs imagined here involves an internal, reciprocal relationship between what is designated by the nominative component ("the Washington monument") and the verbal factor ("is walking")" (42, n. 6).

38. Ibid.

39. Ibid., 58.

40. Ibid., 45.

41. Margaret Mary Kelleher, "Liturgy and the Christian Imagination," *Worship* 66 (March 1992): 127.

42. Thomas H. Troeger, "Tapping Hidden Streams: Receiving the Spirit through the Discipline of Imagination," *The Marten Lecture in Homiletics*, Saint Meinrad Seminary, Saint Meinrad, Indiana, October 6, 1992. It should be recalled that this empathic imagining-how is not a recent discovery within the field of homiletics. Rather, the preacher's empathic imagination was extensively explored by Gregory the Great in his marvelous "Catalogue of Hearers," in *Theories of Preaching: Selected Readings in the Homiletic Tradition*, ed. Richard Lischer (Durham, N.C.: Labyrinth Press, 1987), 261–68.

43. Philip Wheelwright, *The Burning Fountain: A Study in the Language of Symbolism* (Bloomington and London: Indiana Univ. Press, 1968). Notes cited in the text.

44. Anticipating homiletic implications of this insight into imagination theory, we will want to note that the assembly may be invited to

image, imagine-that, or imagine-how. We will not, however, want to design an image system that asks the assembly to achieve more than one of these forms of imagining at one time.

45. Edward L. Murray, "Imagination Theory," in *Imagination and Phenomenological Psychology*, ed. Edward L. Murray (Pittsburgh: Duquesne Univ. Press, 1987), 208.

46. See Richard Kearney's *Poetics*, 134–62, for a survey of the development of Paul Ricoeur's hermeneutics.

47. Paul Ricoeur, *Paul Ricoeur on Biblical Hermeneutics, Semeia 4,* ed. John Dominic Crossan (Missoula, Mont.: Scholars Press, 1975), 77.

48. Ricoeur's nice phrase (*Biblical Hermeneutics,* 77). See Murray, "Theory," 209–10.

49. Bryant, *Play,* 93.

50. Ricoeur, *Biblical Hermeneutics,* 77.

51. Paul Ricoeur, *The Rule of Metaphor: Multidisciplinary Studies of the Creation of Meaning in Language,* trans. Robert Czery (Toronto and Buffalo: Univ. of Toronto Press, 1977), 211.

52. Ricoeur, *Rule,* 211.

53. Paul Ricoeur, "Metaphor and the Central Problem of Hermeneutics," ed. and trans. John B. Thompson, *Hermeneutics and the Human Sciences* (Cambridge, England: Cambridge Univ. Press, 1981), 181.

54. See Ricoeur, "Central Problem," 170–81.

55. Ricoeur, *Rule,* 192.

56. Bryant, *Play,* 96.

57. Ricoeur, *Rule,* 246.

58. Hans-Georg Gadamer, "The Play of Art," in *The Relevance of the Beautiful and Other Essays,* ed. Robert Bernasconi (Cambridge, England: Cambridge Univ. Press, 1986), 124. See Gadamer's *Truth and Method,* 2d rev. ed. (New York: Crossroad, 1989), 101–34, for his central explication of play in relation to his hermeneutics.

59. Bryant, *Play,* 107.

60. Joel C. Weinsheimer, *Gadamer's Hermeneutics: A Reading of Truth and Method* (New Haven: Yale Univ. Press, 1985), 104.

61. Gadamer asserts that play lacks an extrinsic purposive content. "Play," he adds, " is really limited to presenting itself. Thus its mode of being is self-presentation. . . . First and foremost, play is self-presentation." (*Truth and Method,* 108).

62. Ibid., 109.

63. Bryant, *Play,* 113.

64. Ibid., 115.

65. Gadamer, *Truth and Method,* 112.

3

Making the House Our Home:
Narrative and the Perceptual Model

The purpose of this chapter and the next is to locate the various aspects of the theory of imagination within a postliberal narrative hermeneutic. Such a project assumes several tasks along with some methodological directions that will not be followed. Regarding the former, the initial hurdle to locating imagination theory within a narrative hermeneutic context takes the form of Margaret Miles' presented dichotomies between text and image. For the purposes of this project, it will suffice that (1) the "texts" at stake be delimited to texts-as-stories, and (2) that in place of Miles' construal of a relationship of polarity and even opposition, we achieve an alternate portrayal in which story texts and imagery at least may be seen as having an affinity for each other. To the extent that polar opposition persists between narratives and images, the larger task of integrating imagination theory within narrative hermeneutics will be stymied. The door to imagination's house will remain closed and locked.

If this initial hurdle is overcome, the opportunity is then provided to explore the processes of imagining-that and imagining-how as they intersect with a postliberal perspective. Here some rewarding firstfruits of this hermeneutic project may be harvested. However, to shift the metaphor, the "miraculous catch" of these investigations may well be as imagination theory's turn toward the linguistic is explored from the perspective of narrative theology. While homilists in particular have benefited greatly from the analysis of metaphor as an act of the imagination, a significant insight of narrative theology will be that the imaginative act of

76

irony must be seen as a decisive companion to metaphor. Finally, Gadamer's notion of imagination as play will be applied to homiletic performance encompassing both the communal act of preaching and the social role of the preacher.

As alluded above, the location of imagination theory within a postliberal hermeneutic also implies directions that will *not* be taken, particularly those that reside in some sort of foundationist appeal. For example, Garrett Green depicts a hermeneutic that would seek to ground itself in reaction to rationalism's *homo cognitus*—in an anthropology of *homo imaginans*. Such a program, Green comments, would be quite conceivable:

> First of all, the imagination would need to be grounded philosophically as the definitive human faculty and the source of human piety—in short, as the religious a priori and therefore the foundation for theology. An analysis of the structure of *homo imaginans* would then provide the anthropological base with which the truths of revelation could be correlated. Human imagination could then be interpreted as an implicit relation to the divine—no doubt inadequate from a Christian perspective but nevertheless the precondition for faith, the outstretched hand waiting to be filled by the revelation of God, the anthropological question awaiting a theological answer.[1]

Of course, to ground anthropology in such a foundationist construal of imagination would preclude methodologically the priority of biblical narrative among the worlds that shape us; with all the other experiential-expressive approaches, the adequacy of Christian faith would be evaluated according to some prior human experience—in this case, of ourselves as imagining beings.

A second path not taken is that of deconstructing narratives in favor of punning the semiotics of the words of texts. Jacques Derrida and his followers,[2] convinced of narrativity's essential illusion of order and security, have taken up an attack on "logocentrism." Wesley Kort summarizes the (op)position with reference to biblical narrative:

> This kind of move (locating oneself in "The Christian Story") is bound to provoke a postmodern reaction describing our location as on a broad, undifferentiated expanse of writing

and not within the stable borders a coherent narrative would grant. Such identity and location are delusions, as Mark C. Taylor in *Errings* points out (152–53).[3]

By way of deconstruction, there is an imaginative recasting of the text's language into an ur-language of puns and pictographs,[4] which ironically shifts the discourse toward the visual and imagistic pole of Miles' dichotomies. The visual text in its deconstructed form no longer can regain its true ur-language of speech and story. In response, John Haught insists that "we can accept narrative as an ally of the desire to know while at the same time recognizing that narrative funcitons [*sic*] as a meaningful integrator of our lives."[5] And in the way of a rejoinder, Haught suggests, "somewhat paradoxically, that the very basis for (deconstructionism's) courage lies in—stories. . . . In some pre-theoretical way the archetypal story of the hero lies at the very foundation of all suspicion."[6] While we will look with interest on Deconstructionism's imaginative plays on words, our narrative hermeneutic will remain focused primarily on the oral/aural expression of narrative as story and as discourse. Unwilling, then, to resolve the story text within a semiotic category of literary pictograph, we are once more challenged at imagination's door by the oppositions proposed for story and imagery.

Story and Image in Polarity

In the course of the argument in *Image as Insight*, at least three sets of polarities are presented with regard to texts and images. Texts are construed as dynamic (mobile), cognitive, and language-based, while images are presented as static (spatial), offering up affection, and dependent upon vision. As indicated, the challenge is to interpret texts as stories in relation to visual images in such a manner that polarity and exclusion are supplanted by affinity and interplay.

The Dynamic/Static Opposition

There is no desire, on one hand, to restate the nature of narrative such that its temporal mobility and linguistic tensiveness are suppressed. The very dynamics of plot, the richness of character development, and shifts in point of view are all essential to narrative's capacity to offer a world, and they are essential as well for biblical narrative's insistence on the preeminence of its *kosmos* over other *kosmoi*. On the other hand, the visual image seems a case study in immobility and duration through time, happily devoid of story's contingencies. All of the above continues to obtain, while at the same time, each realm (story and imagery) also shares in some of the qualities of the other to their mutual enhancement.

With regard to narratives, there is an increasing appreciation of an inherently spatial dimension to narrative's enactment. At one level, this spatiality is expressed as an aspect of a story's setting. At stake here is much more than the spatial dimensions of a narrative that simply provide a "location" in which various characters may have their plots thickened. In Mark's Gospel, for example, the spatial dimension of the story functions theologically as boundaries are portrayed and overcome in Jesus' ministry and as sacred places are challenged, transformed, or rendered null and void in his passion, death, and resurrection. Referring to Jesus' teaching the crowd (on the shore) from a boat (on the sea) in Mark 4:1, Mark Allen Powell observes that "such images are fraught with possibility for mediation between spatial opposites."[7] In the crossing accounts, not only is the fear and lack of faith in the disciples uncovered; also revealed is a new place of God's reign weaving together Galilee and "the Galilee of the Gentiles." Likewise, spatial settings in Mark become ways of speaking of where the locations of presence and absence of God are now being reversed: the temple's veil is torn as Christ breathes his last on the cross. The spatial dimensions of the Markan narrative clearly and powerfully interact with the oppositions and reversals occurring at other levels of the discourse.

In Stephen Crites' depiction,[8] the spatial dimensions of a narrative extend far beyond matters of its setting. The setting for a narrative is expanded to include its "social space," involving culture; language; and, inevitably, a community. But stories of "depth" center on a vertical axis reaching by way of imagination both up to a "celestial canopy of gods and angels" (105) and down into our personal inner space of the spirit. Crites notes a delightful

homology between these two spaces. The inhabitants of the celestial "are like our inner space, where thoughts and images fly
free and stories pass among us" (106). At the end of the vertical
axis lies for us moderns the twin voids of boundless outer space
and an equally boundless inner space, an "eternal sublimity" of
emptiness and death (108–11). Yet, again, back at the middle is
our "earthly ground," reminder of our bodily existence, which
"grounds every true story" (113). To speak of a narrative having
any truth whatsoever is at least implicitly to recognize these
spatial dimensions as a necessary condition.

Noting, then, an inherent spatial dimension to narrative along
with biblical writers' exploitation of spatial settings, it is now our
task to interrogate imagery with regard to its affinity for mobile
and dynamic expression. That is, we question whether the image
presents itself in any respects other than as a static phenomenon
within our perceptual field. (As my glance in August returns to
February's calendar photo, that beautiful glider is still tied down
snugly next to the runway, its wings layered with snow!) Of course,
we recall at once that the visual construal of imagery is not to
be synonymous with the perceptual model of imagination. "Mobile images" abound in music, for example; and in the case of the
plastic arts and architecture—from a Grecian urn to the lastest
postmodern building—mobility is invited with respect to both
point of view and environmental variables, particularly lighting.
Still, the snow remains on the forlorn glider, and, more uplifting,
Van Gogh's "Starry Night" remains curved around a favorite coffee
mug. Within the realm of visual images, however, and especially
in art and photography, mobility and a sense of contingency are
informed by point of view and environment. The clue here is that
a dynamic sense is located more in the viewer's response, since
the image retains a static character in itself. E. H. Gombrich
underlines this viewer-response contribution to visual perception
by way of noting how various artists actually design-in the necessity for the viewers' imaginative creativity. He suggests that
one painter's works (Gainsborough) "are little more than those
schemata which serve as support for our memory images."[9]

The test case for visual imagery's affinity for some kind of
mobility may be most appopriately that of the icon. Here, as Miles

and others have noted, the iconic image resides well toward the denotive in which every detail "may be 'read' by the worshiper in terms of a particular context of scriptural or historical significance."[10] However, to assume that the interpretation of the icon is exhausted by such a static, denotive description is to misinterpret how the icon functions within the Orthodox community of faith. There is a hermeneutic function of the icon whereby the imagination is illumined so as to properly interpret self, church, and world. Given this capability of "transfiguring" the worshiper's imaginative vision, the dynamic of this interaction of icon and believer is best described as *metanoic*. Static image and the dynamics of faith are at the heart of a viewer response to the icon.

> The icon's form is static and unchanging, faithful to a body of convention that preserves the mind of the church but that discourages too much interpretive "individuality" on the part of the artist. But if the form is static, the effect is not. The icon's intent is not static but kinetic, moving and prodding the Christian imagination to shape and interpret the world anew . . . (it) exerts its dominance over the Christian imagination, moving it to engage the culture of which it is a part and transfigure it.[11]

Here is an insight into imagery's structural analogy to story. If, with Crites, there is a spatial dimension to narrative, the opposite side of the coin is that, with Ugolnik, there is a mobile and tensive dimension to the image as icon.

The Cognition/Affection Impasse

At the center of Miles' programmatic model of interpretation is the disjunction between text and image, related to their relative alignment with a spectrum from the rationalist/conceptual at one pole and the affective/emotive on the other. Moreover, a further signification is layered onto this spectrum with regard to gender. The question confronts us: "Can a world peopled by rationalist, text-bound males and affective, imagistic females ever be reconciled?"[12] Interestingly, this polarity strikes close to home in the recent tradition of the American pulpit. As Charles Rice has noted, a certain schizophrenia has affected modern preaching, with a

sermon's development alternating between discursive, propositional "points" and illustrative material overdone in its emotive
subjectivity. The program never does get close to real life; it trades
either in a "projective-discursive style" or on affective "personality
without personhood."[13]

It is important to recall here, that as imagination theory was
traced from the focus on images through the "turn to the linguistic" and finally to the notion of imaginative play, there was
no erosion in the emphasis on the affective element in the act of
imagination. Whether the play of imagination leads to the production of images or is construed as an interpretive act involving
both *logos* and *eros*, the bodily and affective dimension persists
through it all.[14] As we have seen (and heard), the metaphoric act
of imagination—with its linguistic turn—in no way finds the
affective dimension of its performance diminished as compared
to the more visual imagery. Rather, the issue needs to be redefined
less as one of polarity and impasse and more as one of a spectrum
ranging from concept to image. Here again, Margaret Miles does
allow for the image's "spectrum of meanings"—and an implied
spectrum of affective states in the viewer—but does not extend
such interpretive and affective range to texts. With Garrett Green,
however, we may delineate a span "extending from the pregnant
image, full of implicit or potential application, to the developed
concept, in which the underlying analogy has been articulated
and delimited."[15] Green adds that, with regard to the concept, "the
image has become transparent, unambiguous, precise."[16]

What we do not have, therefore, is a polarity between cognition
and affection paired with an opposition of text and imagery. Indeed, from the perspective of narrative hermeneutics in particular,
an often fluid affinity obtains between texts-as-stories and images.
The former evoke the latter; on the other hand, images imply the
stories within which they were begotten. The issue is rarely that
of affect *or* cognition in polarity, but is one of the *quality* of the
affective dimension of the particular imaginative act. Identifying
that act as visual and imagistic or linguistic and narrative says
nothing a priori as to the respective presence or absence of its
affective element. We will assume at this point that no imaginative

activity is without such affective significance. The question concerns the "truthfulness" of this affective dimension in relation to the narrative world of Scripture and the character of God. Similarly, such a narrative biblical perspective does not orient gender into polarities, especially alongside dichotomies of cognition and affection. Bozarth-Campbell responds to precisely this gender-based stereotyping of the creative and interpretive functions of human imagination:

> In reality I believe there are no "masculine" or "feminine" qualities that cut irrevocably between the two sexes, that permanently exist in dichotomy, and that can define us simplistically along the narrow limits of gender. We are all the intricate sum of all that has gone before us and of the accidents of our cultural experience. I believe there are human qualities that have become distorted, imbalanced, one-sided in our culture. . . . The point is the type of quality one is describing, not that generally speaking and for various reasons it may appear to be more obvious in one sex than in the other.[17]

The Aural-Oral/Visual Impasse

As presented by Miles, this particular dichotomy was construed as opposing images in their visual presentation and texts in their linguistic usage. Again, both sides of the proposed impasse beg further analysis; both sides also stand in need of a fundamental reconstrual. First, notice an essential ambiguity in Miles' employment of "text" as that language-based and cognitively oriented repository of meanings. Already the alignment of "text" and cognition has been called into question, especially since the most central texts of the Christian faith are narratives. Texts as stories, it was observed, may or not be susceptible to a rationalistic hermeneutic—parables precisely and vigorously resist such ideational distillation. Apparently, the interpretive palette from denotive to the affective or tensive will need to be brought to bear on both visual images and on texts as stories as well.

The confusion at the heart of this rendering of "text" in *Image as Insight* is twofold—the text is ubiquitously aligned with persons who are language users (mostly male); moreover, vagueness exists regarding aural imagery and the role of language in all of the above. Regarding the former issue, Ivan Illich's insight into the relatively late emergence (mid-twelfth century) of the text in Western consciousness is of central importance.[18] In fact, one condition of that emergent text is the diminution and loss of the priority of the text as a record of—and visual aid for—speaking and hearing. There is, therefore, a shift in the emergence of the text away from hearing and inevitably toward seeing. Texts now align themselves more in company with visual images than against them![19] Both are grasped in perception as spatial, distant from the subject, and in a relatively static medium. The alternative to visual imagery, more precisely, is texts as stories when reenacted in speech and hearing. The latter may be best construed as the hermeneutic alternative to both literary texts as well as visual images.

The alternation between narrative and imagery, then, leads to Robert Fowler's observation that "although the written word appears to be spatial and particularly in a print culture constitutes a literate visual mode of consciousness, the spoken word is indubitably temporal, and it constitutes an oral-aural mode of consciousness."[20] Here is suggested a fundamental reorientation of the dichotomy presented between text and image. The alternatives first appeared to be those of seeing and hearing, visual and aural images. While that contrast persists within our perception of the world, it persists only by a process of abstraction, first of hearing from speech and then of the oral-aural from story.[21] The perceptual model of imagination, then, will need further refinement; it will also be adequately contexted only as the imaginative turn toward the linguistic is achieved.

Once the alternation is articulated as between oral-aural and visual modes of perception, a striking reversal shifts the notions of relative intimacy and distance. Previously Miles attributed to visual imagery an affective and bodily immediacy. Texts, mostly defined as discursive, serve the specialized programs of language users. If we speak of the oral-aural modality of texts as stories, issues of distance, immediacy, and bodily existence undergo a striking shift. Walter Ong reports:

> In a visual cosmos, the self is an agent; in an aural world it
> is a patient. In the former, the individual is safe, at least for

the moment; in the latter, the individual is always vulnerable. In one world, the self is free; in the other, it is claimed, called to account, and asked to respond to the initiative of others. In one realm, the self is distinguished sharply from its environment; in the other, sounds bind it tightly to its social context and remind it of its contingency. One world contains only surfaces; in the other there are many and various clues to the interiority of selves.[22]

However, this reading of Ong's analysis may lead to a conclusion oddly similar to that of Miles' own position. Both overstate the dichotomy between oral-aural and visual modalities, Ong in favor of the former and Miles of the latter. Viewed from the perspective of biblical narrative—and the particular element of metaphor— image and language disclose an interplay of meaning-producing functions. This interplay offers immediacy and affective significance across the perspectual spectrum. Moreover, on some occasions the dichotomy between the senses is finally overcome in a unitive experience of self, God, and world. A phenomenon exists in which perception extends beyond its mundane compartmentalization—we may "hear colors" or "see sounds." This synesthesia, David Chidester observes, "demonstrates a type of antistructure, a radical breakthrough of the ordinary structural relations between self and world obtaining within an ordinary phenomenology of perception."[23] Given the possibility of such a synesthesia, overdrawn dichotomies between the senses are not only called into question, they are overturned! From the perspective of our narrative hermeneutic groundings, then, the issues now facing us become those of the varied relationships of story and imagery, taking as our point of origin, the priority of the Word, which as the Fourth Gospel attests, was *en arche* (in the beginning).

Narrative and Imagery in Relationship

"The story is logically prior," George Lindbeck proclaims.[24] The image derives from the narrative. Lindbeck, of course, is speaking from the perspective of biblical narrative, adding that "it determines the meaning of images, concepts, doctrines, and theories of the church rather than being determined by them."[25] However, there are at least two senses in which this logical priority of narrative extends to a general theory of imagery as well. Both are equally important to the relationship of story and imagery in Scripture and in their formative power within Christian community. These two dimensions of narrative priority are best understood as "naming" and as "narrative location."

The narrative naming of images has its *locus classicus* in the story of Adam's naming of all the creatures in the garden (Gen. 2:19-20). Such a naming immediately signifies more than the assignment of some word to stand for its object. Upon this narrative naming, a storied relationship with each creature is begun. Ironically, the storied relationship that first gains center stage is with the creature Adam named "serpent." But in a larger context, naming is a narrative function that allows us to speak of images as offering that "floating chain of signifieds"[26] rather than a skein of inchoate experiences. The delightful attribute of imagery pertaining to its multivalence, then, has to do with images being named and consequently being located in some narrative or other. "Apart from stories," David Harned insists, "images grow ambiguous and opaque," and he adds that "images can be named in a variety of ways, but until they are named in one fashion or another they will not divulge their precise significance."[27] There is a world of difference between imagery's multivalence and plain ambiguity (to invent yet another oxymoron). Narratives serve to name and thereby "locate" images such that their meanings remain diverse yet not random, mutually interacting and not simply juxtaposed.

Now if the priority of narrative means that the significance of an image relates to the story(ies) it inhabits, it is also the case that images gain a life of their own. Images are incorrigibly itinerant; they seem to grow tired of their old home within a narrative and strike off on their own. Some migrate to other narrative locations that feel very much like their old homeplace; yet now to speak of this image finds a resonance occurring between otherwise discrete stories. For example, occasions of providence and encounters with the Holy One occur in Genesis so regularly to (1) a woman at (2) a well that the biblically informed reader of John 4 cannot but feel the resonances and contrasts of all those wellside meetings. At its best, then, typological interpretation of Scripture may well represent a quite sophisticated grasp of this particular insight into the multivalence of imagery.[28]

At other times, images have such a powerful place in the narrative that they provide "the adumbrations of, clues to, and canons of interpretation for the story itself."[29] Put simply, an image is spawned within a narrative but grows to take on a life of its own, *still in connection with the story.* At the heart of this dynamic is the mystery of interplay of story and image in a sacrament. The Eucharist involves a community of people who hear and respond to a narrative prayer and who see and receive the icons of bread and wine. Both are needed. The image interprets the narrative and the assembly, which now is revealed as the body. The narrative interprets the image so that what we taste and see is not just bread but the body of Christ. Alternatively, this narrative and imagery dynamic can become impoverished or even rendered impotent. It is an interesting phenomenon in the history of sacramental theology and practice that the widest oscillations in doctrinal meanings of the eucharistic signs of bread and wine came subsequently to the loss of the narrative character of the prayer over the gifts.[30] No longer was there a multivalence within a range of signifieds. Now, in contexts where the narrative Great Thanksgiving is AWOL, we have clergy "talking about" what this bread and wine means, or, even worse, what it doesn't mean!

A final stage in the dynamic of narrative and imagery may now be identified, that of the emergence of master images. Narrative ethicists among others have noted that the view of self and world becomes framed by certain images that provide a hermeneutic function. So Harned insists that the images of self-recognition play a dominant role in shaping our actions in the world and our beliefs and feelings about the "world" within which we live. Such master images are typically implicit, serving more to limit, organize, and name self and world. Like polarized sunglasses, these master images themselves may remain unnoticed, yet all the while they are acting to filter and color our experiences. Likewise, they serve as media through which we hear the stories of the faith and the world, now functioning much like an audio system connected to earphones. Persons hear stories in ways influenced by capacities of their master image "tuners" both to receive and to bias or distort. In psychotherapy, for example, the counselor will be especially alert to the hermeneutic function of a client's master images (perhaps, for instance, organized around the roles of victim, or anxious, vigilant controller). Congregations, too, will carry such implicit master images, again prescribing a sense of "world" and self with all the attendant assets and liabilities regarding faithful life together.[31]

Vision and Narrative

The perceptual model of imagination wants to orient itself around seeing; the ocular mode of perception seems to claim for itself a preeminence among the senses. Yet, as we have seen (!), the imagination's "possibility and potency are rooted in images,"[32] images offered by all the senses. David Harned reminds us of the mystery of synesthesia when he observes, "We derive pictures from the sounds that strike the ear," while adding, "hands can see and speak, even if their possessors are blind or dumb."[33] In this imaginative achievement, however, there is a constant interplay between the senses; perception involves a collegiality among the senses in its business of forming images. "Imagination," Harned notes, "is the bond of the senses, integrating the impressions they afford."[34] We speak of seeing or hearing independently from each other only in abstraction. A related abstraction is to invoke visual or aural perception apart from its connection to bodily experience, "of the self as organism from its own internal richness."[35] With this collegiality in mind, as well as with the awareness that persons orient their seeing of self and world within clusterings of master images, we may now supplant "sight" with the notion of vision. Here the interdependence of sensual perception is acknowledged along with the decisiveness for agency such vision offers or restricts. We are formed as persons and communities by the vision we possess. In turn, this vision is more than simply a matter of perceptual functioning. It is shaped by personal character, informed by emotions, and strongly determined by communities and their language, culture, and narrative traditions.

The notion of vision is critical for an adequate construal of the perceptual model of imagination. It carries with it an insistence on the mediation of all experience and alerts us to the issue of those images serving as hermeneutic lenses on self and world. Vision is also decisive to our speaking of the role of imagination in agency and intention. To speak of vision, moreover, is to acknowledge the powerful and formative role of language. Dykstra encompasses these factors when he speaks of this visional seeing:

> What people see is an indication of what they care about and can care about. It is an indication of the depth and breadth of their compassion, of the scope and quality of their loves and desires, and the intensity with which they feel. Our emotions, evaluations, descriptions, predispositions, and desires are all brought to bear in our seeing.[36]

Therefore, to speak of the elements that serve to constitute vision also implies the opposite side of the coin. Our vision, in turn, shapes the self and its community, providing the scope within which agency becomes a possibility.

To invoke personal and communal character in relation to the imaginative act of vision is to take note of those master images, that "constellation of images of man and world that resides within the household of the self."[37] We envision the world through particular imagistic constellations. These components of vision, then, encompass all of the senses and their image-forming competencies. Included in the achievement of vision, moreover, is the vast and complex symbol system connecting these images and elevating some to the status of hermeneutic lenses. Still, the notion of vision is not fully explored without attending to language and the linguistic turn of imagination. Our vision is shaped as well by the ways in which we imagine-that and imagine-how, and by the metaphors and ironies of our stories. There is a distinctive sense of praxis within narrative hermeneutics that is implicit in these considerations. Christian vision obtains through the practice of the disciplines of a biblical people—prayer, worship, service—all the means of abiding in the Word. To preach this Word, therefore, involves nothing less than exercising and sharpening the vision of persons within the body of Christ. Without a vision the people perish.

"Imagining-That" from a Narrative Perspective

In imagination's turn toward the linguistic, an intermediary position has been detected between the perceptual model, seeing-as, on one hand, and metaphoric and playful imaginative achievement, on the other. This middle ground is frequently overlooked in favor of the imaginative models of perception or metaphor, yet imagining-that and imagining-how constitute an essential location within the entire house of imagination. Here, in this "middle room," imagination may or may not depend on explicit perceptual phenomena, and it now entails at least a proto-linguistic articulation (nouns and verbs are needed to express imagining that and how!). Here, too, the intimate relationship between agency and imagination begins to assert itself. To imagine that a state of affairs exists, invites—or insists—that persons have a relationship, a response to it. To imagine-that is to be called to make a decision of some sort with regard to the state of affairs—there is incredible potential for personal and communal *metanoia* in this invitation.

Perhaps the most articulate and radical statement of this power of imagining-that in biblical perspective is Walter Brueggemann's *Hopeful Imagination*.[38] By way of interpreting the message of 2 Isaiah, Brueggemann cites numerous references to Israel's homecoming from exile. Clearly we may sense along with Brueggemann the remarkable achievement of the poetic imagination in imagining that God declares release from captivity and return, precisely where no signs of the times point in that direction. What may be less clearly grasped, however, is that the naming of the contemporary situation as exile is an equally significant imagining-that without which homecoming settles into cheap grace. "To use the poetry of homecoming without the prior literature of exile," Brueggemann insists, "is an offer of cheap grace" (90). He adds, "It is important that the 'new thing' of 2 Isaiah comes after a long season of exilic discontent" (90).

It is this choice to name one's personal and communal context as exile, however, that is the logical and theological precedent to the announcement of homecoming. "[Exile] is a decision one must make," is Brueggemann's insight (93). Certainly Israel could and did adopt other ways of imagining-that while in captivity—cultural accommodation and death-dealing despair perhaps being the predominant ways! Brueggemann then extends his analysis to link imagination and agency. Each of these self-images involves a decision, an act of imagination. To locate oneself as an exile, though, involved several component beliefs and ways of living among one's captors. "*Exile* is a sense of not belonging, of being in an environment hostile to the values of this community and its vocation. Exile is practiced among those who refuse to accept and be assimilated in the new situation" (102). Within this distinctive imagined-that world, the state of affairs of being in exile realistically faces up to the dominant society's alien definitions of power and authority, and this awareness paradoxically "generates energy for imaginative and faithful living" (93). A decision is made by those in exile to *not* imagine that the dominant definitions of reality prevalent in society are real!

Living as exiles in a foreign land is only possible as an imaginative act, Brueggemann adds, if the community recalls its narrative of God's dealings with Israel in the past. Memory is essential to the capacity to imagine that God will act in the future for the liberation of exiles. Without that specific memory, faithful and liberating imagination is rendered problematic. To nurture Israel's counterconsciousness, the writer of 2 Isaiah hearkened to this narrative meaning of Israel "which is articulated in concise credo, in liberated song and poetry, in liturgical recital, and in the more expansive, reflective literature of the Torah" (113). This capacity to imagine that a new state of affairs was declared from God's side was not born of ad hoc novelty, but of the community's faithfulness in remembering its narrative tradition with this same liberating God.[39]

To announce homecoming to such a people, then, is to speak of a new reality based on the enduring character of their God. This poetic speech is marked by a distinctly illiberal avoidance of the practical matters of getting oneself out of bondage. Rather, the intent of the poetic and prophetic speech is to articulate a new reality already being accomplished in its speaking. Babylon's gods are dethroned, ridiculed, and uncovered as idols. Babylonian power is declared already impotent, its reality null and void. Yet,

> the poetry does not describe what is happening. Rather it evokes images and invites perceptions in Israel that were not

available apart from this poetry. The poetry is not aimed first
of all at external conduct. . . .(It) cuts underneath behavior to
begin to transform the self-image, communal image, and image of historical possibility. (96–97)

Through poetic speech, the writer of 2 Isaiah imagines that God
has announced homecoming to the exiles. In so doing a new social
reality is given. Israel's Judge and Lover has announced pardon;
in a little while God's people will head home through prison doors
flung open and hanging off their hinges.[40]

"Imagining-How" in Narrative Perspective

One distinctive expression of imagining how takes the form of
mental rehearsal, of some sort of sequential anticipation of agency.
Any performance, whether in the fields of engineering, sports, the
arts—even homiletics—will involve some degree of "thinking
through" prior to its enactment. Sometimes persons range through
the entirety of the performance in their imagination—again, taking either a perceptual or a nonperceptual expression. Where the
performance tends to be organically connected in sequence, such
as in activities as diverse as figure skating, surgery, or eucharistic
presidency, the enactment may be imagined numerous times in
a kind of "virtual real time" scenario. As this kind of imagining-
how occurs, without conscious effort the temporal succession of
the performance may undergo expansion or compression, particularly as the more challenging or intricate situations are rehearsed.
To return to the flight metaphor, a student pilot engages in this
type of imagining-how repeatedly in the struggles from first flight
to first solo. Prior to every flight along the way, a mental rehearsal
of the task is undertaken with compression of the maneuvers
where some level of competence has been achieved. Where needed,
though, certain maneuvers, steep turns or stalls, perhaps, may be
imagined-how in a kind of slow-motion expansion. Additionally,
even when competency has been attained, there is a satisfaction
experienced in this sort of anticipatory imagination. One pilot/
author speaks of the joy of flying and explains:

> I like flying. I like getting up early in the morning and looking
> out the window at the sky, the feeling of the breeze on my

face as I preflight the airplane, the look and smell and feel of
the airplane. *I like anticipating the flight and imagining how
it will be.* I like thinking about it afterwards. I like everything
about flying.[41]

In other mental rehearsals, imagining-how will isolate a section
of a performance to hone that enactment to a edge where it no
longer has to be "brought to mind." The skill becomes "automatic"
and less an application of mental effort. In other cases, this focus
on an aspect of the performance may involve imagining how one
element contributes to the whole—an organist may imagine just
the pedal work of a piece of music, an actor may isolate just the
blocking of one scene, a preacher utilizing the Buttrick method
may imagine how just one move will occur. Frequently, a performer's creativity and innovation come to expression precisely
by means of this process of isolating discrete aspects of performance in ahead-of-time imagining. A writer will sometimes come
to a bind in the story's movement and will imagine how one
character leads things in a new direction. Sometimes, then, the
overall performance is shifted by this imaginative focus around
some discrete component.

Finally (if that word may ever be used with regard to imagination theory), imagining-how may perform an abstracting function in its mental rehearsals. Here the "shape" or texture of a
work is elevated and explored on behalf of the performance. It
may be that a musician envisions the dynamics, texture, and tonal
sequence of a composition in an imaginatively abstract fashion.
Sometimes program notes speak of the performance in this fashion, using color, visual and aural imagery, and emotive tone to
describe the experience of hearing the music. Preachers, too, will
utilize such abstractive imagination with reference to shifts in
rhetorical systems or as a way of tracking the homiletical plot.
"Lowry's loop" is one example of this imaginative abstraction
raised to the level of an explicit homiletic method. Preaching a
Lowry sermon will almost certainly involve imagining how the
shape of the homily will proceed.[42] In the tradition of narrative
preaching in the African-American church, such abstraction may
well be needed as the preacher mentally rehearses for an incredibly
rich oral performance. Here a sermon's shape may encompass not

only plot and illustrative systems, but the intended use of many other elements in the black preacher's repertoire.[43] A performance is rarely enacted on the basis of an organic mental rehearsal in its entirety. Rather, an isolation of discrete passages, scenes, moves is undertaken. Preachers abstract sermonic plots; poets, the shape of the poem.

Reviewing the "How" of Imagination

Philip Wheelwright spoke of poetic imagination's creativity as embodying four component activities: the confrontative imagination, imaginative distancing, compositive imagining, and the archetypal imagination. From a theological perspective interested in Hans Frei's approach to narrative hermeneutics and committed to Lindbeck's cultural, linguistic model of doctrine, some sort of theological analog to Wheelwright's schema may well be articulated. That is, an analogous sequence to the "how" of the poetic imagination may well be projected, although the particular interests of the theologian will result in a necessary reworking of Wheelwright's categories. For our purposes, a review of the specific interests of a Christian educator (Craig Dykstra) regarding moral transformation and a teacher concerned about Christian pedagogy (Maria Harris) will be compared to my own interest in a narrative-based homiletic. In each case, Wheelwright's foundational work is essential to the project; in each case it is revised for its new context and application:

Fig. 3.1 The How of Imagination

Poetic Imagination	Moral Imagination	Contemplative Imagination	Homiletic Imagination
1. Confrontative	Conflict	Contemplative	Conformative
2. Distancing	Waiting	Ascetic	Patient
3. Compositive	Insight	Creative	Sermonic
4. Archetypal	Transformation	Sacramental	Paradigmatic

Homiletic imagination is born along with our new birth into the community of faith. Preachers are not first of all—if this vocation is "in Christ"—representatives of some theological or ideological movement. They are those who, like all believers, have gone down into the waters of their baptism, died to self, and are being raised within the body of Christ. The preacher's approach to Scripture, then, is in concert with her or his approach to the practice of Christian life, arising out of this initiation into the church. Whatever subsequent critical, distanced relationships are adopted to facilitate the preacher's calling, the primary invitation is to conform to Scripture and church as a catechumen. Here is the beginning, the birth of Christian imagination, and therefore of homiletic imagination. To speak of this "conformative imagination," however, is not to suggest an absence of "conflict."[44] In fact, we should expect a sense of conflict to be the normative condition of any catechumen making the passage from life in the world to life in Christ. Rather, it is to insist that becoming Christian "is to conform oneself with that tradition,"[45] to learn how to see and feel and think and act as shaped by that tradition. This conformative imagining finds its locus in the assembly's worship life, as the hearers attend to the lections and proclamation and share in the actions of the liturgy. Once baptized, the richness of this conforming to the biblical Word becomes ever more evident. The text is read and heard "not in order to recapture the times when independent tradition units were circulated in Christian communities, but in order to set the pericope we read (or hear) now next to the passion and resurrection of Christ held forth in the supper."[46] Such a hearing and reading, this conforming, comes to fullest expression as a kind of communal attentiveness particularly to the passion and resurrection narratives as the hermeneutic center for all reading of the Bible. Elizabeth Achtemeier summarizes this initial stage of conforming to the Word:

> The practice of church theology is a matter of receiving a traditional, biblical body of Christian understanding—of absorbing that basic theology into one's own bones until it becomes automatically the context and guide of one's own thought and practice, then carrying on a constant dialogue with and critique of one's own society and culture in the light of that Christian understanding.[47]

This conformative imagination also incorporates "the active intensity of the contemplative life, which calls for a totally engaged bodily presence, attending, listening, being-with, and existing fully in the presence of Being."[48] Homiletic imagination begins with a conforming to the Word in community as a catechumen; it involves conflict and invites contemplation.

The next stage in the dynamics of homiletic imagination is that of *patience*. Conforming to the Word is not *ex opere* productive of a corpus of homilies! Rather, the Christian, including the Christian preacher, is called to attend to Scripture equipped with the virtue of patience. As Craig Dykstra notes with regard to moral transformation, the interlude functions to relax old patterns of consciousness: "One lets go of the conflict for a time and waits for something to happen."[49] We are instructed in this essential hermeneutic stance by William F. Lynch:

> The decision to wait is one of the great human acts. It includes, surely, the acceptance of darkness, sometimes its defiance. It includes enlarging one's perspective beyond a present moment, without quite seeing the reason for doing so. Fortitude and endurance are there, to an extent, beyond the merely rational. Waiting is sometimes an absolute, which chooses to wait without seeing a reason for waiting. It does not ignobly accept such pseudo-reasons as "don't worry," "don't fret," "don't be silly," "listen to better judgment," "a Christian knows there is no reason for stress." It simply chooses to wait, and in so doing it gives the future the only chance

it has to emerge. It is, therefore, the most fundamental act,
not the least, of the imagination.[50]

Perhaps the most radically counterculture activity of the American church would be this imaginative waiting while being conformed to the Word.

The dominant culture outside, and inside, the church, however, assigns patient waiting as a passive and therefore irrelevant virtue. Yet such an assessment represents a profound misunderstanding of the dynamic and active character of "waiting upon the Lord." So as she describes the ascetic imagination, Maria Harris emphasizes the activity of patient waiting; it brings with it "all the understandings associated with religious discipline and discipleship."[51] Among the disciplines of patient imagination are those of a recovered *lectio divina* approach to Scripture. Silence is central to this discipline of "spiritual reading." Robert Mulholland cautions:

> It is almost impossible for us to sit down with scripture and immediately be in an inner posture of openness and receptivity toward God. Time must be given to silence the grasping, controlling, manipulative dynamics of our being. We must come to a point of inner release, a deep relinquishment of ourselves and our lives to God.[52]

There is wisdom in the Tradition's insistence on this active waiting in relation to Scripture, this prayerful devotion in the presence of the text. The imagination of the biblical interpreter needs discipline and formation, time for us interpreters to be shaped first by the Word.

The discipline of patience before Scripture also includes the more scholarly investigations commended by historical-critical methodology as well as a strong interest in literary criticism and hearer-response criticism. Notice, however, that our identity as preachers is not that of "objectivity" as assumed in a comparative religions context or one shaped by an ideology of "pluralism." The dynamics of imaginative interpretation are conformed by the praxis of Christian life and by the patience of *lectio divina*. Preachers come to Scripture first and foremost within the community's liturgical life through "the year of grace." They first come as catechumens, conforming themselves to the practice of Christian faith. The Christian imagination is born here; it is honed and exercised in the disciplined patience of waiting and of prayerfully interpreting the scriptural text.

To be "patient" is to be called to suffer. Patience (*patior*) is a kind of suffering, and those called to preach will be called to distinctive forms of suffering as they prayerfully and critically interpret the text. Tom Troeger speaks of a necessary "empathic imagination," while Walter Brueggemann points to a necessary grief, with Jeremiah, in the face of the world's ideologies "of continuity and well-being in which human reality is covered over by slogans."[53] Whether in the *patior* of grief, compassion, or of silent, prayerful waiting, the Christian preacher's imagination is formed by such patience.

The dynamics of proclamation move from patience to the sermonic imagination. Now the process of attending to the text and its preaching is undertaken. Again, imagination is involved. Distinctive roles are played by imagination within any homiletic method in any age. Most homiletics within modernity, however, have located the preacher's imaginative activity in three distinct arenas.[54] First, imagination was construed in its objective, traditional sense of bringing near objects or circumstances that remained otherwise distant. Then, under the influence of the Romantic era, a unique, subjective imagination was invoked that gave the preacher access to sublime truths otherwise not simply distant, but unattainable. Finally, preachers were continually admonished to cultivate a lively "historical imagination" whereby the world behind the text was represented through vivid life-like prose. Through such historical imagination, congregations were taken on trips down dusty paths in old Galilee with a Jesus mirroring our own piety and cultural values.[55]

Now at the end of preaching's modern era, this sermonic imagination is finding itself both reframed and renewed. Most contemporary homileticians continue to acknowledge imagination's role in bringing near those things that are far off, presenting them in the assembly. More accurately, however, this imaginative function now involves a presentation of images and stories out of the lived experience of the congregation. Memory, of course, is the vehicle through which most of these imagined situations are typically "brought near."[56] In any narrative-based approach, the trajectory of sermonic imagination will run along two intersecting trajectories—sermonic plot and image systems. In the former, the shaping of the sermon's structure and movement will be imagined in conjunction with the biblical text's own plot and intention as well as the pastoral interests and needs of the congregation. In the latter instance, focal locations within the homily will be imaged with immediacy—an imagining that or imagining how some situation or other obtains.

What is certainly called into question in postmodern or postliberal homiletics is any notion of "historical imagination." A phenomenological homiletic such as articulated by David Buttrick bypasses historical imagination through that method's fusion of horizons between interpreter and text. The text's offering is an "intending to perform" in some fashion within consciousness, not an opening onto a world behind the text into which homilist and assembly may take an imaginative plunge. For postliberal preachers, imagination's opportunity is to explore the world of the text and to note the interplay, tension, and conflict between that world and our conventional personal and social "worlds."

Over the course of time, preaching week in and week out, baptizing and breaking bread, the homilist anticipates and proclaims *transformation*. With Dykstra, this transformation "comes in the form of a new patterning of the imagination."[57] He comments:

> Often this is a pictorial image in the mind, but it may also
> present itself as a gesture, as a new way of saying something,
> or in a new pattern of action. Whatever the form of the insight,
> it is a creative reorganization of the imagination in which all
> of the elements of the conflict are related in a new gestalt.[58]

We may call such a discovery, this transformation, a shift in the paradigmatic imagination. It catches up in its "creative reorganization" all aspects of the human imagination; by employing the term *paradigmatic*, we point to imagination's pattern-making function. And by emphasizing the totality of a paradigm's scope—"all of the elements"—it is likewise asserted that such patterned organization of a "world" is "a precondition for recognizing the parts *as* parts in the first place."[59] Put simply, persons do not come to an encompassing paradigm through the slow accumulation of elemental sensory data or isolated acts of interpretation. Rather, the experience of self and world is inevitably ordered and shaped by a patterned vision of the whole.

To speak of moral "transformation" (with Dykstra), or arrival of a "sacramental" stage of imaginative learning (with Harris) involves a shift, not just in some aspects of imaginal organization, but in a shift in the paradigmatic imagination itself. Similarly, Christian preaching's goal is not one of adjustments (therapeutic or otherwise) to the personal and communal imagination of the assembly. Christian preaching's *telos* involves a "creative reorganization" of the imagination, now becoming conformed to the world of biblical narrative.

When we speak of such an all-encompassing shift in our imagined world, Thomas Kuhn's work on scientific paradigms and their function in research and practice is particularly illuminating.[60] A paradigm shifts under the pressure of a sensed anomaly, an awareness of growing problems within its interpretive organization of its world. Moreover, Kuhn observes, the "decision to reject one paradigm is always simultaneously the decision to accept another."[61]

Garrett Green expands on Kuhn's insight by speaking of the discontinuity between paradigms; shifts "cannot be made piecemeal since they involve changes in the basic ordering pattern itself."[62] By way of illustration, Green retrieves Wittgenstein's analysis of aspect in *Philosophical Investigations*.[63] There is a gestalt character to our perception such that the same sketching can be interpreted as a rabbit or a duck (see figure 3.2). Here is a shorthand analogy for the paradigmatic imagination as a whole. Our recognition of "rabbit" or "duck" is discontinuous; we see the whole as one or the other.

Figure 3.2 Duck/Rabbit

Even the most rapid, intentional shifts in aspect recognition cannot override the patterning of the whole. Duck or rabbit, we will see one or the other, even argue which it truly is, but will not see both in simultaneity. Green notes this "logical peculiarity of paradigms" and concludes that "the transformation is not gradual and cumulative but logically (and psychologically) discontinuous, like a visual gestalt shift in which the elements of perception suddenly come together in a new and unanticipated configuration."[64]

One other characteristic of paradigms relates to their peculiar logic—that is, their incommensurable quality. By "incommensurable" Kuhn intends to emphasize that the canons of evaluation within one paradigm must not be extended into the world of another. Explanation is an activity pertaining to the intraparadigmatic world, and the one pattern "cannot, therefore, be explained in terms of the other."[65] While rival paradigms may be *compared*, Green insists, they are not arbitrary constructs—what cannot be accomplished is an exploration of any part of one construct on the basis of another. Paradigms may or may not be compatible, and they may or may not be irreversible. Duck and Rabbit are certainly comparable and are reversible as well. We easily shift back and forth once the double pattern is spotted. On the other hand, while Ptolemaic and Copernican astronomy are comparable, they are nevertheless quite irreversible in our experience. Neither of these alternative paradigms, however, are commensurable.

With regard to the ministry of proclamation, this grammar of paradigms and paradigm shifts yields several key insights. Especially in this "age of pluralism," preachers first need to be sensitive to the disruption and confusion evoked within a parish during a pastoral transition when "ducks" suddenly become "rabbits."[66] Whether at Mary Help of Christians Parish, Church of the Redeemer Lutheran, or Second Congregationalist Church, the interpretive paradigms of successive preachers may change with seemingly arbitrary and discontinuous shifts. Today preachers in many communions within the American church may no longer assume continuity or even compatibility of paradigmatic models of interpretation upon arriving at a new pastoral situation. Moreover, those of us called to preach most probably should assume the presence of at least one dominant paradigm that is shaped by the culture's narratives and images within any congregational setting. Even so seemingly central a doctrine as soteriology, for example, may be informed more by America's "solo savior" myth than by the Pauline convictional system regarding Jesus Christ as savior.[67] In such a case, the alternate paradigms are irreversible as well as incommensurable. Transformation (Dykstra), the sacramental imagination (Harris), and the paradigmatic imagination all speak of the gospel's claim of truthfulness and the biblical narrative's insistence on the preeminence of its world. Once the shift is made to the paradigm of Christian faith, one can't go home again to the old world with its paradigms of power and control.

The Empathic Imagination

To imagine-how, we have discovered, is more than mental rehearsal of some enactment or other. It also serves to relocate ourselves creatively into the situation, the state of affairs of another person, social unit, culture, and so on. Imagination, therefore, permits us to live into a context not our own with a developing empathic skill. Thomas Troeger speaks of this empathic imagination as "our ability to enter the world of another."[68] This empathic skill, when employed with sensitivity, also has the capability of changing our own perception of the world, Troeger adds. When we imagine how other individuals, communities, and cultures experience suffering and evil, for example, our own situation is transformed. The empathic imagination, then, is essential to the church's ministry of preaching.

What our analysis of paradigms disclosed, however, is that human experience is not an uninterpreted set of universals as implied in the experiential/expressive model of doctrine. Some kind of patterned interpretive whole—the paradigmatic imagination—inevitably shapes and locates a field of possible meanings for any and all discrete experiences. Our example of suffering is particularly apt here and will be explored in some depth. Initially, suffering must be distinguished from pain. The latter "is a physical sensation that all animals sometimes endure, but suffering is a distinctly human experience because in one way or another is a function of meaning."[69] The quest for this meaning is a frequent component of psychotherapeutic interaction, it is expressed in various interpretations of the horror of the Holocaust in recent Jewish and Christian writings, and it is central to each of the New Testament's various approaches to the theology of the cross. Some paradigm or other, we discover, is present in our images of self and others as sufferers.

The empathic imagination, given this analysis, must be employed with care and precision since it is always couched within a hermeneutic and reaches out to other contexts, possibly with quite distinctive and different patterned images of self and world. For the North American church, we can conclude confidently with Edward Farley that the worlds within which the faithful empathically imagine-how will be either the paradigms of individualism or of the collective/"social-ist."[70] Within the contemporary church situation, as Farley accurately notes, the predominance of individualism especially is manifested in "the newly revitalized evangelical movement and the therapeutically oriented mainline denominations" (244). Here the individual is seen as the most real as compared with groups, and he or she is likewise identified as the fundamental unit of social change. Farley quotes Robert Bellah approvingly when the sociologist announces that in North American culture, "the primary way of experiencing and understanding the world is 'individualism' " (242).[71]

While the most ubiquitous paradigm of the American church is individualism, a second perspective, "social-ism," sees groups of all sorts as the preeminent expression of human existence. Admitting social-ism to be "relatively marginal" in the present religious situation, Farley discovers its habitats to be "in certain intellectual and critical movements (liberation theologies, feminism), in the bureaucracies of mainline denominations, where ecumenism and social justice form a continuing agenda, as a literature within evangelicalism and in the black church which mixes individualism and social-ism in a distinctive form" (244). Within such power-based habitats, the social-ism paradigm has become the "official story" of mainline Protestant churches, an ideology that not only speaks of the power of social and political arrangements, but exercises that power with deft and thorough administrations. Not only do individualism and social-ism construe their worlds in distinct and mutually exclusive ways—as we would expect of such polarities—they have led the churches to a place of heightening division. There is a "great fracture" in most all of our churches between those who hold one or the other of these two paradigms.

Now, however, yet another paradigm has emerged according to Farley, a new dualism. Recognizing that these two postures represent competing views of the world and each continues to possess vast institutional or cultural influence, they have increasingly been combined into a *single* hermeneutic. The operative model here is not, however, merged or integrated. As Farley insists, "The reason this is a *dualism* is that the two abstracted aspects are—like body and soul—juxtaposed in relation to each other, and the juxtaposition is a disrelation, a combination" (246). What is being asserted here is that by virtue of either paradigm's inability to achieve continuing predominance over the other, the "solution" has been to rest in the simultaneous postures of both individualism and social-ism. Increasingly, "a binary hermeneutic structures clergy thinking" about most every facet of the church's life, including worship and preaching (247).[72] The chief asset of this new dualism, for Farley, is that "the *individual* who combines the two hermeneutics and lives in the both-and of the individual and the social is better off than one who embodies the one or the other" (248–49).

From the perspective of imaging-how's empathic move, this analysis, and especially the liabilities of the new dualism, becomes of deep interest for moral philosophy and theology as well as for preaching. Farley's thesis yields an American church locked into a dualistic paradigm best described as "a cognitive failure," "a binary interpretation which separates and sets things out of relation" (249). Invited to an empathic imagining how the other person and the other community lives, the emergence of this dualistic hermeneutic de facto presents us with a distorted vision. Human beings do not experience themselves and their world in such binary, disjunct ways, as if the lives of the individual and of the social world's groups somehow remain formally alienated from each other! Farley tersely comments that "human being is not a *combination* of the individual and the social" (252). Lacking an adequate interpretive posture, the church likewise will offer a "gospel" reflecting the hermeneutic split.

The inadequacy of the new dualism is also revealed to have a second and more profound dimension. Not only does this hermeneutic yield binary abstractions—personal selves without social worlds and social worlds without individual lives and their stories—it builds into its patterned analysis precisely those opposites that restrict and abstract the richness of the biblical narrative. Individualism, for example, finds the notion of covenant rather extraneous to its project of getting individuals saved or well adjusted; social-ism has shown an inability to receive the Christian "scandal of particularity" in light of competing claims from other religious and secular groups. Joining these hermeneutics in a new dualism does not provide the Christian people of our culture with a gain over each one viewed separately. As Farley concludes:

> In theological terms, a mere combination of the individual and the social does not redeem but leaves each side in its autonomy. The dualist can only live in and promote both sides in their separateness. Hence dualism, the both-and combination, promotes each one in its limitation and sin. (249–50)

By way of this conclusion, Farley first restates the hermeneutic challenge of moving beyond this new dualism and alludes to the need for a new paradigm beyond the scope of both individualism and social-ism. He also admits that other corrective dualisms may well follow on the heels of this present bifurcating of human experience and Christian faith. However, in the midst of these musings, Farley finds himself suggesting some conditions that would obtain if the dualism were left behind. First, he rightly claims that "the sphere of the human is an interhuman sphere which is neither individuality nor society" (254). Then he adds that any unitive paradigm serving to interpret what it means to be human and faithful will be marked by reciprocity between previously polar postures. And, in anticipation of these explorations, Farley suggests that a nondualistic stance will need to deal adequately with evil, the reality of human suffering, and with its redemption (254).[73] Beyond the binary distortions of the new dualism, then, emerge (1) the insistence on the interhuman sphere, (2) a notion of reciprocity, and (3) a test of any paradigm's adequacy in dealing with evil and suffering.

One may be tempted to reply to Edward Farley that these conditions for a postdualistic hermeneutic already obtain within the narrative claims of postliberal theology. The latter does not establish itself first upon the formal qualities of narrative—as in Stephen Crites' approach—but in the narratively expressed world of Scripture whose content speaks of a people, their God, and preeminently the life, death, and resurrection of Jesus Christ. From such a perspective, each of Farley's conditions for a unitive hermeneutics will need to be reconstrued. His emphasis on the "interpersonal sphere" may be best renamed with precision as that location within the community of faith and the tradition that forms it. Simply put, there is no such thing in human experience as an "interpersonal sphere"—the notion is as much of an abstraction as those anthropological bifurcations within the new dualism. Only as we speak of a distinctive community and its cultural/linguistic situation can such a term concretely refer to something. Otherwise, Farley slips into the liberal snare of positing universal human experiences prior to a "regional hermeneutics" (to use his term).[74] For those persons formed by the Christian tradition, this "interpersonal sphere" becomes described through images of Word, water, bread and wine; and they in turn connect to the biblical narrative and the person of Jesus. Outside such a story-formed community, an interpersonal sphere could refer to fundamentalist Islam's intense "brotherhood" or New Age cosmic harmonizers! But then, the latter also represent communities of interpretation with their own distinctive images and stories and therefore their own particularity of human experience.

In the second instance, Farley suggests that a postdualism paradigm will be marked by a dynamic of internal reciprocity among its "postures" rather than by opposition and juxtaposition. Here as well, the issue is *which* community and *which* narrative tradition will shape the sense of reciprocity we desire in place of the polarities of the new dualism. An incipient dualism is evoked by any community's religious particularity in distinction from its general social and cultural environment—church and world, Israel and *goyim*, and so on. Reciprocity, interestingly, becomes a possibility only when and where such religious particularity is asserted and lived out in community. For example, in the most "dualistic" gospel, John, precisely the sharpening of dualistic images (light and darkness, sight and blindness, love and hate) sets up the possibility for a reciprocity based on bearing testimony and feeding even the sheep of the Father's other flocks.[75] Ironically, in the name of "inclusiveness" liberal Christians diminish rather than intensify the conditions for true reciprocity. Consequently, the necessary diminishment of Christian particularity in tradition and covenantal life as well as the suppression of the issue of religious communities' truth claims gives the illusion of a posture beyond dualism. In reality, such "inclusiveness" mitigates against reciprocity by deleting the conditions for its enactment.[76]

Finally, it is also necessary, as we have seen, to reconsider Farley's insistence that a postdualistic posture must adequately deal with the realities of evil and human suffering. Certainly his insight is accurate and essential. The old individualism and the old social-ism are most vulnerable to critique precisely in their distorted interpretations of these human realities. Individualism locates evil within the heart of unconverted individuals and thereby defines the Christian stance toward evil as that of converting more souls. Social-ism locates evil within the "isms," those systems and institutions that are corrupted, unjust, and oppressive. Here the stance has become one of opposition and of mobilizing churchly and secular power to eliminate the respective "ism." Farley would immediately add here that in the new dualism, the

rhetorics of both individualism and social-ism are grouped together as evil is first defined and then opposed. We are now in a
season in the church's life when this rhetoric is increasingly becoming the church's new "official story." However, Farley's insight
that a marriage of two deficient religious paradigms does not make
for a new paradigm is to the point here. Neither of the marriage
partners is capable of adequately serving as a hermeneutic stance
for interpreting the biblical witness to power, suffering, and evil.
Together, the pair may even serve less effectively as an adequate
interpretive lens.

It is at this point that the New Testament's language of power
and its interpretation of evil become the necessary grounding for
any paradigm beyond those Farley portrays. In a remarkable trilogy
devoted to this exploration, Walter Wink insists that any such
reconstruction be based on the New Testament witness to the
principalities and powers.[77] Representing power both on earth and
in heaven, involving persons and social structures, encompassing
both the visible persons and institutions wielding power as well
as the inner "spirit" of that embodiment, the principalities and
powers clearly challenge both the old individualism and newer
social-ism. However, this New Testament language about power
is not a ratification of the new dualism, as may be observed when
their characteristics are adequately portrayed. Wink groups these
defining elements under three main headings: the powers are good,
they are fallen, and they must be redeemed.[78] To these, we must
add another characteristic that is critical to their understanding—
namely, that in Christ, all evil powers have been defeated. In fact,
every New Testament reference to the powers in their fallen manifestation is located within a treatment of the mystery of Christ's
work of redemption.[79] In so doing, the primacy of narrative is also
asserted; we do not name, unmask, nor engage the powers apart
from our baptismal sharing in Christ's passion, death, and resurrection. So, with David Buttrick, we must add to Wink's short
list that in Christ, the powers are defeated and no longer have
authority to enslave the world.[80] Otherwise, this biblical paradigm
of power, evil, and redemption may sadly regress to an experi-
ential/expressive model in which Christian faith is one notable
instance of a general notion of human freedom.[81] Once more,

therefore, we are reminded (1) that "all paradigms are not created equal,"[82] and (2) that our experiences of and speech about any dimension of human existence—especially about good and evil— are mediated and formed by some paradigmatic imagination or other, without exception.

Notes

1. Garrett Green, *Imagining God: Theology and the Religious Imagination* (San Franscisco: Harper & Row, 1989), 42.

2. See the bibliography concluding Stephen D. Moore's "Illuminating the Gospels without Benefit of Color," *Journal of the American Academy of Religion* 58 (Winter 1990): 276–79, for a listing of Jacques Derrida's publications. Also see Mark C. Taylor, *Errings: A Post Modern A-Theology* (Chicago: Univ. of Chicago Press, 1987).

3. Wesley A. Kort, " 'Religion and Literature' in Postmodern Contexts," *Journal of the American Academy of Religion* 58 (Winter 1990): 583.

4. See, e.g., Moore, "Illuminating," 257–79.

5. John Haught, "Narrative, Truth, and Illusion," *Religious Studies in Theology* 5 (May 1985): 74.

6. Haught, "Narrative," 74–75. For a critical analysis of the deconstructionist position, see Edward Farley, *Good and Evil: Interpreting a Human Condition* (Minneapolis: Fortress Press, 1990), 22–26.

7. Mark Allen Powell, *What Is Narrative Criticism?* (Minneapolis: Fortress Press, 1990), 71.

8. Stephen Crites, "The Spatial Dimensions of Narrative Truthtelling," in *Scriptural Authority and Narrative Interpretation*, ed. Garrett Green (Philadelphia: Fortress Press, 1987). Hereafter cited in the text.

9. E. H. Gombrich, *Art and Illusion: A Study in the Psychology of Pictorial Representation* (Princeton, N.J.: Princeton Univ. Press, 1969), 200.

10. Margaret Miles, *Image as Insight: Visual Understanding in Western Christianity and Secular Culture* (Boston: Beacon Press, 1985), 34.

11. Anthony Ugolnik, *The Illuminating Icon* (Grand Rapids: Eerdmans, 1989), 62.

12. John W. Dixon comments that this kind of dichotomy along with the related one of language users and nonlanguage users creates more problems than it solves. He adds, "This one undercuts the book's political polemic. In Miles' view, the word is the instrument of definition, of thought, of precision and control; it is the province of men. The image is the instrument of emotion, of intuition, feeling; it is the province of women. Ironically, the result is a caricature of the traditional male chauvinist view of women." Review of *Image as Insight* by Margaret Miles, *Journal of the American Academy of Religion* 58 (Summer 1990): 270.

13. Charles Rice, "The Expressive Style in Preaching," *The Princeton Seminary Review* 64 (March 1971): 39.

14. See Alla Bozarth-Campbell, *The Word's Body: An Incarnational Aesthetic of Interpretation* (Tuscaloosa, Ala.: Univ. of Alabama Press, 1979), 53–65.

15. Green, *Imagining God*, 70–71.

16. Ibid., 71.

17. Bozarth-Campbell, *Word's Body*, 33–34.

18. Ivan Illich, "The Emergence of the Historical Text," *Forum on "A History of Contemporary 'Certainties,'"* Seattle Pacific Univ., February 11, 1988.

19. The medieval practice of illuminating texts is a striking example of this alignment of the text with visual imagery and of the text's growing distance from aural experience.

20. Robert Fowler, *Let the Reader Understand: Reader-Response Criticism and the Gospel of Mark* (Minneapolis: Fortress Press, 1991), 45.

21. David Baily Harned speaks of seeing and hearing as being abstractions in two senses: "of seeing and hearing from their collegiality with one another and with the other senses, and of the self as organism from its own internal richness" (*Images for Self-Recognition: The Christian as Player, Sufferer, and Vandal* [New York: Seabury Press, 1977], 21–22).

22. Walter Ong, *The Presence of the Word* (New Haven: Yale Univ. Press 1967), 6.

23. David Chidester, *Word and Light: Seeing, Hearing, and Religious Discourse* (Urbana and Chicago: Univ. of Chicago Press, 1992), 17. See 17–24 for Chidester's exploration of this intersensory experience of synesthesia.

24. George Lindbeck, "Critical Exegesis and Theological Interpretation," in *Scriptural Authority and Narrative Interpretation*, ed. Garrett Green (Philadelphia: Fortress Press, 1987), 165.

25. Ibid., 165.

26. Roland Barthes, *Image-Music-Text* (New York: Hill & Wang, 1977), 39. Quoted in Margaret Miles, *Insight*, 35.

27. Harned, *Images*, xix–xx.

28. See Robert Alter, *The Art of Biblical Narrative* (New York: Basic Books, 1981), 47–62, for an analysis of biblical type scenes.

29. Harned, *Images*, 155.

30. Historically, the diminishment of the narrative character of the Great Thanksgiving in favor of a more discursive linguistic approach occurred during the same general period of time (seventh–ninth centuries) that the cup began being withheld from the laity and Communion grew less and less frequent. I am not saying that one is causal of the other; rather, I am suggesting that the narrative form of the eucharistic

prayer and the images of the Holy Meal are organically related in sacramental theology and practice.

31. See James F. Hopewell, *Congregation: Stories and Structures*, ed. Barbara G. Wheeler (Philadelphia: Fortress Press, 1987).

32. Craig R. Dykstra, *Vision and Character: A Christian Educator's Alternative to Kohlberg* (New York: Paulist Press, 1981), 77.

33. Harned, *Images*, 13.

34. Ibid., 14.

35. Ibid., 21–22.

36. Dykstra, *Vision*, 51.

37. David Bailey Harned, *Faith and Virtue* (Philadelphia: Pilgrim Press, 1973), 30. Harned offers the master image of "player" as central to a Christian vision of self and world in *Faith and Virtue*. By the writing of *Images for Self-Recognition*, he sees the need to align "player" with "sufferer" and "vandal." This need is largely in response to the desire to provide for a more adequate interpretation of suffering and the problem of evil.

38. Walter Brueggemann, *Hopeful Imagination: Prophetic Voices in Exile* (Philadelphia: Fortress Press, 1986). Hereafter cited in the text. Also see his *The Prophetic Imagination* (Philadelphia: Fortress Press, 1978) and *Finally Comes the Poet: Daring Speech for Proclamation* (Minneapolis: Fortress Press, 1989).

39. See Peter J. Paris, "The Problem of Evil in Black Christian Perspective," *Justice and the Holy: Essays in Honor of Walter Harrelson*, ed. Douglas A. Knight and Peter J. Paris (Atlanta: Scholars Press, 1989), 297–309, for an excellent study of how this biblical narrative became an essential component in the memory of black slaves in the American South.

40. The power of this poetic and prophetic speech is recovered and refocused within another narrative as Jesus reads Isaiah 61 in his hometown synagogue and announces its fulfillment "Today, . . . in your hearing" (Luke 4:21).

41. Stephen Coonts, *The Cannibal Queen: A Flight into the Heart of America* (New York: Pocket Books, 1992), 24. Italics mine.

42. See Eugene Lowry, *The Homiletical Plot: The Sermon as Narrative Art Form* (Nashville: Abingdon Press, 1980). Also see my *A New Hearing: Living Options in Homiletic Method* (Nashville: Abingdon Press, 1987), 75–88.

43. Henry Mitchell is performing an invaluable service in depicting the rich diversity in the black preacher's rhetorical palette. See his *Black Preaching* (San Francisco: Harper & Row, 1979). Also, see my "Henry Mitchell: Narrative in the Black Tradition," *A New Hearing*, 39–63.

44. Dykstra states that the first stage in the dynamics of moral vision is "a period, sometimes extended, of conscious struggle with a conflict"

(*Vision*, 81). Of course, Dykstra most probably would acknowledge that such struggle has as its formal precedent a degree of formation as a Christian, otherwise there would most likely be little or no uneasiness with ourselves and the world.

45. Owen F. Cummings, "Cyril of Jerusalem as a Postliberal Theologian" *Worship* 67 (March 1993): 157.

46. Lathrop, "Rebirth," 296.

47. Elizabeth Achtemeier, *Preaching as Theology and Art* (Nashville: Abingdon Press, 1984), 19.

48. Maria Harris, *Teaching and Religious Imagination: An Essay in the Theology of Teaching* (San Francisco: HarperCollins, 1987), 21.

49. Dykstra, *Vision*, 82.

50. William F. Lynch, *Images of Hope: Imagination as Healer of the Hopeless* (Notre Dame and London: Univ. of Notre Dame Press, 1974), 177–78. Quoted in Dykstra, *Vision*, 83.

51. Harris, *Teaching*, 21.

52. M. Robert Mulholland, Jr., "Spiritual Reading of Scripture," *Weavings* 3 (November/December 1988): 29. See 29–32 for a brief description of the *lectio divina* approach to reading and praying Scripture. Also see Thelma Hall, *Too Deep for Words* (New York and Mahwah: Paulist Press, 1988), 36–56.

53. Brueggemann, *Hopeful Imagination*, 43.

54. See Appendix for an analysis of modern and postmodern homiletic imagination.

55. As with parable interpretation in particular, the portrayal of the Jesus behind the text, as grasped by the "historical imagination," was most typically a projection of the preacher's own theological convictions and the ethos of the preacher's particular tradition. Liberal preachers gave us a young and fearless prophet, conservatives offered an atoning Savior, while pietists imagined us alone in the garden with Jesus.

56. David Buttrick reframes memory within his notion of personal and communal consciousness. The congregation's lived experience is couched in images pertaining to the social world and to that of our own self-awareness. Hence, a congregation's lived experience becomes the field within which we search deeply for "the actualities of consciousness" (*Homiletic: Moves and Structures* [Philadelphia: Fortress Press, 1987], 33).

57. Dykstra, *Vision*, 83.

58. Ibid.

59. Garrett Green, "Fictional Narrative and Scriptural Truth," in *Scriptural Authority and Narrative Interpretation*, ed. Garrett Green (Philadelphia: Fortress Press, 1987), 85. John McClure adds that "the idea of paradigm includes within it the idea of a tradition and a community of

practices. . . . They are formal systems that find their meanings in communities of commonly shared practice" (*The Four Codes of Preaching: Rhetorical Strategies* [Minneapolis: Fortress Press, 1991], 74n).

60. Thomas S. Kuhn, *The Structure of Scientific Revolutions*, 2d ed. (Chicago: Univ. of Chicago Press, 1970).

61. Kuhn, *Revolutions*, 77.

62. Green, "Fictional Narrative," 91.

63. Green, *Imagining God*, 50.

64. Ibid., 47.

65. Ibid., 57.

66. John McClure speaks of such homiletical ducks or rabbits as being a preacher's "rhetorical schema." This schema may include "such things as (the preacher's) definition of preaching, approach to biblical exegesis and interpretation, facility in language and communication, context of ministry and personal understanding of that context, and any number of other personal interests" (*Codes*, 1).

67. See Bernard Brandon Scott, "Towards a Hermeneutics of the Solo Savior: Dirty Harry and Romans 5–8," in *Intersections: Post-Critical Studies in Preaching*, ed. Richard Eslinger (Grand Rapids: Eerdmans, 1994), 123–56. See also Scott's *Hollywood Dreams and Biblical Stories* (Minneapolis: Fortress Press, 1994).

68. Thomas H. Troeger, "Tapping Hidden Streams: Receiving the Spirit through the Discipline of Imagination," *The Marten Lecture in Homiletics*, Saint Meinrad Seminary, Saint Meinrad, Indiana, October 6, 1992.

69. Harned, *Images*, 43

70. "Social-ist" is Edward Farley's term to represent the view that "the most decisive bearers of human reality are not individuals but groups" ("Praxis and Piety," *Justice and the Holy*, 242–43). Hereafter cited in the text. See also his *Good and Evil*.

71. See Robert Bellah et al., *Habits of the Heart: Individualism and Commitment in American Life* (Berkeley: Univ. of California Press, 1985), especially chapter 6.

72. Notice, e.g., this dualism as embodied in a seminary or denomination's continuing education offerings for clergy. The new dualism, moreover, is encoded within recent revisions of mainline denominational hymnals and embodied in the social resolutions of those same ecclesial communities.

73. "Most descriptions of human sin," Farley notes, "fall on the side of the corrupted individual self or the corrupted structures of society" ("Praxis and Piety," 254).

74. Farley begins his analysis of good and evil by way of asking, "In what way does the Hebraic and Christian paradigm of the human condition express the truth of things" (*Good and Evil*, 116). Given his acknowledgment that the personal, interpersonal, and communal experience of good and evil is couched within some paradigm or other, it is

odd to posit a neutral, nonparadigmed place from which biblical faith can be assessed with regard to "the truth of things." Unless Edward Farley has rehabilitated some tradition-independent location for adjudicating "the truth of things," the experiential/expressive assumption is once more being made that human experience comes prior to a cultural, linguistic, and religious contextualization.

75. See Paul Minear, *John: The Martyr's Gospel* (New York: Pilgrim Press, 1984), especially his chapter "No One Comes to the Father but by Me," 103–12.

76. A pastor relates that a liberal colleague became quite baffled when he responded that what was excluded in the celebration of "inclusiveness" was himself and his tradition as a catholic Methodist!

77. See Walter Wink, *Naming the Powers: The Language of Power in the New Testament* (Philadelphia: Fortress Press, 1984); *Unmasking the Powers: The Invisible Forces That Determine Human Existence* (Philadelphia: Fortress Press, 1986); and *Engaging the Powers: Discernment and Resistance in a World of Domination* (Minneapolis: Fortress Press, 1992).

78. Wink, *Engaging*, 3.

79. See Wink, *Naming*, 39–96, for an analysis of "the disputed passages."

80. David Buttrick, *The Mystery and the Passion: A Homiletic Reading of the Gospel Traditions* (Minneapolis: Fortress Press, 1992), 58–60. See p. 59, n. 10, for a listing of recent writing on "the powers that be."

81. Wink tends in this direction at times throughout his three fine volumes. For example, he defines the gospel as "a context-specific remedy for the evils of the Domination System" (*Engaging*, 48). Indefinite articles in such contexts usually will point in an experiential/expressive direction.

82. Green, "Fictional Narrative," 91.

4

Metaphor and Play
in Narrative Perspective

In his turn toward the linguistic, Paul Ricoeur achieved a significant advance within twentieth-century imagination theory. By shifting the imaginative paradigm from perception to linguistics, several decisive advances were achieved. Imagination was no longer construed as primarily reproductive (that is, of what is perceived), but as productive of new meaning within a linguistic world.

Turning toward the Linguistic

In Ricoeur's treatment of metaphor as the preeminent imaginative event within poetics, his hermeneutic enters a new stage. The resulting shift from a focus on the symbol (and therefore on the word or phrase) to this exploration of metaphor now expands the semantic range to at least that of a sentence. In this "semantic impertinence" of metaphor, new meaning is disclosed as prior and dissimilar semantic elements are brought into imaginative alignment. The prior literal meanings self-destruct in this productivity of new meaning so that, "in this sense," Ricoeur states, "a metaphor is an instantaneous creation, a semantic innovation."[1]

At one level, then, the turn to the linguistic in Ricoeur's notion of metaphoric innovation offered what Edward Murray describes as "a new way entirely of understanding the imagination as a new way of languaging and engaging in meaning."[2] However, even more is at stake in Ricoeur's hermeneutics than this description of semantic innovation with regard to the significance of metaphor.

For in this depiction of language's way of creating new meaning, he asserts as well that reality is being created. Metaphor is the imaginative locus for semantic generation of meaning and an ontological revealing of reality. Hence, as Richard Kearney observes of Ricoeur's hermeneutic investigations, "imagination's role in the metaphorical play of language leads Ricoeur to the ontological paradox of creation-as-discovery."[3] Both language and our sense of reality are shattered in the metaphoric achievement, both new meaning and reality undergo a new disclosure, a new transformation.

From the perspective of a narrative hermeneutic, Ricoeur's work on metaphoric productivity remains of keen interest, but with several important provisos. First, the narrative location of metaphors, particularly in the biblical witness, becomes preeminent, with Ricoeur's semantic theory becoming of secondary interest. In other words, our interest is not in a general hermeneutic theory of metaphor that may find illustration in such scriptural genre as parables. Rather, our interest in parables as narrative metaphor stems from their power to disclose the reality of God's dominion and to reflect on the parabler Jesus. This brings us to the second proviso—namely, the concern that the person and preaching of Jesus not become reduced to some new disclosures as to the religious dimensions of human experience. So Frei critically observes:

> in hermeneutic theory one subsumes Jesus' preaching, especially the parables of the Kingdom of God, under a more general reference. In Ricoeur's terms, there is an "extravagance" in the denouement and the main characters that contrasts with the realism of the narrative and constitutes the parables' specific "religious" trait.[4]

Finally, our caution with regard to Ricoeur's hermeneutic turn to the linguistic in the metaphor has to do with the mode in which he construes its ontological role. Even if metaphor functions so as to invite discovery of "world" in its reality, for Frei, Lindbeck, and others, such a world delivered through any general hermeneutics is called into question, caught up in, and possibly transformed by the world of biblical narrative. If the church's interpretation of Scripture reflects the integrity of biblical narrative, then general discoveries of metaphorical meaning and reality may find themselves in dissonance with the meaning of Christ and kingdom. The ontological weight, too, will have to go with the world revealed in biblical narrative, witnessing to the presence and power of Jesus Christ.

The Dynamics of Irony

Reading biblical narrative within Frei's "literal sense," it becomes apparent that metaphor is not the singular device of indirection recent hermeneutics has sought to portray. Rather, there is an increasing appreciation for the role of irony in the witness of Scripture, to the point that it will need to be placed alongside metaphor as an essential vehicle for conveying the world of the text and the character of God. Why is it, we may ask, that the writers of many of the narratives in Hebrew Scripture and especially Mark and John among the Gospels rely so thoroughly on irony in their rendering of these stories?[5] Much more seems at stake here than simply the employment of yet another trope for textual decoration. In fact, given the scope of the recent work on irony by biblical scholars, Wayne C. Booth is right to observe that both metaphor and irony, beginning as "minute oratorical device(s)," have risen to "imperialistic world conqueror(s)."[6] But that is to put Frei's cart before the horse again. First, imagination's turn to the linguistic in metaphor's companion, irony, must be explored.[7]

Elements of Irony

The meaning of irony was learned back in school from the large dictionary resting securely on its oak stand in the library. Irony, it told, was saying one thing and meaning another. However, as Wayne Booth remarks, "There is nothing especially wrong with this view, except that it still radically obscures the complexity of what we do, and how we manage to do it."[8] The initial question is one of discernment: How does irony move us from that place which at first seemed stable enough? To answer that question and to gain competence in discerning situations of irony, Booth offers "a practical preliminary notion of irony" (5), which he then elaborates into a thoroughgoing depiction of stable irony. Irony is *intended, covert, stable or fixed,* and *finite in application* (5–6).[9] We will now explore each of these steps with Booth in some depth:

1. Ironies are *intended.* They are "deliberately created by human beings to be heard or read and understood with some precision by other human beings" (5). Implied here is an ironist with skill in shaping the complex workings of an irony. Also implied is an audience, a group of people expected to share a level of competence in spotting ironies. This ironic transaction is made to order for reader response criticism. Lacking an audience equipped with an ironic vision, there is no movement from the first and insecure location of the literal meaning.

2. Ironies are *covert.* The surface meaning is signaled as false and in need of repudiation. Still, this signaling must be subtle and mostly hidden. The most typical means of retaining this sense of the covert is by having the initial surface meaning stated or believed by some person or literary character and by the initial meaning's easy recognition as part of a larger, social structure of meaning. Put conversely, irony cannot obtain if a patently and explicitly false assertion is first made with everyone involved being knowledgeable of its falsehood.[10]

3. Ironies are *stable* or *fixed.* In the discernment of the surface meaning's unreliability, the hearer or reader is now confronted with the task of reconstructing a meaning akin to that intended by the ironist. Booth adds that "once a reconstruction of meaning has been made, the reader is not then invited to undermine it with further demolitions and reconstructions" (6). This decision to reconstruct and then rest with that newly built meaning is what defines stable irony. Implied here is some rather close "fit" between the ironist's intended real meaning and the auditor's reconstructed meaning. Lacking such proximity, the irony would be rendered unstable. Therefore, Booth insists: "Whether a given word or passage or work is ironic depends . . . not on the ingenuity of the reader but on the intentions that constitute the creative act. And whether it is seen as ironic depends on the reader's catching the proper clues to those intentions" (91).

4. Ironies are all *finite* in application. It is inherent in the dynamics of irony that if recognition is to occur in the face of this covert ironic presentation, then the ironist and reader will need to share in a particular community's "language game," codes, and norms. Moreover, the required reconstruction also is undertaken utilizing those same resources, but with some new meaning. Ironies, then, do not travel well; they are usually "local" to a context and relate with effectiveness only within a specific cultural and linguistic setting.

Ironic Reconstruction

Given these four preliminary steps in the achievement of irony, it may be startling to discover such complexity to this process of saying one thing and meaning another! Readers must possess a necessary competence in order to reject the surface meaning along with its attendant and implied worldview. Then the readers (or hearers) must be imaginatively engaged in the tasks of proposing alternate meanings, assessing the adequacy of each, and of deciding for a new place to build upon this preferred understanding. Booth both analyzes this complex irony dynamic and proposes the metaphor of "reconstruction" to speak of this intricate reader response. "Conscious of a loss in grace and warmth," Booth confesses, "I turn to the building trades, to 'reconstruction,' implying the tearing down of one habitation and the building of another one on a different spot" (33). However, it must be reemphasized that this activity of building on another spot is predicated on an imaginatively grasped awareness that the surface meaning is one built on sand. Only when that judgment has occurred may reconstruction begin.

Once the literal meaning is rejected, reconstruction begins by sampling rival meanings and by chasing down their rival cultural and linguistic "worlds." (Irony insists that we view single meanings in their larger, social contexts!) These alternate meanings, Booth observes, "are tried out—or rather, in the usual case of quick recognition, come flooding in" (11). For irony to work, however, a decision regarding the new place for meaning reconstruction is made in conjunction with the awareness that the author is speaking ironically and that she or he does possess knowledge and beliefs about the true but hidden meaning. In the absence of the former—a sense of irony at work—we may simply "not get it" or attribute the surface meaning to the author. A friend asks, "Think it will rain?" Standing there dripping wet, we conclude that we are either in the presence of irony or a very dumb friend. On the other hand, when it is assumed that the author's true beliefs are other than those of the surface meaning, we may find ourselves in that awkward revelatory moment when we realize that no irony was intended in spite of our having rejected the presented surface meaning. We think, or even blurt out, "You can't mean that!"[11]

Once the situation has been discovered as having an ironic character and the convictions of the speaker have been discerned, reconstruction now involves a decision regarding the new place of meaning *and our own response to it*. This stage in the process introduces the element of agency into ironic interpretation. To decide to build the new house of meaning in favor of remaining in the old habitation of the surface meaning is to decide as well to live in that new place, perhaps with its new people, beliefs, and customs. Notice, however, that this communal dimension to ironic discernment began in that complex activity leading to an awareness of the real authorial convictional system. Reconstruction, then, "completes a more astonishing, communal achievement than most accounts have recognized" (13).

Irony and Metaphor

A particularly handy comparison is provided by Wayne Booth between the two "imperial conquerors," metaphor and irony. Along the way, he notes that metaphor, of the two, has attracted a predominance of attention in the modern era. By way of comparing these prime figures of indirection, Booth lists four major points of dissimilarity between the two. Implied is an awareness that both irony and metaphor are not to be taken simply on a literal level and that both involve doublet systems of reference or meaning. Booth's points of comparison include:

1. With metaphor as with irony, the interpreter is pushed beyond the presented surface meaning, though in the case of metaphor, "what is rejected is primarily the grammatical form of the claim" (22–23).

2. With irony, we are pushed to explore alternate meanings of the literal and must be alert throughout that process to the author's own true beliefs and convictions. In metaphor we are given permission to add other unspoken meanings "with or without further words from the author" (23). Added meanings may enhance the richness of metaphoric discourse, and we are forced to retreat "only if and when we come to meanings that are incongruous" (23).

3. Given this fundamentally additive process, metaphor involves no strongly shaped decision regarding the author's beliefs and convictions. This is not to say that no decisions are made in the course of metaphoric imagining; rather, it is to single out irony as that context within which decision is a central and necessary element in interpretation.

4. Related to the above, and admitting that decisions may be needed in the metaphoric process, Booth still grants decision as an intrinsic component only to irony. With metaphor "it may not be disastrous if no decision is made at all" (23), but the same can never be said of irony.

Dramatic Irony

In stable irony as developed by Wayne Booth and others, a clear and delineable sequence proceeds from a sense of dissonance to one of resolution by way of reconstruction. In the beginning is the discovery of two levels of meaning, one that is the surface, literal meaning, and the other residing at a deeper level of the rhetorical situation. Moreover, Booth, Muecke and others insist that irony "requires that there be dissonance or tension between the two levels."[12] As regards this dissonance, it is further required that one party—narrator, character, crowd, or other—be innocent of the inherent tension. Hence, there is the need for the "ironic victim." What thus confronts the reader is an invitation to respond as a "knowing" and therefore responsible agent in favor of the deeper, more truthful level of the irony. Here Booth applies his metaphor of reconstruction. Having rejected the false world represented by the surface meaning, the reader is then required to rebuild a world based on the more solid foundation of the deeper meaning.

It is at this point of invoking his model of reconstruction, however, that Booth has attracted criticism from other scholars investigating the dynamics of irony. As these interpreters view the problem, it is Booth's celebration of the *stable* character of the reconstruction that is most problematic. Gary J. Handwerk, for example, notes approvingly that Booth initially speaks of irony as an "intricate intellectual dance," while later on "the dance metaphor finds itself increasingly pushed aside by the more mechanical metaphor of irony as reconstruction."[13] The distinction invoked by the critics of the reconstruction metaphor relates to the rhetorical context of the irony. If we speak only of verbal ironies, then perhaps a resolution is possible in a meaning location that remains stable and in which we may "rest secure." Within a narrative context, however, dramatic ironies rarely come to such stable and secure resolutions within the discourse; for such dramatic irony, "Booth's language of reconstruction, which suggests that the resolution of the irony is complete and final is much too strong for use here."[14]

The issue, then, is to differentiate the literary device of verbal irony from the narrative-based genre of dramatic irony. First, and most insistently argued, is the precisely nonstable, even dialectic interplay between reader and the story where dramatic narrative is at stake. Robert Fowler observes:

> Because dramatic irony involves the audience in perceiving incongruity that the characters in the story do not perceive, it always has a two-layered structure to it, a built-in dialectical relationship between what is not understood within the story and what is understoood in the audience's encounter with the story. . . . After the audience comprehends the distance opened up between it and the undiscerning characters, the irony continues to reverberate in the gap between the story and the audience. Dramatic irony is inherently revelatory.[15]

If for verbal irony, a reader's discernment may result in a stable and finite reconstruction; for dramatic irony, the reverse obtains. Ironies once presented from the viewpoint of characters or narrator rarely come to rest within the scriptural narrative context. With Fowler, I admit to ongoing "incongruous reverberations" between the story and the reader that remain insecure and unstable.[16]

One of the most fruitful case studies for insights into the dynamics of dramatic irony may well be the Gospel of Mark (with John running at least "neck and neck"; see John 20:4). In Mark, dramatic irony abounds, rendered chiefly through the dissonance, if not conflict, between the knowledge and point of view of a variety of characters within the story and the point of view and knowledge accorded the reader/hearer. At a formal level, this dissonance is achieved by the conflicts between Mark's story (the "what of a narrative") and Mark's discourse (the "how of the narrative").[17] The so-called messianic secret, for example, operates at the story level, especially with regard to the disciples' persistent lack of faith (vision). On the other hand, we have already been given Jesus' true identity in the first verse of the Gospel! While Fowler is specifically commenting on the Walking on the Water account (Mark 6:45-52), the observation may be expanded to include almost all of the dramatic irony in Mark:

> Of all the characters in the story, only Jesus is included consistently within the circle of intimacy occupied by narrator and narratee. . . . The ironies and other indirect moves shared by the narrator and the narratee operate at the expense of virtually all characters in the story except Jesus and put distance between us and them. (80)

The effect on the reader is profound!

Mark's skill in achieving this ironic tension and reverberation between story and discourse persists and grows even more intense in the concluding passion narratives. Repeatedly, through strategies of exclusion (information is shared with us that is unavailable or unreceived by the characters relating to Jesus), we find ourselves called to decide between the point of view regarding Jesus provided for us and those offered by others in the story. And while the revelation of Jesus' identity remains hidden to most of those same characters, we are let in on the true identity of Jesus from the beginning. Remarking on these Markan rhetorical devices of "exclusionary strategies" and "veiled revelations," Camery-Hoggatt notes that it is the narrator's purpose that we take a position, declare ourselves.[18] Mark's dramatic irony places us in a highly unsettled and conflicted context: Are we to believe the banal viewpoint of the disciples or the fuller vision of Jesus already shared with us by the narrator? Such a decision, moreover, does not remain one of only intellectual significance. To decide for our own privileged point of view as hearers and readers "must be an activity of personal response as well as an activity of intellectual assent." Thus, "the ironic dimensions of the passion may *effect* the kind of commitment which for Mark lies at the core of discipleship."[19]

Within either stable or dramatic irony there is an inherent call for decision. The surface or conventional meaning is never presented as simply an alternative to the covert, deeper meaning. Rather, "the superiority of the new meaning is an aggressive or competitive superiority—the rejected meaning is in some real sense a rival or a threat."[20] The ironies offered by Mark or the other Gospel narrators involve not only intellectual decisions regarding these rival meanings but choices regarding social affiliation and disaffiliation as well. To decide *against* the meanings of Jesus' opponents is also an invitation to decide *for* a new community capable of seeing the truth. Irony's "exclusionary strategies," therefore, also function by indirection to beckon the reader to include him- or herself within the community of disciples. So Fowler maintains that "all persons reading the Gospel, to the extent that they see through the irony, become a community—a community not bound together by ties of race, culture, or politics but by the common experience of reading and coming to terms with Mark's irony."[21]

An irony lies latent within this biblical dynamic of irony. Viewed from a surface, and liberal, point of view, such ironies "exclude" and must therefore be set aside in favor of a more "inclusive" interpretation of Christ and church. The irony in this avoidance of dramatic irony's exclusionary strategy in the Gospels is that the deeper and more radical meaning is thereby abandoned as well. And as Booth perceptively notes, there is a "peculiarity" about this community formed by a shared ironic vision. He observes that "it seems clear that Mark's irony builds a larger community of readers than any possible literal statement of his beliefs could have done."[22] Booth adds that such a community "is often a larger community, with fewer outsiders, than would have been built by non-ironic statement."[23] Here is "the irony of ironies"; a truly inclusive community in Christ is one shaped by the exclusionary strategies of biblical narrative, confronted with decisions about truth and discipleship, and comprised of those who recognize themselves as having become excluded outsiders in so choosing.

Given these dynamics of irony within biblical narrative, we are struck by several features that speak directly to our concern for a postliberal theology. First, this apparently essential role of dramatic irony in Scripture underscores Hauerwas's insistence that any adequate hermeneutic must include the church as well as the Bible. Although not directly speaking to the role of dramatic irony, Hauerwas is on target when he insists:

> Part of the difficulty with the rediscovery of the significance of narrative for theological reflection has been too much attention on texts *qua* texts. . . . But the emphasis on narrative can only result in scholarly narcissism if narrative texts are abstracted from the concrete people who acknowledge the authority of the Bible.[24]

As we have seen, the ironies within a Gospel text are not adequately described as fully located in that literary context. Irony in its fullest expression as discernment of competing levels of meaning, decision, and personal and communal dis- and re-identification all involve the role of the reader. In this way irony is not as much "a property resident within the text," but is "somehow resident within the reaction of the reader."[25]

A related implication for postliberal theology is the hermeneutic importance of personal and communal virtues. Equipped with the insights of reader-response criticism, it is notable how frequently the Gospel narrators invite the reader in on points of view and privileged information inaccessible to many of the characters who surround Jesus. So the assembly of the faithful may spot that the soldiers guarding the tomb following the "great earthquake" (Matt. 28:2) plus the appearance of the apocalyptic angel "were shaken and became as if dead" (28:4),[26] thus, in fact, literally "trembling before the Lord" (see Ps. 99:1). As for the guards, they remained innocent of the irony here, unconscious of it, actually!

Notice, however, that several competencies are assumed of the readers/hearers by the Gospel writers when they perform a dramatic irony. One obvious assumption is that Christian readers have conformed themselves to the biblical witness and that their praxis includes praying psalms. People who are illiterate of the Bible will rarely, if ever, spot its ironies! Another competency assumed by the Gospels is that readers/hearers are equipped "with resources of evaluation which are different from those available to their characters."[27] The same resurrection story in Matthew that treats the guards with continuing irony also tells of the resources for true evaluation of the resurrection—a relationship in community with the risen Christ, worship of the Lord, and obedience to his command to proclaim the gospel to all the world (28:16-20).

Finally, the identification of irony along with metaphor as the two central "devices of indirection" in Scripture shifts the interpreter to the question of competencies that must be gained. How do Christian readers of their Scriptures discern that the presented surface meaning of a text is an invitation to an ironic vision? Moreover, how are they to know that their decisions regarding the deeper meanings of dramatic irony are either in concert with the intent of the author(s) or in accord with the gospel? Clearly, irony in the biblical narratives involves more than literary technique; a healing of our blindness and recovery of sight is implied. So Fowler speaks of irony "as the experience of seeing and seeing through an incongruity."[28] Ironic vision is an acquired virtue of the community of believers and is based on several convictions, some of which are the following.

1. Christians live in numerous worlds, all shaped by storied traditions and their attended skein of imagery.

2. These worlds inevitably shape us, may equip us with certain virtues, and just as surely may limit our vision to their own construals of the real and the true.

3. These worlds often are in tension with each other and with themselves, hence the occasion for irony emerges.

4. These worlds are inherently in tension with the biblical world and with the character of God and Christ revealed through its narratives and images. Ironic vision is "trained" as the community

learns to perceive the dissonance and contradictions between story and discourse within biblical narrative.

5. Some world or other will function to shape the paradigmatic imagination such that rival interpretations are either rejected or re-visioned.

6. Discerning the ironies within the biblical narrative invites decision as to truth and performance as disciples.

Homiletic Performance

Each successive construal of imagination—the perceptual model, pragmatic imagining, the linguistic turn of metaphor and irony—has expanded its horizon while implicitly showing forth prior inadequacies as well. As significant as the turn toward the linguistic is for an adequate notion of imagination, the advance represented in Gadamer's model of play culminates this sequence of imagination theory. Here personal embodiment, with or without a linguistic expression, added a key element to the growing matrix of imagination theory. As each successive construal of imagination has been located within a narrative-based postliberal theology, however, the need has emerged to reshape the prior theory. With regard to this notion of the play of imagination as well, we will gratefully welcome the advances made to imagination theory; we will also expect to find similar adjustments necessary by virtue of our interest in preaching and the preacher.

Among the primary facets of Gadamer's notion of play, three have been celebrated in a number of diverse arenas—(1) the immediacy and movement of play as primary, (2) the immediacy and self-forgetfulness of the players, and (3) the location of play as art within a tradition. Each of these components bears review from theological perspective grounded in biblical narrative.

1. The dynamics of play. One of Gadamer's insights regards the primacy of play with respect to its players. Noting the back-and-forth dynamic of play, particularly in nature, he reverses conventional wisdom by insisting that "the primordial sense of playing is the medial one."[29] That is, there is an "ease," a "movement," a "purposelessness" to play such that the player is one who is

played. This structure of play "absorbs the player into itself" (105), and therefore significantly diminishes the player's self-consciousness. We lose ourselves in play; actually, the game plays us.

So familiar is this experience among those called to preach, that in many respects, the word *play* could be substituted by *preach* and *game* by *sermon* or *homily* with a natural and playful ease. In so doing, David Bryant's description of this dynamic of play easily becomes the insight that "the essence of [preaching] is located not in the consciousness of the [preacher] but in the movement of the [sermon] itself."[30] Another Bryant quote speaks nicely to this aspect of homiletic imagination. Again, we replace "play" and "player" so he reads, "When preachers preach, they are preached by the sermon."[31] A homily is the play of movement, and the homilist is "played" in its enactment.

2. Closely related to this player-as-played dynamic is the self-forgetfulness of the one who loses him- or herself in the movement. Gadamer observes that there is "the primacy of play over the consciousness of the player" (104). To give oneself over to the game is to relinquish a mundane sense of control or mastery over oneself. Rather, this relinquishment has to do both with the characteristic "spirit" and "structure" of each respective game (as forms of play). There are "rules and regulations that prescribe the way the field of the game is filled . . . whenever there is a game" (107). These regulated patterns of activity, then, both insist on their hegemony over the players—otherwise a "zebra" might call a foul—and allow an imaginative participation in which self-conscious behavior is more or less out of place.[32]

Viewed from a homiletic perspective, this language of the game would appear to resonate more fully with the imaginative act of preaching than simply play. On one hand, the absence of *telos* within pure play does not fit well with the intentionality of a sermon's movement. As soon as we say with David Buttrick that a homily is a structured shaping of language with regard to certain intentions of a pericope, we are more aligned with the language of game rather than play. On the other hand, Gadamer's remarks concerning the role of a game's patterned "field" in diminishing the self-consciousness of the player likewise speaks to preaching. A preacher may break the homily's rules by all sorts of "fouls."

Then, too, the spirit of the homiletic game may be violated by the intrusion of excessive self-consciousness in the pulpit. In either case, the assembly is deprived of their movement with the homilist in the game.

3. Play as representation. When play shifts to the context of music, theater, sports, or the liturgy, "the closed world of play lets down one of its walls, as it were" (108). Gadamer explains:

> A religious rite and a play in a theater obviously do not represent in the same sense as a child playing. Their being is not exhausted by the act that they present themselves, for at the same time they point beyond themselves to the audience which participates by watching. Play here is no longer the mere self-representation of an ordered movement, nor mere representation in which the child playing is totally absorbed, but it is "representing for someone." (108–9)

What Gadamer asserts here first is that by letting down play's wall, the audience becomes part of the performance. A child lost in play loses that playfulness and becomes self-conscious upon being discovered. Such primordial play admits of no spectators! Within the enactment of a drama, however, the actors represent not only their roles to an audience, but thereby invite the audience to be the completion of the play. The wall goes up once again— this boundary between players and those not in the play—but it now encloses both actors and audience within its field. Preaching is this imaginative representation par excellence. What is represented is out of the biblical "script," which has already evoked in the present the roles of the preacher and the congregation. To say that preaching is representative play is to retain the self-forgetfulness of the homiletic player. It is also to say that the preacher in some heightened way represents in that preaching a focused and unified embodiment of the gospel for a community of faith. And this play as representation further highlights the essentially communal context for the enactment. The wall goes up again, now including preacher, sermon, and people all within its boundary.[33]

Beginning with the notion of imagination as play, Gadamer has blazed a trail that leads to the game metaphor and finally that of

performance. Here, at last, we find a location best suited for homiletic imagination. Of course, what is not meant by "performance"
is any sense of the old "pulpit prince" performing before a passive
"audience" in the dimmed sanctuary. Nor do we mean the more
contemporary expressions of "performance" in the excessively
self-conscious personal disclosures of preacherly affect. In both
cases, inappropriate self-consciousness intrudes on the highly
complex imaginative act of preaching. Still, the homilist does play,
is played within a game, and enacts a performance. A performer,
however, is aware of the spirit and the rules of this patterned play.

The notion of imagination construed as homiletic performance
encompasses preacher and congregation and is additionally shaped
by such factors as denominational and regional traditions, as well
as by the congregation's own distinctive history. The liturgical
event of preaching occurs never in a vacuum but within "horizons
of assent"[34] of shared expectations and commonly held experiences. A kind of distinctive "currency" is extended by an assembly
that gives or withholds permission for the homiletic performance.
This currency may be spoken of as a church's "norms," but as it
comes time for the sermon, these norms become enlivened into
a highly imaginative communal event. Even such an obvious issue
as the sermon's location in the order of worship reflects these
norms even while they are enacted within the imagined world
of that liturgy. This imaginal currency of homiletic performance
may be spoken of as having three primary "denominations": the
temporal, the spatial, and that pertaining to a homily's "rhetorical
stretch."

The temporal aspect of homiletical performance. Most every
preacher since the apostle Paul has "lost" one of his or her sleeping
congregants out a window as the realities of a congregation's expectations regarding sermon length were exceeded. Pastor and
parish usually come to share the norms regarding the length of a
homily, and within these parameters, the preacher and parish give
permission for the sermon to be spoken and heard. Such a temporal
expectation may be the eight to ten minutes for a homily during
Mass or a quite extended period in some traditions, within parts
of the African-American church, for instance. Notice here, though,

that it is not simply how many minutes elapse that is determinative. "Getting through too soon" may be as much of an offense to a congregation as "talking too long." Moreover, the particular liturgical event, season, or pastoral context may qualify this temporal expectation.

This (mostly) shared sense of expectation between preacher and community is articulated as an imaginative activity in much the same way Gadamer speaks of the patterns of shared play as imaginative. There is "time" for the game—sometimes brutally shown on the clock above the basketball court or ice hockey rink. There is "time" for the drama as an audience collects and settles for the theater production. And there is "time" for the homily before we move on to hymn, creed, prayer, and the Meal (to assume an ecumenical pattern of the liturgy). Interestingly, this time for the performance with its somewhat structured expectations is a necessary condition for that occasion's sense of timelessness in play and preaching. Here *chronos* and *kairos* are not polarities; rather, the former provides a shared imaginal "house" for the performance's possibility of becoming *kairos*.

The spatial dimension of homiletic performance. Typically, there is a space for preaching, reified in the location of pulpit or ambo. Once more, the particulars of that space are shaped by a host of considerations, yet certain dynamics are at work regardless of the particulars within any church setting. First, the space for preaching is imagined as one distinct from, but in relationship to, the hearers. This location serves to free the assembly to attend imaginatively to the homily without other factors intruding on the performance. Also, this spatial distance and more or less predictable location of the preaching expresses and reinforces the community's shared perception of the pastor's identity. Being "set apart" as a pastor/preacher has been critiqued for its often too lofty location with regard to the worship place of the laity and their ministry. So quite appropriately, the spatial locations for preaching have been moved in many churches to reflect a less hierarchical and more collegial ecclesiology. Still, there will typically be a new place for the sermon, and some distance will be maintained.[35]

This spatial dimension to the performance of preaching, as with the temporal, serves paradoxically to define parameters in order to free. The actor is "blocked" with respect to location, movement, and even gesture. Then the actor has something to work with in the creation of a character. The audience extends quite a bit of latitude regarding the play's location. Still, the audience both comes with assumptions as to this "space" of the play and must perform certain adjustments of its imagined spatial sense each time a play begins.[36] Analogously, congregations, along with their preacher, also reassemble their particular spatial imaging of the homiletical performance at each new occasion.

The rhetorical "stretch" of homiletic performance. Within the horizon of assent of preacher and parish, there will be found a dominant and persisting rhetorical code shaping the expectations and imaginative possibilities of that community. John McClure identifies four primary codes of preaching, each having a number of possible specific expressions.[37] Viewed from our perspective of homiletical performance and the imagination, what is interesting about McClure's schema is that the imaginative "stretch" of a homily does not vary so much among the four codes as within them. That is, operating within the scriptural code, a preacher may adopt *translation* as a strategy telling us what "the Bible says." Imaginative stretch—that capability of preacher and parish to engage together with mobility and tensive meanings—is thereby severely restricted. Other preachers operating out of the same code may *transpose* the biblical story into a plotted sequence of meanings related to the intention of the text and imaged out of contemporary congregational experience. According to the skill of the preacher in imagining such a homiletical plot and its attendant image systems, such a homily would represent a quantum leap in rhetorical stretch.[38] Similar ranges of breadth in the imaginative horizon within each of the other codes' subtypes also obtain. At any given time, however, it is to be assumed that a pastor and parish's horizon of assent will center on one rhetorical code type and perhaps one subtype. Other codes may be visited, and this is encouraged by McClure, but the tendency will be to locate a "code-home" as one rhetorical imaginative space.[39]

From the perspective of postliberal narrative theology, homiletic performance will delight in the incredible riches of biblical anamnesis, whatever the particular homiletic method. Once again we are confronted by this paradox of the faithful imagination: freedom comes most fully within a community conformed to the narrative of Israel, its God, and the new Israel in Jesus Christ. Ironically, it is liberalism's experiment of attempting to retain community severed from tradition that has left us with an American church unduly hardened and polarized within the respective "horizons of *assertion*" of individualism and social-ism. Stanley Hauerwas's insight speaks directly to this issue:

> Liberalism, in its many forms and versions, presupposes that society can be organized without any narrative that is commonly held to be true. As a result it tempts us to believe that freedom and rationality are independent of narrative—i.e., we are free to the extent that we have no story. Liberalism is, therefore, particularly pernicious to the extent it prevents us from understanding how deeply we are captured by its account of existence.[40]

If that perniciousness is disclosed in the church's understanding of its social role in America, its effects are by now even more evident in the ecclesial disintegration resulting from this experiment of sustaining community apart from a narrative-formed tradition. What was seen as a liberating, casting-off of the disciplines (read "constraints") of the biblical tradition has resulted in churches and bureaucratic structures increasingly (and ironically) hardened in their imaginative stretch. Implied in the emergence of the new dualism spotted by Farley are at least two symptoms of this brittleness in Christian imagination. First, the new dualism represents an adoption of two previous paradigms having different ideological roots as one new paradigm. Since the two constructs with their prior historical and intellectual developments are mutually incompatible, this new dualism represents a tacit arrangement to forgo Christian conversation in favor of an institutional truce. Second, the new dualism's "both-and" hermeneutic represents an admission by the adherents of individualism and social-ism that institutional power has not carried the day for their cause. As a consequence of this admission, the new dualism is adopted and thereby focuses unresolved anger and blame internal to one's primary ecclesial location rather than external to it. The resultant "hardening" of imaginative stretch is quite analogous to those families who have internalized contradictory stances and behaviors within an uneasy truce. Psychologists speak of such dualism in family systems with a language of addiction and codependence. In fact, Rabbi Friedman has shown the immediate applicability of an analysis of such "hardened" families to the dynamics of religious communities.[41] However, these congregations, at least, should not be underestimated in their ability to recover their faith tradition and once more to stretch their horizons of assent. How preaching may move communities in that direction is now both the challenge and opportunity.

Notes

1. Paul Ricoeur, *Interpretation Theory: Discourse and the Surplus of Meaning* (Fort Worth, Tex.: Texas Christian Univ. Press, 1976), 51.

2. Edward L. Murray, "Imagination Theory," in *Imagination and Phenomenological Psychology*, ed. Edward L. Murray (Pittsburgh: Duquesne Univ. Press, 1987), 205.

3. Richard Kearney, *Poetics of Imagining: From Husserl to Lyotard* (London: HarperCollinsAcademic, 1991), 152.

4. Hans Frei, " 'Literal Reading' of Biblical Narrative in Christian Tradition," *The Bible and the Narrative Tradition*, ed. Frank McConnell (New York: Oxford Univ. Press, 1986), 48.

5. See Robert Alter, *The Art of Biblical Narrative* (New York: Basic Books, 1981), and the index in Meir Sternberg, *The Poetics of Biblical Narrative: Ideological Literature and the Drama of Reading* (Bloomington: Indiana Univ. Press), 555–56, for treatments of irony in Hebrew Scripture. In New Testament studies, see Alan Culpepper, *Anatomy of the Fourth Gospel: A Study in Literary Design* (Philadelphia: Fortress Press, 1983), and Gail R. O'Day, *Revelation in the Fourth Gospel: Narrative Mode and Theological Claim* (Philadelphia: Fortress Press, 1986), for irony in the Gospel of John. See also Jerry Camery-Hoggatt, *Irony in Mark's Gospel: Text and Subtext* (Cambridge, England: Cambridge Univ. Press, 1992), 183–84, for an extensive reference to recent studies of irony in Scripture by a variety of scholars.

6. Wayne C. Booth, *A Rhetoric of Irony* (Chicago: Univ. of Chicago Press, 1974), 177.

7. In this exploration, we are following a path trod by Søren Kierkegaard in his seminal work, *The Concept of Irony*, trans. Lee M. Capel (New

York: Harper & Row, 1965). This achievement was Kierkegaard's thesis for his master of arts submitted in 1841.

8. Booth, *Irony*, 35. Hereafter cited in the text.

9. Alan Wilde begs to differ with Booth's notion of stable irony. For Wilde, Booth's work "is a book that in many ways is more a defence of civility than a study of Irony" (*Horizons of Assent: Modernism, Postmodernism, and the Ironic Imagination* [Baltimore: Johns Hopkins Univ. Press, 1981], 3).

10. It is this necessity for the covert that often creates the need for a "victim(s)" of an irony. Such may be characters or real persons who tell surface meanings without guile and who present themselves as sharing in the conventional ideology such meanings reflect (cf. Booth, 27–28).

11. In a recent homily retelling the parable of the good Samaritan with that compassionate helper portrayed as an alien and even as our enemy, some members of the congregation were shocked and angered. Others, though, did not see through the surface meaning, one of their number commenting, "I guess you can't believe everything you read in the newspaper."

12. Camery-Hoggatt, *Irony*, 61. See D. C. Muecke, *The Compass of Irony* (London: Methuen Press, 1970), 19ff.

13. Gary Hardwerk, *Irony and Ethics in Narrative from Schlegel to Lacan* (New Haven: Yale Univ. Press, 1985), 6.

14. Robert M. Fowler, *Let the Reader Understand: Reader-Response Criticism and the Gospel of Mark* (Minneapolis: Fortress Press, 1991), 14.

15. Ibid., 13–14.

16. Ibid., 46.

17. Ibid., 16. See Seymour Chatman, *Story and Discourse: Narrative Structure in Fiction and Film* (Ithaca, N.Y., and London: Cornell Univ. Press, 1978).

18. See Camery-Hoggatt, *Irony*, 10.

19. Ibid.

20. Booth, *Irony*, 40.

21. Fowler, *Reader*, 12.

22. Booth, *Irony*, 29.

23. Ibid. Jerry Camery-Hoggatt describes one aspect of this community formation role of irony as "the camaraderie of the shared joke" (*Irony*, 26).

24. Stanley Hauerwas, "The Church as God's New Language," in *Scriptural Authority and Narrative Interpretation*, ed. Garrett Green (Philadelphia: Fortress Press, 1987), 188.

25. Camery-Hoggatt, *Irony*, x.

26. David Buttrick's translation in *The Mystery and the Passion: A Homiletic Reading of the Gospel Traditions* (Minneapolis: Fortress Press, 1992), 69.

27. Camery-Hoggatt, *Irony*, 39.

28. Fowler, *Reader*, 164.

29. Hans-Georg Gadamer, *Truth and Method*, 2d rev. ed. (New York: Crossroad, 1989), 103. Hereafter cited in the text.

30. David J. Bryant, *Faith and the Play of Imagination: On the Role of the Imagination in Religion* (Macon, Ga.: Mercer Univ. Press, 1989), 106.

31. Ibid.

32. Intruding such self-consciousness onto the field of the game thereby violates one of play's central norms. A player is censured not for violating the rules but for violating the spirit of the game. Fan disapproval is readily displayed for such "hot dogs" who intrude themselves inappropriately into the game.

33. Edward L. Murray notes "the tremendous symbolism" that characterizes a preacher's office and performance. Given such potential imaginative power, Murray laments that preachers may "imagine their efforts as fruitless, if not futile." He adds, "The truth of the matter is, it is easy for them to forget who they are and the powerful influence they actually do wield in human lives, on the human scene" (*Imaginative Thinking*, 243).

34. Alan Wilde's fine phrase. He explains, "I have chosen the word *assent* deliberately to suggest a response that partakes of neither the passivity of acquiesence nor, quite, the force of assertion." Wilde adds that the Latin root in its verb form derives from *assentire:* "to join in feeling, which expresses precisely the notion I want to convey" (*Assent,* 15). This notion is also the precise sense in which preacher and community engage in homiletic performance.

35. Keith Hackett, a pastoral counselor, has strenuously objected to the tactic of preaching along an aisle in the nave as a way of "being down with the people." The therapist responds that pastoral identity cannot be given away and in the context of worship must not intrude on the space of the congregation. The preacher inevitably will be located within some imaginative space on behalf of the emotional well-being of the assembly.

36. This relative expansiveness in the dramatic imagination's sense of place and movement is achieved by virtue of the defining function of character. The "space" between audience and character is retained even if a "cat" begins to nuzzle our hand prior to the overture of *Cats.* This is why a preacher gains considerable imaginative space if she puts a cloth about her head and performs an "I, Deborah," kind of sermon. The congregation shifts in its communal imagination to the self-awareness of an audience. If there is a gain in imaginative space, notice that it is at the expense of the distinctive interactions of the homiletic performance. *All* parties must shift their identities when the preacher becomes actor!

37. John S. McClure, *The Four Codes of Preaching: Rhetorical Strategies* (Minneapolis: Fortress Press, 1991). McClure identifies the four

codes as the scriptural, the cultural, the semantic, and the theosymbolic. "A code," McClure explains, "is a system of signs, words, or ciphers that becomes a way of organizing a particular level or aspect of human interaction" (8).

38. See the description of David Buttrick's notion of the homiletic imagination in the Appendix.

39. Particularly abrupt shifts in codes are most likely to occur at times of pastoral transition. If the incoming preacher is inattentive to the congregation's dominant or preferred code and subtypes, a relocation within a common horizon of assent simply may not be achieved.

40. Stanley Hauerwas, *A Community of Character: Toward a Constructive Christian Social Ethic* (Notre Dame, Ind.: Univ. of Notre Dame Press, 1981), 12.

41. See Edwin H. Friedman, *Generation to Generation: Family Process in Church and Synagogue* (New York and London: Guilford Press, 1985).

Part Two

Practice

5

Preaching Narrative and Imagery: An Exploration of Homiletic Method

Whatever else, imagination has to do with the production of images. To perceive involves at least the possibility of reproducing images; moreover, this potential of the imagination possesses epistemological significance. Images "do not take the place of objects of perception, of a world transcending our subjectivity, but mediate between the world and the self in a way that opens the self to the world."[1] It has also been demonstrated that a distinctive relationship obtains between images and the stories within which they reside. Images gain some meaning or other, yield some affective state or other, by virtue of the narratives to which they belong. When viewed from a communal perspective, images become decisive as hermeneutic lenses through which self and world are envisioned. The common thread uniting all of these functions of the image is the role of mediation: between the perceiver and the object, between the auditor and the narrative, and between the community and its members and themselves and their vision of "world." Images mediate all the time.

Now in the turn toward methodological considerations for preaching, these epistemological and hermeneutic rules will need to be translated into procedures for homiletic performance. In other words, at issue now is how best to exploit these profound imagistic functions in our preaching week in and week out. Fortunately, the schema Mary Warnock developed with reference to images and perception translates nicely into a format for explicating the role of the image in a homily. Warnock construed images as enabling our recognition of the world as familiar, as allowing

us on a particular aspect of what we experience, and as
1ew insights into our world through the adoption of al-
.... points of view.[2] With these categories in mind, the challenge is to apply Warnock's considerations within the field of
homiletic method.

1. *Images allow us to recognize everyday objects as everyday.*
In spite of this foundational insight, many preachers depend overly
much on story illustrations to achieve this recognition of the
everyday world by the congregation. "Illustrating" some meaning
within a sermon almost inevitably has come to involve a casting
about by the preacher for some anecdote or other. To be honest,
preachers have become so thoroughly formed to think of "illustrating" as appending stories to "points" that "a good story" cir-
culates among preachers like baseball cards among preadolescent
boys. Two difficulties, among many, with this dynamic are that,
first, as these stories are excessively imported into sermons, this
overuse ironically tends to diminish their impact. Second, when
such stories are used to illustrate the everyday world of the congregation, the meaning tends to become more narrowly focused
and less encompassing in its scope. The "I once met a man . . ."
type of sermonic anecdote almost immediately works to de-
generalize the issue in question—gender, chronological age, cultural experience; all these and more serve to exclude portions of
the worshiping community from the sermon.[3]

Recalling that images connect to narratives, the homilist has
a happy option in many cases of imaging the meaning at stake
rather than providing a full-blown anecdotal illustration. By (the
mixed) virtue of most any congregation's exposure to vast amounts
of television programming, images of the culture and the world
are readily available. Since television advertising depends increasingly on an image-ladened format, our culture's images of success,
happiness, and popularity are constantly being stockpiled in the
congregational consciousness. If, for example, a homily's text is
the powerfully ironic story of the request of the sons of Zebedee
in Mark 10:35ff., all sorts of comfortable and easy "baptisms" are
offered by the culture, all susceptible to being imaged. Moreover,
an additional advantage to utilizing images from television beyond
their ubiquity in social consciousness is that point of view is

nicely built in.[4] That is, the imperative to provide a perspective along with the image is cared for by simply locating the assembly before the television set.

> *So we flop down in our favorite chair after supper, reach for the remote control, and flip on the TV. Suddenly, we're at this happy party, everyone being joyfully "baptized" in a swimming pool with the Budweiser logo painted on the bottom. What fun! This is really living! What fun! Are we able, Jesus? You betcha!*

At other times, the narratives to be imaged may be more regional in character, but still with the need to include the entire congregation within the sermon's "location." It is not important in these cases that every person have the experience being imaged, since an effective image developed with strong point of view can invite everyone to "see" the same way. What is decisive here is that the image and its attendant point of view not unintentionally preclude its being shared by any constituency within the congregation. The empathic imagination of a Christian assembly has considerable breadth, especially as formation within the world of biblical narrative matures. Still, the preacher may want to offer a multiple image set in order to provide the kind of pastoral and cultural coverage needed to include most all of the hearers. So, for example, in imaging an early "move"[5] in an Easter sermon on Matthew 28:1-10, preacher-exegetes may notice that the two Marys do not go to the tomb with a functional purpose in mind (to anoint the body as in Luke). Rather, the purpose seems to be simply that of "being there"; the sepulchre is their "station" as much as it is for the guards. They come to their station to get close to their memories and to regain some sense of "being near" while "being there." For a rural parish, one possible image might be:

> *We all need at one time or another to return to the old home place. Not to do anything, really. Just to go down the path to the old place and stand before the collapsed walls, tangled now with vines. Only the stone chimney still stands—a kind of headstone over the ruins. And we just need to come and be near this memory place, to see it for ourselves, just to be there.*

If, however, an image set is provided on behalf of an interest in having everyone included, each image will be more terse than the above example. Three images most probably will be used (twos do not hold in congregational hearing), and a little rhetorical system may be devised to tie them together. One such possible system could be a recurring tag line following each of three images: *"And just like the women at dawn, something moves us just to be there at our station, guarding memories in silence."* It is important to note in regard to such image sets that the preacher does not have a similar opportunity regarding illustrations (that is, more extended anecdotal material). "Multiple illustrations," cautions David Buttrick, "will always weaken analogy, and thereby make understanding even more difficult."[6]

2. *Images allow us to focus on a particular aspect of what we experience.* The converse of the insight that narratives evoke images is that the presentation of an image will invoke the narrative that gave it birth. One difficulty here, as David Harned detected, is that images are slippery and may relate to more than one narrative simultaneously. To complicate matters even more, there is nothing that guarantees that these multiple stories be compatible in meaning. In fact, they may stand in opposition to each other. On the other hand, images developed with precision and well-focused point of view may bring into immediacy one particular facet of personal and communal experience with amazing power. Within a suburban, largely young adult congregation, the apostle Paul's reference to "pressing on to the prize" might be imaged *"by the whirring of a Stairmaster as we watch the red dots mount up across the computer screen."* An urban parish's "fortress mentality" in a now changed neighborhood might be imaged as a *"locked and silent building each night, the only light a red glow from the armed security system's control box, keeping its vigil."* In both cases, notice, a red light is presented as the visual image, yet each distinct context serves to keep that red light focused as regards its function as analogy and as description. (What will most probably not function effectively is the utilization of both of these "technological red dot" images within a single sermon. The two image systems will most likely collapse together in congregational hearing.) Properly contextualized, however, an image can readily

focus on distinctive and quite particular aspects of personal and communal experience.

3. *Images can serve to provide new insights through a shift in perspective.* The most obvious example here relates to narrative shifts in point of view regarding characters. From what perspective, or whose, a narrative is developed in a homily can dramatically shift the assembly's experience and insight. Within the field of parable study, Robert Funk's insistence that the parable of the good Samaritan (Luke 10:30-35) have as its primary point of view our solidarity with *the man robbed and beaten, lying helpless in the ditch* dramatically shifts the entire force and movement of the sermon.[7] The church's "conventional imagination" of the story typically has been determined by a point of view in common with the helper, the good Samaritan. With the church imaged as "good Samaritan," some encouragements to good works and compassion are certainly obtainable. Imaged from the point of view of the one robbed and beaten, however, a hated alien becomes the instrument of grace, "mercy comes from the quarter from which it is least expected."[8] Shifts in point of view have the potential to reinterpret the biblical narrative as well as the manner in which it becomes the world of the hearers. This use of imagery to provide for new insight relates to this focus on an image's "hitherto hidden or largely ignored features."[9] Shifts in character point of view, as with the parable of the good Samaritan, are rich with potential for new insight and even new hearings of the biblical narrative.

Beyond character shifts in point of view, however, a variety of other alternatives are available to the preacher as well. As with the lumberjack and the birdwatcher looking at a tree, our perspectuality on the same image can vary widely (or wildly). Here, the image is retained but reinterpreted by other perspectual factors and experiences. The alternate mode of re-envisioning involves retaining a consistent point of view while shifting the image offered within it. For example, we could image the space shuttle lifting off at Cape Canaveral (point of view: watching television) or image that awesome but awful explosion of Challenger against the blue Florida sky (same point of view, different content). Affective and symbolic significance shifts drastically between these two imagings. Seeking for "hitherto hidden or largely ignored features"[10] of our experience and of Scripture has become the special vocation of feminist and liberation theologians. Where a commitment to the integrity of the biblical narrative persists, albeit with a hermeneutics of suspicion, powerful and fresh images derived from the tradition challenge the conventional imagination. Catherine and Justo González comment on the Pentecost story in Acts and alert us to a hitherto hidden role of the Spirit, as "each of us, in our own native language" (2:8) hears the Good News. The commentators add:

> In Pentecost, God's intervention confuses the unities that empire has built. What is new about Pentecost is not that they all speak the same tongue. They do not. What is new about Pentecost is that God blesses every language on earth as a means of divine revelation, and makes communication possible even while preserving the integrity of languages and cultures.[11]

A homily for Pentecost imaged from this perspective offers a new vision on a familiar Bible story, calls into question conventional readings, and invites the assembly into the world of the text with a new way of hearing and seeing ourselves and the world.

A User's Guide to Imagery

If images within a sermon will typically function in ways suggested by Mary Warnock, the challenge to the preacher now becomes that of effectively employing images in order that they will function as intended. What follows, then, is an abbreviated "user's guide" to images as utilized within the sermon. It is based on several models related to the praxis of homiletic imaging: in the "camera model," "the video camera model," and that of a "simulator" (as in "flight simulator"). Each model provides a series of possibilities and constraints regarding the use of images in preaching. Each is chosen to supplement rather than supplant the others.

The Camera Model

Developed by David Buttrick in *Homiletic*,[12] the camera model is basic to any user's guide to sermonic images. The dominant, and essential, character of images in their homiletic usage is that of point of view. We look through a camera's viewfinder until we get the image we want; conversely, the image we "get" is always retrievable with a specific point of view. When preaching, then, point of view will need to be built into every image provided. Moreover, preachers will be especially cautious about expecting congregations readily to follow rapid shifts in point of view. We will build point of view into every image; we will shift point of view with care and caution.

Given the camera model, Buttrick notes that "alterations in focal field, lens depth, and focal depth can be managed with ease."[13] "Focal field" invites preachers to notice that they may image within a range from expansively wide to tightly narrow. Some images call for a widened focus—i.e., inviting an assembly to look out on a Kansas wheat field in mid-summer. Other images need a much narrower focus—*"Scan a display in the bookstore and suddenly one title pops out*—Adult Children of Alcoholics. *We stare and think, 'Good grief, somebody's written about me!'* " Lens depth deals with "the degree of self-engagement involved in point of view."[14] How removed or near is the image to us, along with the affective element it conveys? *"The med students slip into the theater seats and look down on the surgery going on. They watch carefully. Dr. Green is an artist* (or) *You're a surgical nurse. You look on carefully. The patient was your Sunday school teacher when you were really needing a friend."*

By "focal depth," Buttrick means "how far we may be seeing *into* things and people."[15] This degree of penetration exercises the preacher's empathic imagination on behalf of the congregation. Clearly we can focus near the surface of people, places, and objects, imagining perhaps a tranquil scene of people receiving the bread and wine before the altar. Deepened focus may invite the assembly to the point of view of a man or woman (we will need to specify in the sermon) receiving the sacrament for the first time since a divorce some fifteen years ago. "Imagine yourself as a homiletic camera" is Buttrick's advice to preachers; and he always reminds as well, "and don't forget point of view!"

The Video Camera Model

At least two elements are gained by setting down the homiletic camera and picking up its video camera counterpart. First, and most obvious, we now are dealing in a mode of imaging that allows movement while still retaining control over point of view. Our camera can give us the image of the space shuttle sitting on the pad, frozen in suspended flight, or exploding. The video camera model invites us to consider images that have mobility as one of their components. Point of view shifts, and our face turns up as we watch the shuttle move off above us. The second element gained is sound—the video camera is equipped with a microphone, too! So all can watch the shuttle move upward until we lose sight of it and only the rumble of its rockets echoes through the viewing area. With the video camera model of imaging, then, the preacher is capable of inviting the congregation to be driving down the street while a black limousine with darkened windows streaks by, or to be watching a salmon leap up a rapids, or to be seeing the desperate reaction of the sick when the pool of Bethesda is troubled by the angel. The community can see and hear the news of continued artillery shelling in Sarajevo or recall Kunta Kinte in *Roots* holding up his crying infant to the sky.

Moving images or static images?—in a variety of homiletic situations, that is the question. Should the preacher have that shuttle sitting there on the pad or roaring off into the heavens? This question, interestingly, will rarely be one of aesthetics only. Something will often be at stake regarding the meaning of the image in this decision for static or mobile portrayal. In some cases, communal memory will provide the cue, and the preacher will interrogate how persons in the congregation first perceived the image or what particular rendering strikes a certain chord. As kids, most of us first saw a goose as a drawing in a child's book. As youth, we may have gazed at a flight of geese and wondered about the mystery of our life's journey. In some circumstances, a static image will connote more of a sense of stable foundation and permanence. Homiletically, looking at a rock familiar to the members of a church will connect to the affirmation in Psalms that "God is the rock of our salvation" (Ps. 95:1). Conversely, mobility may suggest the trivial and bothersome (flies swarming around) or the impermanent (the University of Washington stadium's steel girders slowly collapsing into what looks like a gigantic tangle of spaghetti). Special attention needs to be addressed to the kind of mobility represented in computer games. What does our child's control of Super-Mario darting about the TV screen imply? Preachers, along with theologians, educators, and ethicists will need to take seriously the "world" of Nintendo and all the other computer games that now are shaping the lives of millions of persons in contemporary culture.

Another whole field of meaning exists, however, in which the opposite values entirely are attributed to mobility and static states or conditions. Here the mobile image invites a sense of potential and of actual change, even *metanoia:* "I will arise and go to my father," says the prodigal son (Luke 15:18); "when [one of the ten lepers] saw that he was healed, [he] turned back, praising God with a loud voice" (Luke 17:15). Within this symbolic universe, the mobile is charged with thoughts and feelings of the new and the redemptive. Also within this particular world, the static connotes the unredemptive—all that is flat, tasteless, and incapable of change. (It is no accident that Tennessee Williams names Maggie's impotent husband in *Cat on a Hot Tin Roof*, "Brick.") The preacher, then, will need to keep all these things in mind as he or she considers the use of static and mobile images. More is at stake than meets the eye.

The Simulator Model

A pilot checks her heading given by San Francisco flight control. "United two seven, maintain eight thousand feet on heading zero niner, two hundred-fifty knots." "Eight thousand at two-fifty on zero niner," she replies. Off the left side of the plane, the Golden Gate Bridge slips behind and, looking ahead, the Bay is plied by some ships heading in and out. "United two seven, come to heading five five, begin descent to three thousand five hundred feet. Maintain two-fifty knots." "Roger, San Francisco." Pushing the yoke forward, she inches back on the throttle. The whine from the two engines on the 737 changes pitch.

Imagine being strapped into the pilot's seat of a commercial jet. All of the sights, sounds, and bodily feelings attendant to the task are present, including your own emotions and bodily reactions. Yet you are not flying a *real* aircraft; the real cockpit is at the center of a huge flight simulator. More than the imagistic model of the camera with its achievement of a static "seeing as" and more than the video camera with its audio component and its (at times now) mobile imagery, the simulator model introduces bodily sensation and the full spectrum of perceptual faculties.

For preaching, this model first invites an attentiveness to biblical language that speaks of the bodily ingredient in emotions and motives. For example, John speaks of Jesus' being "greatly disturbed in spirit and deeply moved" at the sight of the grieving friends at Lazarus's tomb (John 11:33, NRSV), the full bodily dimensions of *enebrimesato to pneumati* are implied.[16] Moreover, if the preacher is eager to image the full range of the lived experience of a congregation, kinesthetic images as well as visual and aural will be explored. The temptation, of course, is to try to convey these "bodily images" by means of colorful adjectives and adverbs along with the rather generic verbs in the homily. Two difficulties thwart this strategy. On one hand, this adjectival elaboration of matters in general and of bodily sensation in particular actually distances description from lived experience. We would do well to heed Eugene Lowry's caution at this point:

> When in English composition class, I thought "being descriptive" meant using a lot of adjectives and adverbs. But typically, the use of a modifier does what the term suggests—it *modifies*. That is, it alters or shapes. Most of us are not greatly impacted by an alteration. We are impacted by a radically new and different image. To do that, one needs the power of nouns and verbs. Moreover, modifiers clutter, complicate the sentence structure, which again tends to dilute the power. They call attention to the sentence and hence to the speaker.[17]

An immediacy is gained by a rich, imaginative deployment of verbs when speaking of emotional and kinesthetic experience.

Beyond the strategy of going for a more imaginative palette of verbs in the language of our preaching, the simulator model also highlights the importance of appropriate analogy in our illustrative systems. Here again, the simulator model is suggestive. To return to John 11, a homily on the raising of Lazarus may be concluded with the point of view being that of entombment—and of being called out.

> We are called by name by Jesus, the stone is rolled away. Now we stagger out into the sunlight. "Unbind!" orders the Lord, and they're taking our grave clothes off like a nurse unwrapping a freshly healed wound.

Notice that all of the attendant feelings and thoughts associated with being unbandaged do not need to be described. Rather, the image itself will be trusted to convey the senses of new life and gratitude implied in the Lazarus story's ending.

Finally, David Buttrick observes that homiletic imaging can provide for perceptual immediacy plus a secondary appeal to another state of awareness. Retaining a focus on a hungry child, the homilist can also introduce an internal reflective awareness, recalling the words of Jesus, remembering our own childhood suppers, or introducing an emotional or physiological reaction.

> The TV screen holds our attention on the refugee children having their first meal in days, just after the UN trucks have brought them to safety. We watch and begin to feel our stomach knot up. While they devour the soup and bread, we can no longer think of eating a thing.

Not every image used in a homily will operate at this more complex level of primary focus and secondary awareness. When the right occasion presents itself, however, the preacher will invite the congregation to become aware of another experience that serves to interpret the one provided in the image itself. Such awareness may entail recall of Scripture, association of the image with personal or communal memories, and the depiction of internal feelings or bodily states in relation to the focus on the imagery.

Preaching Narrative and Imagery

Narratives give birth to images, images that may subsequently function for anamnesis—of the originating narrative as well as others. This interplay of narrative and imagery suggests a span of possible homiletic strategies related to the scriptural narratives and the biblical images. Although a myriad of variations may be detected, there is a sweep in method from one pole in which the narrative plot of the homily is preeminent to the other in which the image system itself serves as the organizing agent. In the former circumstance, the homiletical plot will more or less adhere to the biblical narrative's own movement and intention, although nonnarrative texts may also be preached utilizing a narrative homiletic method. The latter context is one in which the images themselves determine the shape of the homiletical plot. In the center, narrative and imagery interact with a relative equity of influence. So a schema emerges that may be portrayed as taking the form of a chiasmus. At each pole, narrative or imagery predominates with regard to the sermonic movement. In the center, each move must be imaged in some way, as articulated in David Buttrick's homiletic (see figure 5.1).

Figure 5.1 Narrative-Imagery Scheme

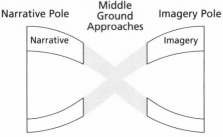

The Narrative Pole

A number of strategies obtain for preaching biblical narrative. Eugene Lowry offers four alternatives in his book *How to Preach a Parable* and a fifth approach in his prior work, *The Homiletical Plot*. With regard to the Hebrew Bible, John Holbert lists five general categories of narrative sermons.[18] David Buttrick's "mode of immediacy" relates easily to biblical narrative since the movement and structure of the sermon more or less replicates that of the text.[19] Henry Mitchell carefully interprets the typical components of narrative preaching in the African-American church.[20] Buttrick speaks for all of these homileticians by asking, "How do we preach a story?"[21] John Holbert answers for them all: "In my judgment the primary gift that a preacher and congregation may receive from the narrative style is the basic union of form and content in the sermon. The best expression of a narrative is a narrative."[22] Within all of these, and other, homiletic methods hovering near the narrative pole, several primary tasks are at stake. A homily will be shaped in such a manner that the form and intention of the narrative text will be maintained in the hearing of the assembly. Moreover, each of these options of the narrative pole will embody one or more tactics for contemporizing the narrative text in order that it may become our world *now* as well as Scripture's world *then*. Finally, each of these approaches will stand or fall as the preacher either trusts that the narrative will do its formative work among its hearers or loses faith and begins to sink back into the old illustrative mentality in which every story must have an ideational payoff. To achieve these primary tasks, the preacher will need to learn a repertoire of narrative techniques, unless she or he has been blessed by formation within a church tradition steeped in narrative preaching. In the latter case, these techniques are more "caught" than "taught."

"Running the story." Seen in its most traditional form in the narrative preaching tradition of the African-American church, the option of "running the story" (Lowry's term) achieves the primary task of fidelity to the text's plot by adopting it as the homiletic plot. That is, the movement and intention of scriptural narrative and homily become coterminous. The sermon begins, continues, and concludes in alignment with the pericope. An initial challenge for the preacher, therefore, is that of establishing the parameters of the narrative and identifying the "lexies," or scenic organization, of the plot. Once the overall surface structure of the text's movement is established, particular attention is devoted to the imagery located within its story. Next comes the critical decision regarding contemporization, with several alternatives presenting

themselves. They are (1) periodic excursi, (2) contemporizing cues, and (3) modern recasting.

By "periodic excursi" is meant those occasions in the narrative plot that the preacher designates as places to pause in the story and open out into the contemporary situation of the hearers and their world. These excursi may be spoken of as the narrative sermon's "gateways," and typically more such locations will be spotted than will be used. At each gateway, the narrative development will be put on "pause." Rhetorical devices such as restatement will serve to bring the congregation's sense of narrative movement to a temporary halt.[23] Then some technique for signaling this entry into the world of the hearers will be employed. Often, in narrative preaching within the African-American church, for instance, the preacher will tell a personal experience. However, it is crucial to observe that this device will function as intended only within traditions and churches where the preacher retains considerable currency as an imaginative representative of the congregation. Otherwise, such first-person references wind up focusing the assembly's point of view on the preacher, rather than on their common experience. Eugene Lowry typically softens the first-person homiletic problem by setting up the issue at stake in the biblical narrative and commenting, "Now I don't know about you, but this troubles [worries, raises some questions for, bothers] me." At any rate, the preacher will signal in some fashion that he or she is pausing the narrative flow and exploring the contemporary context in relation to this place in the narrative. Often, a strong image in the text will both offer the place to make an excursus and provide the interpretive lens through which our own world is seen. Following a time of contemporary analysis, the preacher will "release the pause button on the story" and lead the assembly back through the gateway, resuming the narrative. It is critical in a narrative sermon that such excursi do not expand into an embolism created by a too-extensive story illustration. The hearers are all too likely to get stuck in that story world of the illustration and be unable to return to the narrative.

To illustrate the device of narrative excursus, let us use the parable of the prodigal son (Luke 15:11-32) as a narrative test case. Practically every line in the parable can become a "gateway" occasion, but let us select verse 13: "The younger son gathered all he had and took his journey into a far country." Perhaps we might reiterate, *"He didn't just go to town, he went off to a far country."* Now, at the gateway, a question may be posed: *"Ever been to a far country—a place distinctly 'not home'?"* Probably a second sentence is needed to put the congregation's narrative consciousness on hold: *"We're not talking about some trip whose destination is already known, such as Grandma's place out in the country. No, leaving for the far country is to leave behind everything that is familiar."* Then some exploration of this image can proceed. *"You don't need a spotters' guide to tell when you're in a far country. It feels new, exciting, maybe a little scary. You take risks there, try on a different lifestyle, do things you'd never do back at home."* Now the exploration is particularized for the specific pastoral context. *"Read the new data on married men and women who check yes on the question, 'Have you had a relationship with someone other than your marriage partner?' It's amazing how many check yes. Now here's a far country—feel new, leave the old cares behind for a while, maybe even enjoy being scared as part of the attraction."* To tell a story illustration here would be to create a dangerous embolism. It is better to universalize off the infidelity image and reenter the narrative. *"I don't know—but look, 'far country' can mean a million things. It is a kind of escape, and we always know it when we get there. So now this younger son has made good his escape from home. 'Welcome to the far country,' the sign says; 'you're going to love it here.' "*

Contemporizing cues. Assuming the same initial work as in the excursus strategy, another option is to bring the hearers into a more recognizable "our own" world throughout the sermon. This approach, though, does not attempt a complete recasting of the text into a contemporary one; rather, it intends to "seed" the biblical story with cues that it is really *our* narrative world. These proleptic elements will typically not be scattered through the homily at random but located deftly to bring the hearers into a particular context that is within their own personal or communal experience. Staying with the parable, the preacher and hearers might travel with the younger son on the journey until a sign up ahead reads, "*Welcome to the Far Country. You can't even phone home from here!*" In a sermon on Noah, Dennis Willis adopts this "contemporizing cue" approach as he runs the story.[24] Imaging Noah's postflood drunkenness, Willis tells us that "there in a corner face down is a plaque to Captain Noah. 'We would sail with you anywhere,' and he dares not see that" (44). Later Willis tells us of a Gatlin Brothers song about some winos who sing, "Will there be Mogen David up in heaven? Oh, Lord, that's all I want to know" (46). The preacher also seeds the sermon with remarks like, "Maybe, Lord, maybe, I just peaked early" (47). Only the song is hanging somewhat outside the story, but not by much! Used with imagination and discipline, these kinds of cues work with subtle effectiveness to locate the hearer within the narrative. Lowry comments that a contemporary paraphrase "has the effect of saying to the listeners, 'This story is close at hand, not remote and hence difficult to comprehend.' "[25]

The narrative frame. A prevalent device for achieving the primary tasks of maintaining the integrity of the biblical narrative as well as locating its contemporary context involves what Holbert terms a "narrative frame."[26] Here the preacher may delay the introduction of the narrative while developing present-day situations and issues to which it is addressed. Lowry terms this device "delaying the story," adding that the text will serve as a response to some pastoral need.[27] Other alternative methods of framing the narrative involve "suspending the story" (Lowry's term) and adding a postnarrative "tag." The chief danger in the former strategy (suspending the story) is that the intercalated material may become too pervasive or powerful on its own, precluding a successful resumption of the biblical story. In this case, the homily suffers a major embolism that might well be fatal! The potential liability in the postscript "tag" is that the preacher takes this extranarrative occasion to explain what the story means. Holbert remarks that a postscript to a narrative involves "a conclusion that focuses the narrative for the congregation" and adds:

> By *focuses the narrative*, I do not mean "explains" the narrative. The story is not an extended illustration for a point to be made at the sermon's end. After telling a story, the preacher should never lean over the pulpit and say, "Now, for

all of you here who did not get the point of the story I have just told you, here it is." That sort of tactic is not a part of narrative preaching as I am defining it.[28]

A more complex situation emerges for the preacher and his or her hearers if the material employed to frame the biblical narrative is also narrative in form. Options here, as advocated by Richard L. Thulin include (a) "the nonbiblical as context," (b) "the nonbiblical as conclusion," and (c) "interweaving the biblical and nonbiblical."[29] Thulin indicates the first option (a) as providing "a context in which the biblical narrative can be heard with a sense of immediacy" (13). His "b" option allows for the conclusions of the biblical narrative to be "tested in the crucible of a nonbiblical story" (15). Finally, the "c" option, which Thulin confesses to be the most challenging, seeks to interweave the biblical and nonbiblical narratives forming "one story from beginning to end" (17). The options may be diagrammed as in figure 5.2.

Figure 5.2 Thulin Methodological Options

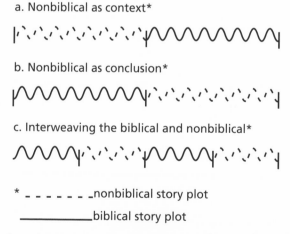

a. Nonbiblical as context*

b. Nonbiblical as conclusion*

c. Interweaving the biblical and nonbiblical*

* – – – – – – –nonbiblical story plot

————————biblical story plot

The crucial, and in many cases insurmountable, problem with these bifocal narrative options is that of first establishing a narrative world for the assembly involving plot, character, setting, and tone and then shifting to a different story with its own distinctive narrative elements. Told well—as is the case with Thulin's example of option (a), in which a scene from the film *Raging*

Bull is the context (14)—it will be a major challenge simply to extricate the congregation from the contemporary story and have them pick up the biblical one without tripping. Moreover, this dual narrative schema assumes that the congregation will not only hear and retain both narratives, but will also make the connections and interactions intended by the preacher. Perhaps in some percentage of cases the "context" or "conclusion" tactics will function successfully by being simultaneously retained. (My own experience with such sermons is that one of the narratives will inevitably take center stage in our hearing, leaving the other only on the periphery of consciousness.) Given the multivalence of narratives in general, however, it remains problematic whether the preacher's own connections and interactions will replicate themselves in the hearing of the sermon. Certainly these first two bifocal options involve a rather high-risk strategy for narrative preaching!

If Thulin's first two options involve homiletical risk, the tactic of interweaving two stories in a sermon will almost always abort. To expect a congregation to (1) assemble one story world within the communal consciousness, (2) set it temporarily aside while another is assembled, and (3) continue this oscillation with an interaction intended by the preacher, is to have those expectations frustrated. At least, the congregation will stay with the narrative developed with the clearest imagery and characterization—typically the contemporary story—and totally lose the other as it is being heard. The diagnosis of this almost inevitable loss of one of the two story lines is provided by David Buttrick: what the preacher has created is a doublet sermonic plot, two systems of meaning and point of view having equal status (such doublets can be word doublets, illustrative doublets, or in this case sermonic plot doublets). One of the rival systems will always drop out of communal consciousness, or the entire homily may remain confusing and scattered.[30] Fortunately, in both Thulin's case and Lowry's as well, when it comes to illustrating this "interweaving" tactic, the homilies in fact represent other, far more successful, narrative methods. Thulin's sermon, "Boy, Does That Taste Good!"[31] and Fred Craddock's "Praying Through Clenched Teeth"[32] both exemplify well-told contemporary narratives in which images resonate with Scripture. Both retain contemporary perspectuality throughout. Craddock nicely adds a brief portrayal of Saul of Tarsus to others he has assembled to cluster around an image system of bitterness. In neither case, however, do stories alternate in tense or point of view between the contemporary and the biblical. In fact, these two homilies illustrate quite readily the next alternative for narrative preaching—recasting the narrative.

Recasting the narrative. The mirror image of "running the story" is the strategy of recasting it in a contemporary setting. Sources for such recastings may come from the preacher's own creativity, authors (Frederick Buechner, Flannery O'Conner, and others), film and theater, or current events. The initial challenge here is that there be a proximate congruence between the meanings and intention of the story sermon and the biblical text. Occasional parallels of plot or character or several shared image systems will not provide an adequate rendering of the biblical world and the character of God. Such "proximate incongruence" fails in its faithfulness to the integrity of scriptural narrative. However, a growing number of homiletic recastings of the biblical text accrue week by week in the churches. Preachers adopting this strategy, however, do have methodological resources available that parallel those of the biblical narrative sermon, only in reverse! That is, instead of providing excursi *forward* into the contemporary world, the homilist may now carefully shape an excursus *back* into the biblical world. "Contemporary cues" construed within a recast story become "scriptural cues." The same considerations obtain whether an excursus dips back or plunges forward—putting the narrative on hold, locating the gateway, exploring the outside-the-narrative situation, and returning to the homily's narrative. Similarly, a contemporary story may be framed by considerations raised in the lection.

At its simplest, a contemporary recasting may involve nothing more or less than a paraphrase of the biblical narrative. Parables are particularly susceptible to this strategy of paraphrase, although the strategy probably should not be overworked in frequency. The formula here is to retain the biblical plot, character traits, and tone, and develop an analogous setting. Then proceed with recognizable contemporary characters, shifting the setting as appropriate. Notice, however, that the biblical plot and the tone of the biblical narrative must be retained.[33] Beyond paraphrase, sermons may recast the pericope as a contemporary story utilizing any of the narrative strategies deemed appropriate. An exclusionary clause must be added here however: "providing the resulting story sermon is theologically congruent with the biblical text." The use of films as story sermons frequently violates this proviso by the introduction of other values, meanings, images, and plots. Moreover, the hearers' response to or identification with various actors in the film may serve to subvert this strategy.[34] Films are not necessarily inappropriate within narrative sermons, but most films cannot *in themselves* provide a theologically congruent recasting of the biblical text. For example, we may try to image sacrificial love in a sermon by a scene from the movie *Platoon*.

> The troopers scramble onto the choppers, loading their dead and wounded. At the loading zone, it's a madhouse of shouting, explosions, helicopters lifting off. The door gunners are shooting like mad. Just then, one of the men shouts, "Look, it's Sergeant Elias!" Sure, enough, he has held off the attack and is alive! We watch him being chased by the enemy; he takes hits, falls to his knees with his arms extended. We think of the cross and sacrificial love. Greater love has no one than this.

Now as this homily was assessed, the hearers all reported being deeply moved by the image. Some did make the analogy to cross and sacrifice. Others reported feelings of rage rekindled that the door gunners could not prevent Elias's being cut down! On the other hand, cinematic images with their points of view, short cuts of dialogue, and numerous other resources are abundantly available to preachers. The challenge is to retrieve the scene or dialogue from the film while devising means to keep the now awakened cinematic imagination of the hearers from chasing off into other aspects of that experience to the detriment of the sermon.

Nonstory Narrative Plots

As our attention is shifted toward the middle ground of our schema of homiletic methods involving narrative and imagery, we can readily observe that the dependence on narrative scriptural texts no longer obtains. That is, in the central section of the schema, narrative and imagery are in varying relationships to each other, but the sermonic method is no longer coupled necessarily to a narrative text. Rather, this middle ground is one where, as John McClure notes, the sermon employs narrative "at the level of plot."[35] The sermon will most definitely embody a homiletical plot, though this structure is neither dependent upon narrative texts (although a narrative text may be shaped according to such a plot) nor under any pressure for that sermonic plot to be based on a story. Within such nonstory narrative plots, images are typically deployed within the "scenic" units of the homily. Several models of these middle-ground plotted sermons are available to the preacher.

The first nonstory but plot-based approach is that of David Buttrick's "mode of reflection." Here "the original sequence of a text is no longer crucial. . . . The movement of a sermon in the reflective mode of consciousness is movement around a structured field of meaning, a moving from one contemporary meaning to another."[36] This structured field of meaning is one formed and informed by the biblical text or a network of texts, though not dependent upon any text's original sequence and intention.[37] Alternatively, this mode of reflection also focuses contemporary lived experience, yet envisioned *through* the relevant field of meaning. As reflective consciousness engages in its work, a structured sequence of theological meaning emerges, which becomes the basis for the homiletical plot. Akin to the mode of immediacy, the sermon will be comprised of a succession of "moves" designed to form in communal consciousness with a logic of movement. "We will not end up," Buttrick growls, "with a distilled topic or a propositional truth—stuff from which sermons are frequently shaped" (324). Each of the component moves, moreover, will be imaged out of the lived experience of the hearers; these images are likely to be drawn more from contemporary experience rather than the biblical text, or texts. A dominant image of a text, however, may well serve to coordinate the images deployed within each move. (It would be odd, for example, that a sermon reflecting on 2 Corinthians 4:7-11 not have its image system informed by Paul's image of "this treasure in earthen vessels.")

Eugene Lowry's "homiletical plot" represents a second model for nonstory narrative preaching.[38] Here the notion of a sermonic plot has an affinity with "movie or television plots."[39] Evident in such sermons will be any plot's characteristics of continuity or movement and the "working through of a sensed discrepancy" (16). In fact, Lowry's model is dependent on this sense of discrepancy or homiletic bind; without a bind, without "trouble," the preacher and the hearers cannot move toward any resolution. The movement of the sermon, therefore, will travel from an initial stated bind, a "felt discrepancy," toward a resolution of ambiguity, "from problem to solution, from itch to scratch" (23). A careful analysis of this general plot form yields five stages that take the congregation from the bind to its resolution. "Lowry's loop" represents this homiletic plot and its sequential stages (see figure 5.3).

Figure 5.3 Lowry Loop

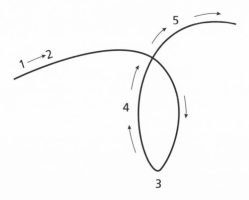

The stages in this sequence include "1) upsetting the equilibrium, 2) analyzing the discrepancy, 3) disclosing the clue to resolution, 4) experiencing the gospel, 5) anticipating the consequences" (25). Again, the warning about reducing Scripture to propositions in a sermon constructed of ideational components is sounded. Like Buttrick, Lowry insists that a plot with its mobility and structured succession shape the sermon. A sermon, Lowry proclaims, "is a plot" (15).

To reiterate, in this plot-based middle ground of our methodological schema, the sermon does not depend on the story-form of a specific text for its shape and movement. A text *may* be a biblical narrative, but even here the text's plot need not replicate itself as the sermonic plot. For example, the preacher may develop issues from the biblical story within the first stage of the "loop" (upsetting the equilibrium). Notice, however, that a nonstory text can serve this purpose with equal alacrity.[40] The biblical text, though, may be located in any of the stages of the homiletic plot or may function in different ways in more than one stage. As with Buttrick's mode of reflection, there need not be any specific reference to the text as long as the theological field of meaning it articulates does present itself (although, as Buttrick comments, such a practice would be "unlikely") (325).

Two primary senses in which the image functions in a Lowry homiletic plot may now be articulated. The first is congruent with the manifestations of biblical and contemporary images previously detected in narrative preaching. In some instances, the image embodied in the text serves to orient a whole section or stage of the homily. Then, too, Lowry also reaches for contemporary imagery to provide a focus on the hearers' "felt discrepancy" or bind. Both biblical and contemporary images are at the service of the preacher at any stage in the sermonic plot. However, there is a second sense in which image comes to expression in a Lowry sermon—the very plot of the sermon itself is experienced as an image! Here is represented a move toward the right-hand side of the narrative-imagery schema. When the "premeditated plot" of the preacher is enacted with effectiveness, the congregation will retain an image of the "loop" itself, that distinctive shape of the bind-become-resolution. This second sense of the sermonic image is analogous to that described by Peter Brook with regard to experiencing a drama:

> The event scorches into the memory an outline, a taste, a trace, a smell—a picture. It is the play's central image that remains, its silhouette, and if the elements are rightly blended this silhouette will be its meaning, this shape will be the essence of what it has to say.[41]

Now the sermonic shape itself can be construed as an image. We move toward those approaches that represent the inversion of the narrative-dominated pole. At the opposite side, the image itself becomes the organizing dynamic of the sermon, its movement and its intention.

Image-Shaped Homiletic Plots

At the alternate pole in our methodological schema reside sermonic approaches shaped by images and image systems. Here narrative is either implicit in the images themselves—the biblical stories that gave rise to these now dominant images—or narrative becomes explicit as it clusters about the imagery. The notion of a homiletic plot still obtains, and with it, the characteristic elements of mobility, structure, and a sequential logic. Such a logic at this methodological pole, however, will not necessarily reflect a narrative plotting, although we will explore one expression of these image-shaped plots where an underlying narrative structure is discernible. (See figure 5.4 on the parable of the mustard seed.) Other types of plotting offer themselves based on the way images connect to each other in conscious reflection and on a version of the typological approach to interpretation. In all instances, it must be insisted, these images are not randomly assembled by the preacher, but are located with reference to the images of Scripture and their implicit narratives.

Biblical Imagery and Homiletic Plots

Among the variety of image-based homiletical plots, an approach commends itself in which the dominant image system of the biblical text becomes the structure of the homily. Within a number of pericopes, the structure and movement of the plot is guided by one or more master images, often involving some significant shift in point of view. Several examples may be found in the parables, with "mustard seed" (Mark 4:30-32) being exemplary of the type. If the analysis of Crossan, Funk, Perkins, and Scott is accepted in place of the old notion of evolutionary growth of a moralistic sort, then two images form the possible referents to the kingdom. On one hand, there is the cedar of Lebanon, the Great Tree, planted by God, which is the eschatological image for Israel (Ps. 104:16-17; Ezek. 17:23). On the other hand, Jesus offers up a mustard shrub that serves to call that triumphalist cedar image into question and replace it with a much more humble sign of God's reign. Pheme Perkins points out the significance of the shift in imagery:

> Cedars do not even grow in Israel. They had to be brought from Lebanon. But mustard bushes could grow up in anyone's field. Here's your national identity, then—a mustard bush. Not as grand or glorious as the cedar, but consider what happens to all the dilemmas about the rule of God and national identity if the nation is a mustard bush. It still can shelter the birds. The rule of God in the world is only a problem for those who think that his people have to be "top cedar." Mustard bush—that they already are.[42]

A sermon organized around the mustard seed image may have a logic of exploring those two master images along with a nexus of contemporary images located around cedar and shrub.

Figure 5.4 Mustard Seed Imagery

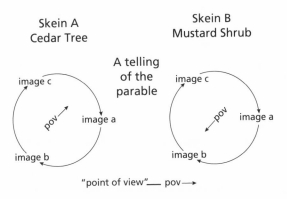

In each skein of images, the selected contemporary images will operate within a common theological field. A central consideration for the selection of images in each case will be not only their theological affinity with the master image (irony: labeling mustard shrub a "master" image!), but the consistent utilization of point of view. The hearers will need to strain the eyes of their imaginations upward to envision the noble cedar, the Washington Monument, a downtown First Church steeple, and so on. While exploring the mustard shrub and its attendant images, we will all be looking downward at such activities as footwashing, nursing an infant, or even a pastor sitting with a group of young palm bearers at the beginning of the Holy Week liturgies. The shift from skein A to skein B may involve the telling of the parable.

Other rich sources for image-based homilies are the prophetic books of the Old Testament and various apocalyptic texts. The prophetic writings frequently organize oracles according to images and even more complex image systems. A notable example of how the latter manifests itself is found in the Book of Joel. Here the plague of locusts is the master image, and the prophet appeals to a variety of perceptual analogies to represent the power of the locusts. They are like charging warhorses (2:4); God's people hear this "rumbling" and "crackling" and feel themselves grow weak and pale (2:6). Attached to the dominant image are two attendant images, an impotent priesthood ("the grain is destroyed, the wine dries up, the oil fails" 1:10, NRSV) and the calling of a fast (ironically called in the midst of a famine!). When the situation shifts by virtue of God's grace and mercy, the image system is transformed, from plague to plenty; from impotent sacrifice to abundance of God-given grain, wine, and oil; and from fasting to feasting on both a rich harvest and an outpoured spirit. In dealing with this pericope, one method for organizing these reversed image systems would be a sequence of moves in Buttrick's approach, in which the plot of the sermon follows this shift from locust plague to Pentecost. Apocalyptic literature can work in much the same way (the Joel passage is, after all, apocalyptic). Typically, the logic of apocalyptic progresses by a sequence of master images with their attendant image systems. And, as with Joel, the preacher will develop contemporary analogies as each image system is built and possibly transformed or reversed.

Typological Method and Imagery

Biblical narratives yield images that in certain instances have the capacity of organizing other narratives as a key hermeneutic function. Within this scriptural dynamic, the images themselves may be altered or even transformed by their location within a new narrative context—we recall Gail Ramshaw's analysis of the "rock" image for God provided in Psalm 95 and elsewhere. Not only do we detect that yes-no-yes pattern to the rock image's journey through the biblical narrative, we also detect layers of meaning—multivalence—built up through these successive stories. What results, Ramshaw notes, is a "chain of metaphors" now centered for the Christian community in Christ the rock. Simon the apostle becomes *petros*, thereby describing both Peter's faith and the church's foundation on the Rock. Ramshaw adds:

> The epistle of 1 Peter carries this metaphor even further. Christ is the rock, and we are stones fixed next to Christ and thus creating the house of God (1 Pet. 2:5). And more: Christ as the rock is also the stumbling block, the rejected stone, the scandal to trip up the religious world (1 Pet. 2:7-8). For if religions in ancient times depicted the great god or goddess as a sacred rock, those religions trip over the rock at the door of Christ's tomb, the crucifixion and resurrection breaking sacred metaphor.[43]

On the other hand, the narrative ethicists have assisted the church in seeing how images may shape personal and communal vision, providing the faithful with indispensable lenses for seeing themselves and their world. Contemporary experience is never apprehended without mediation (liberal doctrine and interpretation to the contrary!). The decisive locus of mediation for a Christian is the "world" rendered by biblical narrative and its attendant imagery. At the heart of the church's sacramental life resides this insight—we make anamnesis of the saving narrative and locate that story in conjunction with the sacramental images of water, bread, and wine. In turn, narratives and their images provide a *habitus* within which the community is formed in its character and endowed with virtues that are essential to its life and work. Through this conforming discipleship, Christians also look at the world with a distinctive image-shaped vision.

Given both the multivalence of biblical imagery as well as its capacity to shape Christian vision, a range of homiletic approaches is suggested. Several methods have been analyzed for shaping the homily informed by the text's own image system or its dynamic of imagistic transformation. However, there also are suggested a repertoire of other homiletic strategies based on this central hermeneutic function of biblical imagery. At least three options result from the respective ways in which these images provide us with a way of envisioning self, church, and world. First, a variety of contemporary experiences may be assembled that are exemplary of the biblical image and its respective narrative. Here the emphasis would be on a sense of compatibility and mutual resonance. The preacher, as it were, is inviting the people to look "here, there, and even over there" for ways in which the biblical image or image system grants us a positive slant on contemporary experiences. Preaching on the saints, in fact, is most often this kind of pointing toward models of Christian discipleship oriented around key scriptural images. One homiletic approach utilizing this mode of positive resonance aligns a series of narratives from contemporary experience and the tradition with a dominant biblical image. The resulting sermon may be envisioned as a sequence of narratives become "transparencies" built up as on an overhead projector. The organizing principle is the biblical image; the multivalence is provided by the depth of narratives seen as exemplary of that image. We may imagine the sermon to express the schema in figure 5.5:

Figure 5.5 Biblical Imagery as Organizing Form

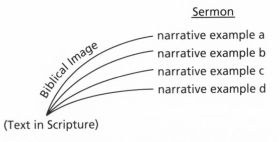

As is the case in the Craddock sermon, "Praying Through Clenched Teeth,"[44] the biblical narrative itself may show up as one of the sequential narrative examples. Critical to the success of this approach, it must be emphasized, is that the narrative examples resonate with the biblical imagery and locate easily within the theological field of the biblical text. This approach, when used with care and integrity, may well be labeled "typological preaching." The core assumption is that the character of God remains consistent and that contemporary analogies to Scripture are both possible and edifying.

Juxtaposition and Affinity in Imagery

A whole sweep of other contemporary experiences and examples exist in the tradition in which precisely the reverse occurs. When envisioned by virtue of the biblical imagery, these stories, situations, and signs stand in opposition to the world of Scripture. Here the relationship is one of contrary juxtaposition. Such experiences abound, for the world is still the world and, therefore, remains in need of redemption.[45] Ironically, a favorite tactic of those conformed to the world is to camouflage its unredeemed and death-dealing artifacts and practices with religious or moral mimicry. MX missiles were labeled "Peacemakers," and now genocide is wrapped in the guise of "ethnic cleansing." A homily employing this relationship of opposition to Scripture and its narratives and images would not look quite like a series of layered "transparencies." Rather, we could envision the preacher's homiletic video camera or simulator checking out a series of claimants for peace or cleansing. Each exploration could be placed against the biblical image and evaluated from its perspective. At some point, however, the preacher will turn to gospel and invite the congregation to envision missile silos now become grain storehouses or the cleansing of peoples imaged as a swimming pool filled with Serbian, Croatian, and Bosnian children, all reveling in the splashing waters and in their enjoyment of each other. Such a homily would perhaps raise the issue presented by the biblical image and conclude sequentially "Not this," "Not this," "Not this"—"This!"

Since the preaching of the gospel cannot remain in a mode of opposition, of contrary juxtaposition, the imagery of biblical faith points toward transformation. (There is assuredly a "This!" to which we must point in Christ.) At the heart of the matter, the cross speaks both of the world's opposition to God's purposes in

Christ and of God's vindication of Jesus and the gospel. As Karl
Barth reminded the church, the cross represents the world's no
to Christ; it also manifests God's yes to the world![46] Images of
transformation, then, will be located in sermons where images of
opposition and juxtaposition have been explored. The homiletic
logic is one of exodus, of movement from bondage to freedom and
from death to resurrection.[47] So in a sermon embodying imagery
in the mode of transformation, our missile silo become grain silo
now is transformed into the eucharistic image of bread made of
finest wheat. The homily begun with the image of opposition
dealing with ethnic cleansing shifts to our pool of frolicking children of the warring factions. Now that image is transformed into
one of the cleansing of the baptismal waters and of our exodus in
Christ from death to life.

It is in this reflection on an image-based mode of transformation
that a dynamic emerges that will necessarily adjust the entire
schema of narrative and imagery in homiletic method. What orig-
inally seemed a polar model (narrative predominating on one side
and imagery on the other) must give way to a more tensive and
mobile understanding. This shift becomes necessary as this mode
of transformation is discovered at the image pole of the model.
Yet we recall that the fullest expression of transformation is to
be found in the biblical narrative with its movement of plot and
revelations of character. So what seemed a static location at the
image pole, this mode of transformation, actually propels the
church back to its narratives which gave birth to the image in the
first place. Now our model shapes itself more like a Möbius strip
with a figure-eight twist (see figure 5.6).

Figure 5.6 Narrative-Imagery Loop

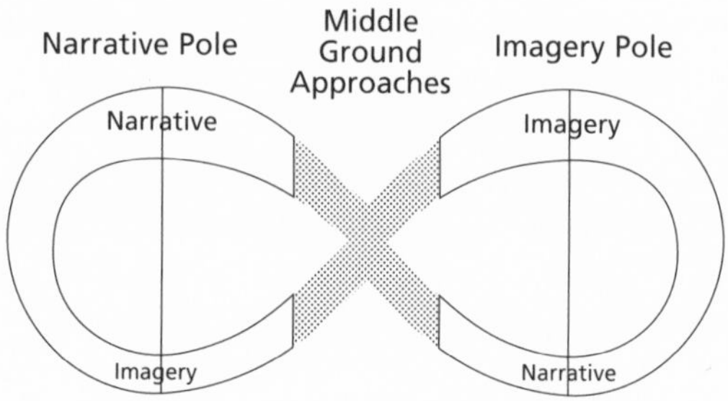

So, preaching biblical narrative and the imagery of biblical faith methodologically comes to have no end; the narratives and the images of our faith turn and return in a dance-like weaving. And that dance will come to a resting place only at the end of the age.

Notes

1. David J. Bryant, *Faith and the Play of Imagination: On the Role of the Imagination in Religion* (Macon, Ga.: Mercer Univ. Press, 1989), 90.

2. Mary Warnock, *Imagination* (Berkeley and Los Angeles: Univ. of California Press, 1976), 172ff.

3. Robert Howard observes that the image systems of most sermons today are from an "overwhelmingly patriarchal point of view" (37). The resulting distortion is one of "immasculation." Women are both compelled to adopt a male perspective in order to hear the illustration and implicitly urged to believe "this masculine point of view to be *the* human one" ("Gender and Point of View in the Imagery of Preaching," *Papers of the Annual Meeting*, Academy of Homiletics, 1992, 39).

4. For an extensive treatment of point of view, see David Buttrick, *Homiletic Moves and Structures* (Philadelphia: Fortress Press, 1987), 55–68.

5. Buttrick's term for an imaged location of single meaning within the homiletical plot. See part 1 of *Homiletic* for his development of move theory.

6. Buttrick, *Homiletic*, 135–36.

7. Robert W. Funk, *Parables and Presence: Forms of the New Testament Tradition* (Philadelphia: Fortress Press, 1982), 29–34. See also John Dominic Crossan, *In Parables: The Challenge of the Historical Jesus* (New York: Harper & Row, 1973), 57–66; and Bernard Brandon Scott, *Hear Then the Parable: A Commentary on the Parables of Jesus* (Minneapolis: Fortress Press, 1989), 189–202. Scott observes, "What commentators have failed to notice is that the Israelite is excluded from being the parable's hero. To remain in the story the hearer cannot play hero but must become a victim" (200).

8. Funk, *Parables*, 65.

9. Bryant, *Play*, 91.

10. Ibid., 91.

11. Catherine and Justo González, "Babel and Empire: Pentecost and Empire," *Journal for Preachers* 16 (Pentecost 1993): 24.

12. See Buttrick, *Homiletic*, 55–68.

13. Ibid., 63.

14. Ibid., 59.

15. Ibid., 60.

16. Extrascriptural usages included to "quake," "seethe," and "throw up"!

17. Eugene Lowry, *How to Preach a Parable: Designs for Narrative Sermons* (Nashville: Abingdon Press, 1989), 163.

18. John C. Holbert, *Preaching the Old Testament: Proclamation and Narrative in the Hebrew Bible* (Nashville: Abingdon Press, 1991).

19. Buttrick, *Homiletic*, 333–63.

20. Henry Mitchell, *Black Preaching* (San Francisco: Harper & Row, 1979).

21. Buttrick, *Homiletic*, 333.

22. Holbert, *Preaching*, 47.

23. When using excursi within a narrative homily it is critical that enough attention is provided to putting the movement of the plot "on hold." One phrase such as "Just as with Abraham, it is also true for us today . . ." will not do. The preacher will want to design a holding or pausing system with the same care and much of the same technique as Buttrick recommends for a closure system for a move. See *Homiletic*, 50–53.

24. "Noah Was a Good Man," by Dennis Willis, in Lowry, *How to Preach a Parable*, 42–49. Hereafter cited in the text.

25. Lowry, *Parable*, 121.

26. Holbert, *Preaching*, 43.

27. Lowry, *Parable*, 79ff.

28. Holbert, *Preaching*, 43–44.

29. Richard L. Thulin, "Retelling Biblical Narratives as the Foundation for Preaching," in *Journeys toward Narrative Preaching*, ed. Wayne Bradley Robinson (New York: Pilgrim Press, 1990), 13–18. Hereafter cited in the text.

30. See my *A New Hearing: Living Options in Homiletic Method* (Nashville: Abingdon Press, 1987), 213–16, for an elaboration of Buttrick's critique of sermonic doublets. The difficulties related to syntactical doublets also obtain for these "then-now" tense doublets with the compounded problem of rapid shift in point of view.

31. Robinson, *Journeys*, 19–22.

32. Lowry, *Parable*, 142–48.

33. So in recasting the parable of the ungrateful servant (Matt. 18:23-34), that servant may become a postal service worker. The grandiosity of the debt, ten thousand talents (18:24), may be recast as a letter he receives from the IRS demanding that he pay $3,487,693.07, his portion of the national debt, due in thirty days. The letter concludes, "Failure to comply with the provisions of the National Debt Reduction Act will result in significant fines and/or imprisonment." Our servant will need to appear before the deputy commissioner of the regional IRS office and plead to her, "Have patience with me, and I will pay you everything"

(18:26). And the deputy commissioner will have pity and forgive the debt. Then the servant will need to go to another—perhaps a migrant worker who owes him money he borrowed to buy a shovel. Needless to say, the servant will not have pity, the deputy commissioner does hear about this ingratitude, and for that servant the recast parable will have its "tragic" ending.

34. In one sermon, a scene from *Pretty Woman* was used as an illustration. In the discussion that followed it was discovered that for most of the hearers, the reference brought to mind either Julia Roberts or Richard Gere!

35. John S. McClure, *The Four Codes of Preaching: Rhetorical Strategies* (Minneapolis: Fortress Press, 1991), 188.

36. Buttrick, *Homiletic*, 325. Hereafter cited in the text.

37. Buttrick states that "preaching in the reflective mode is particularly suited to Pauline passages, to teachings of Jesus, apocalyptic visions, allegories, wisdom literature, and some prophetic passages" (*Homiletic*, 326).

38. Eugene Lowry, *The Homiletical Plot: The Sermon as Narrative Art Form* (Atlanta: John Knox Press, 1980). Hereafter cited in the text. See my *Hearing*, 64–88.

39. McClure, *Codes*, 67.

40. When the biblical text appears in the early stages of a "Lowry loop" homily, it is usually because the preacher has spotted something in it that is "strange" or "weird" or represents "trouble." Lowry invites preachers to approach the text with such a probing in mind ("Workshop on Preaching," *Jubilate Festival of Worship and the Arts*, Seattle, Washington, July 1990).

41. Peter Brook, *The Empty Space* (New York: Avon, 1968), 124. Quoted in Robert G. Hughes, "Narrative as Plot," *Journeys*, 51.

42. Pheme Perkins, *Hearing the Parables of Jesus* (New York: Paulist Press, 1981), 87–88.

43. Ramshaw, *Christ in Sacred Speech: The Meaning of Liturgical Language* (Philadelphia: Fortress Press, 1986), 43.

44. In Lowry, *Parable*, 142–48.

45. Stanley Hauerwas, *A Community of Character: Toward a Constructive Christian Social Ethic* (Notre Dame, Ind.: Univ. of Notre Dame Press, 1981), 72–86.

46. Karl Barth, *Church Dogmatics: A Selection*, ed. G. W. Bromiley (New York: Harper & Row, 1961), 123–33.

47. This exodus typology may be seen in the New Testament, for example, in Luke's Transfiguration account in which Jesus speaks with Moses and Elijah about his departure—*ten exodon autou* (9:31)—and

Luke's ascension pericope in which Jesus "led out" his disciples (24:50).
The verb *exagein*, Fitzmyer notes, is the verb "used in the LXX for Yahweh
leading his people out of Egyptian bondage in the exodus." Joseph A.
Fitzmyer, *The Gospel according to Luke (X–XXIV)* (New York: Doubleday, 1985), 1589.

6

Preaching from the Middle:
Three Sermons and Commentary

As narrative and imagery intersect each other in our methodological schema, neither dominates the sermonic plot. That is, we
do not expect to "run the story" here in "sermons from the
middle," nor do we anticipate the employment of a purely image-
based sermon structure. Rather, each of the following homilies is
related to a narrative biblical text, but each adopts differing strategies for combining the narrative and imagistic features of the
text. William Turner's sermon, "Divine Appearance and Erecting
Altars," gives an initial appearance of "running the story" but
breaks from a close following of the biblical story through a sequence of reflective moves interfolded with sections based on the
text's master image system. The "Storm in the Boat" homily is
designed with David Buttrick's approach in mind and deals in the
mode of immediacy for the first two moves—that is, these first
moves follow with an immediacy the movement and structure of
the text. Then the homily shifts to Buttrick's reflective mode for
the last three moves, informed especially by a hearer-response
criticism of the text. The sermon by Deneise Deter-Rankin, "Follow Me," relates a sequence of contemporary scenes to elements
in the narrative until it arrives at the threefold question-and-
answer portion of the Johannine epilogue. At that point, the scenes
begin to orient themselves to that image system rather than to
elements of the narrative text's own plot.

What we have here are three sermons that all move with some
kind of structured "logic," although none is designed to follow
the story plot of the text closely. In these "sermons from the

middle," however, the preacher is capable of reaching to both the narrative and image poles of our schema for a variety of homiletic strategies. Two issues are of concern as such an approach is taken. First, the plotted sequence of the homiletical plot must remain easily followed by the hearers, meaning that we will not overdo shifts in homiletic strategies. (The three sermons employ a maximum of three strategic approaches—with Turner—and two with the others.) Second, whether based on the text's movement or its image system on one hand or operating in a reflective mode off of these components of the biblical text, it remains the world of Scripture that is preached. In that regard, preaching from the middle is as disciplined in its fidelity to the scriptural world as sermons at the narrative or the imagery poles. This middle range, where narrative and imagery interplay with a rough equity, will offer preachers perhaps the widest possible options of homiletic approach. In a way, more freedom in homiletic strategy is granted; along with that freedom comes both risk and responsibility.

Genesis 12:6-7: "Divine Appearances and Erecting Altars"

by William F. Turner

Sermon	Commentary
Places and events are hardly separable.... There are places that are foreboding, charged with unhappy memories, or utterly depressing. No matter how excited and enthused we are beforehand, when we arrive at such places the spirit sinks, nerve begins to fail, and the utter preoccupation is with departure. Again, there are those places that possess their own enchantment, mystery, and healing for the spirit.	*The sermon could begin simply in the narrative. Instead, Turner has chosen to explore with the hearers the interplay between place and event. They are connected, for better or for worse.*

No matter what the mood, arrival at such places is the greatest remedy that could ever be imagined. But the nature of any place where the Lord appears is such that it occasions the erection of an altar and the utter transformation of not only the place, but all that abides therein.

By the introduction's finish, the hearers may well be waiting to decide about the place and the event to come. "Altar" and "transformation" suggest which direction things will go.

In this text we find the account of how God called Abram to leave his country, his kinsmen, and his father's house to go to a country that the Lord promised. To those who have become familiar with life in ancient Palestine, it seems like a somewhat routine matter that a wandering Aramean would relocate to another spot with his herd. But closer inspection reveals that this was quite a radical move. For just as Abram would pass on his earthly possessions to his son Isaac, so he stood to receive his father's inheritance had he remained with him. In addition, this was a dangerous territory; at any moment there was the threat of attack from people within the land who were not anxious to have intruders wandering about. So in moving out at the command of the Lord, Abram risked losing his inheritance, forfeiting protection, and subjecting all who depended on

Now we enter the narrative.

The primary attention now is given to the spatial dimension of the story. One critic has charged that spatiality is generally underplayed in preaching biblical narrative. Here, at least, that is not the case.

him to a precarious and un-certain future. But it was in the course of such a journey that the Lord appeared and gave the occasion for erecting an altar.

In terms of longitude and lat-itude the place where God ap-peared to Abram was just an-other section of space—just a plain. Indeed, the place was so nondescript that it did not have a name. Following the appearance of the Lord, the place was simply referred to as "there." It was in the middle of nowhere—as we used to say, "ditty wa ditty, no town and no city." All that gave it distinction was that God appeared.

One can imagine Isaac and Lot asking for more information in days that followed concern-ing where God first appeared to Abram. Perhaps they asked whether it was between Beth-el and Ai . . . an altar was built there. But that was not the first appearance. If pressed to account for the first appear-ance, Abraham would have to have said: "It was beyond Shechem, over by the tere-binth tree, over on the plain of Moreh, that God first appeared occasioning the erection of an altar. It was by a desert scrub,

The sermon speaks of risk in this journey by Abram. Again, "altar" is mentioned, this time in conjunction with "journey."

A no-name place is given a nice touch of contemporiza-tion in the folk rhyme. But no-tice that having made the place as nondescript as pos-sible, the preacher adds that "God appeared." Now, the co-ordinates of the sermon inter-sect: "altar," "journey," "transformation," and an ap-pearance of the Lord.

Turner "fast forwards" to an imagined time when Isaac and Lot will ask about this place and this meeting. The prolepsis serves two func-tions—to link the hearers with biblical people who have never stopped asking about the story and to begin ex-panding on the story's setting.

by a turpentine bush—it was there!"

Now the precondition for the appearance of the Lord, which allows for the building of an altar, is the journey of faith. The appearance of the Lord to Abram was not the beginning of God's dealings with him. Indeed, Abram was making this journey to the Negeb precisely because the Lord had spoken, calling him out from home and kindred. God had even made the promise to bless him, to make his name great, to make him a great nation, to curse those who cursed him, and to establish a line through him for the blessing of all the families of the earth. But it was only after the journey began that the Lord appeared permitting the erection of an altar.

In a very Buttrick-like move, a reflective issue is raised, that of the relationship between the altar and the journey. The latter's beginning must precede the former's building.

An appearance of the Lord does not signify the beginning of God's existence or presence in the world; neither does it necessarily indicate the initial presence of the Lord in a given place. Our God does not become real in the moment that we feel him, in the instant when a solution to our problem is given, or in that epiphany when the eyes of our understanding come open. Similarly, God is not absent

Notice that a facility with the design of a move is not restricted to preaching only "moves and structures." Here, a Buttrick-type move allows a necessary "bracketing" of the biblical issues of place and journey. With those issues "on hold," this important question may be explored.

At this point in the move, Buttrick would urge that an image be presented with its attendant point of view.

from places or epochs because we do not sense divine presence in the mannner we prefer. No, the appearance of the Lord that permits the erection of an altar requires simply that we journey to a land God is showing us.

There are many to whom God does not appear, for they refuse to make the journey, and for that reason they have no altars. There is even the child of God, the minister of the gospel, or the student in seminary who passes through life in such a state of deprivation. Some may affirm their faith with the precision of historic creeds: and they may know how to account for all that has been promised through the Spirit. But there has been no divine appearance, and consequently they have no altar. In such a case there is no journey and there is no joy.

Again, there are those who desire to live at an altar erected on some previous occasion; so they despise the journey when it entails patient, disciplined study and application. But a despising attitude toward the journey causes ministry to be tedious, onerous, unfulfilled labor; it makes seminary a dull, dead experience that is

Again, a lengthy story illustration will not do; it may form an embolism precluding our movement beyond the move.

Another Buttrick-like move, this one related in sequence with the former. The examples are designed to speak to the hearers—seminarians at chapel. Notice that Turner concludes each of these moves with a strong closure system that reiterates the opening's single meaning.

the mere requirement of some judicatory.

The journey is from the safety, comfort, and inheritance of Haran, and it is toward the appearance of the Lord and the altar God permits. No matter what the journey may be, embrace it with enthusiasm, affirm it with confidence, and embark upon it with joy. God will appear and give a place and an occasion for erecting an altar. At this place of meeting, we are forced to sing "We praise thee O God, we acknowledge thee to be the Lord." Break your weariness: leave Haran, and start on your journey!

The hearers, along with Abram, are encouraged to take the journey. This little sequence is in the form of a summary of the preceding sections. It concludes in doxology. With such an ending, the sermon must now "begin again," possibly in some new direction.

The one appropriate response to divine appearance is the erecting of an altar in praise and thanksgiving. However, the erection of an altar is an action that is not radically disjunct from all the other things of life. Instead, it deepens the meaning of life; aspects of daily existence comprise the content of which altars are erected.

The journey motif is now picked up in a positive sense. The sequence is established— journey leads to appearance and appearance leads to altar.

Contrast the building of the altar with the more elaborate building schemes of ancient times. Countless hours of labor were required for the perfect cutting of stones from the

This central interest in the "how" of altar-building will provide the leverage for Turner to contemporize the sermon. He begins this analysis, not with the text's image of an altar

quarry to build Solomon's
temple without the sound of
a chisel being heard. But no
such requirements were involved in Abram's altar to the
Lord. We see no evidence that
Abram made any procure-
ments or hired any additional
servants for the task. He simply looked around and picked
roughly shaped stones for
erecting an altar to the Lord.

A rationale for the simplicity
is not given in this text, but in
subsequent books we are told
of the prohibition against the
use of iron instruments in
building an altar to God. The
stones to be used were not to
be shaped, cut, or tampered
with in any way: altars were
for forgiveness while iron was
for punishment; the altar pro-
longed life, but iron cut it
short. But beyond that, the altar was not to call attention to
itself; those unsightly, asymmetrical, jagged stones were to
be heaped together in such a
way that they forced the on-
looker to ask why they were
there and what the reason was
for their presence. The altar,
the place where the gift to God
was sanctified and sacrificed,
was the occasion for telling a
story, giving a testimony, for
making the divine appearance
public knowledge to the
world. Abram and those in his

*of rough-shaped stones, but
with its alternative. Beginning
in a contrapuntal mode, we
move from what Abram's altar
is not to what it will be.*

*Information is provided that
gives some of the background
on the rationale for Abram's
altar with its "unsightly,
asymmetrical, jagged stones."
This Ebenezer is for testimony. The vivid description of
the stones also is designed to
resonate with the contemporization. Homiletically, a
"template" is being established here which will be applied to the hearers' own
situations in the following
section.*

company simply collected stones scattered over the landscape to let the world know that the Lord had appeared.

The altar that cherishes the Lord's presence also cultivates sensitivity and indicates a welcome to him. The altar testifies to the depth of life not accessible to the merely rational, dominating, or aggressive means. It produces the environment in which even the faint and veiled presence of the Lord cannot go unnoticed. The altar need not be elaborate or meticulous: it need only be related to divine appearance. Utter care and precision may be required in preparing the masterpiece that is to be delivered to the preacher-critics on Sunday, but altars can be erected from spontaneous words of praise. Skill, insight, and imagination are appropriate in writing papers and doing other assignments, but the uncalculated flow of love is a fit stone also. Don't spend too much time planning how the altar will look; just grab a stone where the Lord appears and witness to how that place of visitation is already transformed.

There is no plain or wilderness in life that is so barren that stones cannot be found for the

Here Turner provides a contrapuntal to his positive move that follows. We are now given the image system that will become the central one for the sermon. Our rough-shaped stones will be used to build an altar.

The master image is now explored. And a further significance is attached to altar. The stones we heap up will be for a witness. Questions by others as to their meaning will become the occasion for testimony.

Now the preacher makes a move that "celebrates" the building of the altar. A series

erection of an altar. Why, that stone we are close to cursing for being a stumbling block in our way corresponds perfectly to an empty spot in our altar. Academic pressures, stresses in family and community life, and upheaval in the parish come at the time when faith seems to be at its lowest ebb. Specters of racism, reckless leadership, and gleeful callousness in the execution of death-row inmates can be for us stones that litter the way. But when we embrace the journey the Lord has called us to pursue, we see raw material for an altar that celebrates his appearance and on which our lives can be sacrificed. Altars for God are completed by the stones that naturally lie along the path of the journey.

Through Jesus Christ the God who appeared to Abram is ever with us and the life that has been transformed by the Spirit is ever suited for an altar. Indeed, the Christian journey, the walk in the Spirit, the pilgrimage to the city is not less than living in the presence of the Lord. The offering we make of ourselves is not less than giving ourselves upon the altar. The God who appeared to Abram and our fathers and mothers in the faith has now

of "need not be this . . . only this" statements creates a rhetorical system that conveys a growing affective significance. Notice that the system does not attempt to add a great deal of new information or insight at each step. Rather, the interest is to convey that "depth of life" sense of divine appearance. Each statement in the system, then, explores another facet of the same issue without introducing other issues.

Now, with the image of altar stone established, it is reframed in a way that both allows contemporization and, at a subtle level, introduces a New Testament perspective on "journey," "appearance," and "altar." Our stumbling block either can remain so or become an altar stone! Again, we detect most all of the elements comprising a Buttrick-type move here. Also, Turner has now shifted from a narrative sermonic plot to one based on imagery. It is the image of altar and stumbling block that will lead us now to consider Christ. With the New Testament witness introduced almost subliminally in given the Spirit's abiding presence to those who are born from above.

St. John tells us that God appeared and gave himself to the world. We beheld his glory, for the Son was made manifest. And this appearance is for the whole world. Even in the most nondescript places God is present. Permission is given to erect an altar wherever the Spirit has given life. Indeed, the most nondescript of places is transformed into a shrine; ordinary life is touched by glory. Any place is great if the Lord has appeared there and an altar has been assembled from its stones.

This is the meaning of the Table—each time we eat the bread and drink the cup we testify to the appearing of God. The celebration is an epiclesis. It is an invitation for the Holy Spirit to come upon the bread and the wine, and to fill us. When we come to the table we remember Jesus who laid himself upon the altar and poured out his life's blood for our sins. But we have not come to the table in truth, sincerity, and earnestness unless our lives are being offered to him continually on the altar we erect in response to his appearance

the previous move, the place of Jesus Christ in the Christian's journey is proclaimed.

Once the vectors of the sermon have been established as journey, appearance, altar, and transformation, the preacher is able to move naturally between them. The main proviso is that enough attention is devoted to the newly introduced aspect of the sequence. Now our attention is shifted to that of appearance, transformed now to the appearance of Jesus Christ.

The homily is preached at a eucharistic liturgy in the seminary community. Two closing sections now witness to this altar and this place of meeting.

and from the stones that lie along the path of our journey.

But the Table is more. It is a sign of that eternal altar upon which the blood of the new covenant poured. This is the reason stones that formerly caused us to stumble cannot hurt us when placed upon the altar. You see, our Savior is exalted by the Father from a rejected stone to the head of the corner, and a stone to trip those who refuse to believe. Get that burden on the altar. If you can't lift it, drag it; if you can't drag it by yourself, get a friend to help you. But by all means, get it to the altar. Every now and then we need to just lay something down on the altar. This is why we come to the Table. There is GOOD NEWS here in this place.

The "more" of this altar is announced, and the other images of stones are aligned with our master image of altar stone. Now "journey" is again mentioned, though this time, the short one to the altar. A little rhetorical system urges the hearers to take that significant journey.

Mark 8:11-21: "Storm in the Boat"

by Richard Eslinger

Sermon	Commentary

A second feeding has occurred in the wilderness. Jesus has again taken an offering of the meager loaves and fish, given thanks, and shared abundance. "They ate and were filled," Mark says. All four thousand people, fed in the wilderness. And once more

Introduction. The initial segment of the introduction serves to orient the hearers. We are coming in on the end of the second feeding story. Also, this initial section will become the necessary background for the disciples' reaction to discovering only one loaf in the boat.

the remaining pieces are collected and tallied—"seven baskets full!" So this crowd of Gentiles begins the journey home with the news, with the Good News.

"Gentiles" is emphasized. Later on an image of "Gentile feeding" will be developed.

Now moving against the flow of all those satisfied Gentiles are some very unsatisfied Pharisees. They want a sign from Jesus, "to test him." Jesus pauses and heaves a sigh like an ocean swell in the North Atlantic. When it subsides, he announces to them, "No sign! No sign will be given!" Only that of his leaving in the boat with the disciples. Time for another sea crossing. Then a new crisis on board. Jesus' disciples discover that nobody thought to bring along any bread. Only one loaf for this journey. Two crossings, two storms, and now this. Only one loaf.

Attention is devoted to Pharisees who move against the flow.

The challenge is to image anastenaxas to pneumati. "Sigh" will not do. Utilizing the simulator model, an "ocean swell" does the job and also resonates with the sea crossing "storm."

As a "Buttrick" sermon, the introduction is pushing the limits for length. Whatever else, for Buttrick, the introduction must set up a readiness to hear the first move.

The disciples fret and worry over their lack of bread out there on the water. "Only one loaf," they complain to each other. Their meager provision becomes the topic of conversation, overheard, of course, by Jesus. Twice before they have worried about bread. Two times before Jesus had asked them to inventory their resources, and both times the answer had come back—"Not

Move I. *The disciples worry over a lack of bread. The motif of "not enough" is developed. Several sentences establish the single meaning at stake in the move. Such an opening system is essential to form the move within a communal consciousness.*

enough, Lord, not nearly enough." Listening to the complaints, you wonder if Jesus feels like he has interrupted a support group of "adult children," deprived somehow when they were young. Now, even grown up, there is always a sense of anxiety, of need. Listening to their stories, you realize that no matter what the issue, there's never enough. Never enough food, or possessions. Even in the love department, they whine that there's never enough. Problem is, what they do receive doesn't "add up." It's like they start with an empty calculator each day. Every day, all the need is there again, . . . and again. So the disciples out there in the boat worry about bread. One loaf isn't enough, not nearly enough. Look at anxiety afloat—a boatload of worry and care.

Then Jesus rebukes the Twelve, rebukes their dulled senses, their forgetfulness. "Are your hearts hardened?" asks Jesus. Only a sigh for the Pharisees, but the disciples get an earful! First a list of grievances—eyes and no seeing, ears and no hearing. Jesus likens them to the idols old Isaiah mocked and scorned. "Do you not perceive or understand?" he asks. No answer

This first move operates within Buttrick's "mode of immediacy" with regard to the text. Acting childish, an image of always needy "adult children" is chosen. The point of view for the hearers is imagining Jesus interrupting a support group session. The sense of children in the image is important. We will build our image system around it.

A move also needs a closing system, Buttrick insists. Mostly by reiteration the single meaning is again stated in several sentences.

Move II. *Jesus turns and rebukes the Twelve for their worry, really their forgetfulness. An allusion is made to a recurring prophetic indictment of Israel involving idolatry. Since the image of the move comes later, this Old Testament reference cannot be much elaborated. Just a touch for those who have eyes to see and ears to hear! The second move also travels in* from the Twelve. Then Jesus tries a quiz, questions designed to jog their memory, awaken understanding. "When I broke the five loaves for the five thousand, how many baskets of broken pieces did you collect?" "Twelve," they blurt out. "And seven for the four thousand—how many baskets?" "Seven," comes the answer.

"Twelve" and "seven." That's all they have to report. Facts, numbers, but no interpretation. Could have been "eight" and "nineteen" or, well, you pick a number. But no memory that yields understanding. It's like those test results you read about in the paper—high school students who don't have a clue about their history. "Who fought at the battle of Shiloh?" Among the multiple choices, some pick "Spain and Sweden"! No memory, no understanding. Just a vast amnesia—no idea who you are and where you're going if you don't know where you've been. Even getting the numbers right, the disciples have no interpretation. "Do you not yet understand?" questions Jesus. Silence. Only waves slapping against the boat. No answers come; no, they really don't understand.

immediacy with the text. A simple sequence is designed—the disciples worry about their meager provision, (Move I) and Jesus rebukes them for their lack of faith (Move II).

After the quiz (we will invite the hearers to be quizzed in the conclusion), the image of high school exams is presented. A battle in the Civil War at a place with the biblical name of Shiloh is deliberately picked to bring into consciousness an alignment of civil warfare and a church (named Shiloh!). The point of view is reading a newspaper.

Since seeing and hearing are the text's two perceptual models, we play with the aural image of silence except for the waves slapping against the boat. Again, a need for a closure—no faith, no understanding.

Now our anger rises against the disciples. How can those people not remember! How can they be so dull! Why does Jesus even put up with them? They are impossible. Look, they were there at both feedings, distributed the bread and the fish—gathered up the leftovers, too. They get the numbers right but no comprehension. Oblivious to who Jesus is and therefore who they are. What an irony—the Pharisees ask for a sign and get none. These disciples, though, did see the signs. More, they were part of the sign each time they distributed and gathered all that bread. Oh, we would like to be there! We could give Jesus the answer he wants. Instead he's got this boatful of leftovers called "The Twelve." Ever sit in Sunday school when you were a kid? The teacher asks a question, and you know the answer and wave your hand like mad. Mrs. Buchanan looks around and asks Terry—and you know he can't give the right answer. Still, why didn't she ask us, we would have got it right. Not like "The Twelve." We would have got it right. What a bunch. Makes you wonder—why did Jesus go and pick them?

Move III. Anger rises against the disciples for their dulled understanding. The perspectuality of the entire move is in the reflective mode. Our hearer-response is anger, perhaps mixed with a bit of jealousy that Jesus chose the Twelve. Given this response, a child's thoughts and feelings are chosen to image. Assumed is the probability that most people still carry such a child-response around, though well hidden most of the time!

One of the ironies in the text is specifically mentioned— that of sign/no sign. It will be picked up again in a contemporized move.

The point of view is an imagined Sunday School class when we were young.

The rhetoric of the move is designed to match the petulant thoughts of the child presented in the image.

Of course, the sign has been given to us, too. Like the disciples we know there is one loaf in the boat. But we also know the story, celebrate that we are part of the sign. Gathered once more with Jesus, we rejoice that there is the One Loaf in our boat, and that it is sufficient for any need. We see and hear, and by God's grace, understand. Imagine a city church—with so many homeless people on the streets, it's time to start a weekly drop-in center. There's a meal, safety, and a chance to relax and talk with church members, with each other. On Drop-in Night the line of hungry folks stretches around the side of the old church hall and out the door, even families with little children standing there in line. As the pastor comes by the serving station, one hot, cheery member looks up from scooping sauce onto heaping plates of spaghetti. "Just like loaves and fishes, huh, 'Rev'?" Yeah, just like loaves and fishes. Always enough with the One Loaf in the boat. The next Sunday, bread is offered, thanks is given, and it is broken and shared. The choir and people sing, "One Bread, One Body." The spaghetti server joins those to receive Christ. As he opens his hands, the pastor smiles a smile of recognition. "Just like loaves and

Move IV. The sign is given to us, too. Another reflective move.

The presence of Christ in the church is imaged through a sequence of two feeding stories. Only a necessary fragment of each one is given, but the interest is for them to connect by virtue of the recurring line "Just like the loaves and fishes" and the tag line "Always enough." "Little children" are brought into the image of the homeless outsiders (Gentiles?) being fed.

The two-part image (both visual and aural) is designed with the video camera model in mind. Visual elements— the people in the food line, the spaghetti serving, the open hands of the server-now-receiver at the Eucharist—are combined with the "Just like loaves and fishes."

fishes," she thinks. Always enough with the One Loaf in the boat. Oh, yes, we have seen the sign. Much more, we have become part of it. One bread, one body.

Wonder, then, why we worry so much in our boat with Jesus? So much care and anxiety in our church, in the churches. "If we die . . . ," you hear people say, whether the topic is the budget or the building or church attendance. Which roughly translates, "When we die. . . ." Ever wonder why we are so filled with care when the One Loaf is here with us in the boat? Maybe we're more like the disciples than we'd want to admit, at times. We have seen the signs, been part of them. And in spite of that seeing and hearing, we grow anxious. Again and again. Like a church treasurer who tells the organist at the start of each year's finance drive, "Don't know if we'll be able to afford all this music program next year." Anxious treasurer, anxious organist—and all those anxious people. Maybe when you've been through all those crises— all those stormy crossings— it's hard to accept that this season will be without its storm. And so the temptation is to create one in the boat. Look,

Move V. Why, then, do we have so much worry and care? Another reflective move playing off the positive seeing and hearing expressed in Move IV.

A little example is given of the spread of anxiety throughout a parish. What is important is that this image be designed to convey chronic anxiety within the church family system. It is a sickness as well as a faithless stance. Also, a suggestion is made that this storm in the boat may be self-made, given all the crises most any church has encountered.

it's hard to be secure with only one loaf in the boat, even if that one is Jesus. We worry and we are anxious, just like the Twelve.

So it's time for the questions once more. Each Lord's Day the time for exercising our memory comes—about who delivered us from slavery and led us through the wilderness; about who feeds us with that heavenly manna. And then that one about our baptism, about how we died and in whom we live. Oh, and always comes the question about provision: "How many loaves in our boat?" we are asked. With faith, we respond, "One, Lord." And that is always enough.

Conclusion. *It is time to return to the faithful stance of true seeing and hearing, which always entails memory. Also, we now find ourselves quizzed along with the disciples. Knowing, faithful answers are assumed. These questions are out of the baptismal liturgy and the Easter Vigil. "Provision" is again mentioned. The disciples' "never enough" becomes our "always enough."*

John 21:1-19: "Follow Me"

by Deneise Deter-Rankin

Sermon

It's been a while since he pulled one like this. Wining and dining a few clients, a business dinner turns upside down after ordering too many rounds of drinks. He and his two partners and four clients close down the restaurant well past midnight, wheeling and dealing over remnants of a couple of nice steaks turned

Commentary

Scene 1. *A narrative begins, thick with detail of the "binge dinner." There is a shift to the businessman's family then back. We are searching for meaning by this time. What is this scene about?*

cold and gray, glazed in con-
gealed fat. Potato skins, dried
rolls, and parsley. An army of
drained cocktail and wine
glasses wink at them in the
low-burning candlelight. It's
been a while since he resorted
to earning a living under these
conditions. His kids are
asleep. His wife is waiting up.
The key has been removed
from under the mat. She is
wondering what he will bring
home with him tonight. The
pack of aging entrepreneurs
helps each other into cabs,
leaving briefcases and un-
signed contracts in the coat
check booth, forgotten. They
rely on the kindness of cab-
drivers to deliver each of them
safely home.

*Simon said to them, "I am go-
ing fishing." They said to him,
"We will go with you." They
went out and got into the
boat. But that night, they
caught nothing.*

The mirror image of his own
face is fuzzy. Beard growth.
Red eyes, so prickly sore he
could   rub   them   raw.
It's been almost a week of no
sleep. Rain's been so scarce,
the hay was hardly knee-high
when the weatherman called
for sudden rain. And now it
won't quit long enough to cut
the hay that isn't beaten to the

*Notice that as the little nar-
rative develops, there is no in-
dication whether it will extend into the full homily or
come to a terse ending.*

*Then comes the interjection
of the beginning of another
narrative that ends with the
announcement that "they
caught nothing." Possibly that
ending is shared by both
narratives, but we hold our
judgment.*

Scene 2. *Focus is on the face.
We find out that it belongs to
a farmer, worn out by worry
and a rain-drenched crop. At
first we want to hear this
scene as a continuation of
Scene 1. References to the*

ground by the rain. Been trying to scrape up what they could and lay it out in barns to dry. It's like a tide from heaven. Or from hell. If he doesn't make this hay, then there's no way to pay what he owes from the last failed crop. Not to mention this year's bills. If he doesn't get out from under— God knows.

weather and a hay harvest serve to establish this second scene as a different narrative.

His dad used to sneak up on him at the shaving mirror and point his finger over his son's shoulder at his reflection in the mirror. "You'd better like that face, son. Cuz every time you shave it or slap it awake with a pail of pump water, it'll be there. Holding you accountable. To your self. Your family. Your debts. God." Then his dad would turn on his heels and be gone.

A flashback occurs here. Point of view remains the same— looking in the mirror.

Then Dad's voice interrupts the scene with words about the face in the mirror and accountability.

Just as day was breaking, Jesus stood on the beach, yet the disciples did not know it was Jesus. Jesus said to them, "Children, have you any fish?" They answered him, "No."

Again the scene is interrupted, the voice is now that of Jesus. Accountability remains the issue. "No" is the answer. No fish have been caught.

Bumper to fender, inching her way along the boulevard from work to the apartment, she is riding on an all-time high. Not the promotion or the raise she'd been dreaming of. But a smooth landing in the safety

Scene 3. This is a fast-moving narrative, more than either of the first two. In spite of the traffic jam, high morale is signaled. At work and with the car, things are doing good.

net. By crackey, she'd made it!
She had escaped the bloodbath
at work and still had a job. A
future. Income! Plus, her car's
been acting a little strange
lately, and after some tin-
kering around under the hood
(a mechanic friend suggested
trying a thingamajig on the
right side of the carburetor instead of the left) it works like
a charm! In fact, she even
made a few sales calls and
didn't have to leave it running
for fear it would fink out on
her, wrote up two whole new
orders and one increase on old
customers. Things are perco-
lating! Enough to make her believe she's been living right after all. When she lost the baby,
all that miscarriage mess
made it downright hard to believe there could be a kind and
good God to let so many awful
things happen. To her. In the
world. Maybe she should start
going back to church again.

*He said to them, "Cast the net
on the right side of the boat
and you will find some." So
they cast it, and now they
were not able to haul it in, for
the quantity of fish. That disciple who loved Jesus said to
Peter, "It is the Lord!"*

When they bring him home
from the hospital, his drafty
old house smells like yeast

*Describing this mood of rel-
ative well-being and excite-
ment, the rhetoric becomes a
chatty kind of discourse—a
distinct shift from the rhetorical tone of the previous scene.*

*We are let in on her past ex-
perience of a miscarriage. Two
statements stand out: "she's
been living right after all" and
"Maybe she should start going
back to church again."*

*Then the biblical narrative
once more is interjected. The
reference is to the miraculous
catch of fish and the beloved
disciple's recognition of
Christ. By this time we are expecting such a shift and may
even begin anticipating connections. Perhaps we will now
be ready to hear the next narrative system in light of the
biblical one. While these in-
terjections follow the sequence of the biblical text,
they are not designed to form
as a narrative system in com-*

rolls and fresh-brewed tea. The picnic basket on the kitchen counter spills over with fruit and cakes and chips. The warm oven and a note taped over the sink is signed with a smiley face. "Welcome Home!" and for a week, rows of baskets and casseroles march into his kitchen, stuffing his refrigerator until he is sure the old thing is gonna bust wide open with as many different flavors and dishes as people in his church family. A green jello salad is covered over with a crayon picture drawing that reads, "God bless you!"

When they got out on land they saw a charcoal fire there, with fish lying on it, and bread. Jesus said to them, "Bring some of the fish you have just caught." . . . and although there were so many, the net was not torn.

Your husband has been screaming for what seems like hours in the wee hours of the morning, "I see the head! I see the head! Dark hair! Black, like mine! I see the head!" And, if you could speak, you might suggest that he or the doctor, one, grab it by a fistful of hair and pull it out! The pain is too much to speak. Every inch of your body gives in

munal hearing. Only the contemporary scenes will serve in that respect.

Scene 4. Another story fragment. A return from the hospital. Questions form in the hearer's mind. Is this an old man, and with what problem? One thing is clear, some people at church care for him very much. We expect the reference to the meal on the beach with Jesus. "God bless you," reads the crayon drawing on the green jello.

We still hear that "God bless you!" echo at fireside there on the beach with the risen Christ.

Scene 5. At first the hearer isn't sure what the screaming is about. Then it hits. A baby is being born. Point of view is strongly shaped—the wife is giving birth, is a mother. The husband is crying and praying, as a father being born. Whatever else, the scene screams of birth.

and gives way and gives out and you see blue pink white skin and everyone holds his or her breath. Waiting. For the first sounds of this—life. And there is that scream like no other scream in the sweet spasms that fill your ears, and you breathe, and someone says, "It's a boy!" and you don't know you are weeping until you see your husband is weeping, too, while he counts, moving his lips, ten fingers and ten toes. And it looks like he's praying. Amen.

Jesus said to them, "Come and have breakfast." Now none of the disciples dared ask him, "Who are you?" They knew it was the Lord.

One morning over bagels and bran flakes, sipping muddy coffee all alone (it's Saturday and the kids are somewhere else) she looks him square in the eyeballs, then says, "Do you love me?" And in the bottom of his "This Is the First Day of the Rest of Your Life" mug, coffee grounds make fickle patterns for him to study—intently—while he remembers what it was like when they met. Not once had he given any thought to "settling down." Life was just one big sea he rowed in his boat, dragging the tempting waters

The recognition scene in the epilogue breaks in. "It is the Lord," the disciples realize. For us, this has something to do with new life—birth and recognition of a child.
Scene 6. A Saturday a.m. scene. The question is immediately recognizable at this level and in the biblical narrative. We learn more about the man's lack of purpose and direction until the question is posed—"Do you love me?" This is the first time in the homily that the biblical text has appeared directly in the contemporary narratives. We now begin to look for an answer to the question as the scene develops.

with his net to see what variety, what shapes and sizes and colors he could haul in. It was a smorgasbord. A parade of hormones and moods and passing fancies. Until that gentle command, her crooked finger beckoning him, "Follow me," dragged him into the future.

And he wakes up ten years later to the person across the breakfast table asking, "Do you love me?" and he wants to say, "What do you want from me? We're married. Two kids. Two cars. Two-car garage. Two TVs. Bills paid. A VCR. Camper. Disney World. Myrtle Beach. . . ."

Still, his answer is not adequate. It is a mental rehearsal of acquisitions, of possessions.

When they had finished breakfast, Jesus said to Simon Peter, "Simon, son of John, do you love me more than these?" He said to him, "Yes; Lord, you know that I love you."

She gave thousands. Nobody knows how many thousands. Well, almost nobody. Somebody has to know. Because she wrote the check and wrote a note to whomever she doesn't know who knows she wrote the check for thousands and said, "This is an anonymous donation." She gave thousands to her church to build the new

The shift to the question to Peter brings along this sense of "not really getting it" about love. Notice that for the first time, the contemporary scene informs the biblical. We bring convictions and feelings from the former to the latter.

Scene 7. *We know now that this image will relate to Jesus' continued question to Peter. We are given a benefactor, anonymous donor of thousands of dollars for the ministry of the church. "For Jesus" is the reason. This active giving, then, has to do with answering Jesus' question. We wait to determine* gymnasium. The Baptists and Methodists have one. And they say they let poor people use it, too. Besides, you want your kids and grandkids to have one. A safe place. To play basketball and volleyball. For Jesus.

And she writes another note, suggesting, merely suggesting, mind you, that the walls be painted a certain color. That the hardwood floor patterns go like this (hand drawing included). That the light fixtures be this kind of light fixture (photo attached). These are anonymous suggestions. She doesn't want to interfere. But thousands of dollars is a lot of money. And she wants to see the church do right. By her. By it. Certainly.

A second time he said to him, "Simon, son of John, do you love me?" He said to him, "Yes, Lord; you know that I love you."

Some days he thinks that if he has to look inside another ear or nose, or down another throat, he'll scream. Or laugh. Or walk right out the Fire Exit Only door and never come back. His mother was the one who wanted him to be a doctor. Because she had wanted to marry a doctor and couldn't

the adequacy of this character's love.

Still, we have reservation; the woman wants too much control along with her giving. This, too, is a case of "not really getting it" when it comes to love.

Once more, we bring reservations to Peter's second response to Jesus' questions.

Scene 8. *We immediately are given a doctor, learn he's a dissatisfied doctor, and learn about his mother, learn about his love for nature. Where will "Do you love me?" intersect with this narrative?*

find one who would have her.
So she married a car salesman
and bore a son and willed him
to be a doctor. Even though he
lived out of doors. Worshiped
plant life and animals and
wore the soles off his shoes
hiking miles and miles of for-
ests and streams and hills.

His best friend suggested a
psychiatrist for depression.
What do doctors know? Med-
ication pulled him deeper into
the tunnel of screaming babies
and bratty kids and finally sick
children who wouldn't live to
walk the soles off their shoes
to watch tadpoles and follow
baby rabbits home. It is harder
to get up in the mornings.
Harder to sleep. Ever. Nothing
to look forward to. Except
dreams. When he can go spe-
lunking, rapelling, mountain
climbing, camping under the
night owls. Singing. Until he
wakes up. And feels like he
is dying. As somebody else's
doctor.

Things get worse for the doc-
tor, his depression, his
vocation.

Only in dreams does that real
love-life come through.

He said to him a third time,
"Simon, son of John, do you
love me?" Peter was grieved
because he said to him a third
time, "Do you love me?" And
he said to him, . . . "Lord, you
know I love you."

Again the question of Jesus to
Peter. What does it have to do
with the doctor? Perhaps he
needs to be converted into be-
ing his father's son? Only then
will his response be fully au-
thentic.

In the barber shop you wait
your turn for a chair behind a

Scene 9. Barbershop. We view
"a slight man," clearly elderly,

slight man in a yellow button-up sweater. In the May air, its light weight must be just enough between his brown, spotted skin and the breeze. Moving to take his place in the swivel bucket chair awaiting him, he seems amazed that his legs carry him there. Under the barber's green cape, he is smaller. His unshaven chin quivers and his watering brown eyes meet yours and stare. Wide. Smiling, somehow? While scissors and razors shape his white hair to look almost the same as it did before he took his seat, he looks through you and out the window beyond your shaggy head. He has seen things you have never seen before. Eight dollars between his fingers, he reaches toward the barber's shirt pocket to put the money where he has always put it. He smiles without looking into anyone's face. The barber takes one elbow in his hand and walks with his customer to the door. Still smiling, bobbing "good day" to you as he passes by, touching two fingers to a cap that is not on his head, he seems to float out the door. His legs and arms moving a beat or two or three behind, out of synch with his wide, smiling eyes.

"Truly, truly, I say to you, when you were young, you

and we gradually discover that he is "not all there."

The old man makes allusions to a past, though, to things seen, a cap, rituals with a smile.

Now we again question and hear the words about "when

girded yourself and walked where you would; but when you are old, you will stretch out your hands, and another will gird you and carry you where you did not wish to go." . . . and, after this he said to him, "Follow me."

you are old." They conclude in spite of this proleptic vision: "Follow me."

Epilogue

To juxtapose narrative and imagination on behalf of homiletics is to raise, as we have seen, several clusters of concerns. First the question of narrative theology must be addressed, including the fact that there are various types of narrative theology, not all easily compatible. Second, it is now incumbent on reflective practitioners in homiletics to engage the dynamics of imagination theory more comprehensively than ever before. Finally, the particular juxtaposition of narrative hermeneutics and construal of imagination theory attempted in these pages has raised questions about the quality of the relationship as well as the fruitfulness of the interaction. In other words, we are asking about the character of the relationship between narrative and imagination, along with the always important practical question, "So what?" Each of these aspects of our explorations now invites some retrospective remarks, in the way both of concluding and of indicating issues that command further attention.

Types of Narrative Theology

"Narrative theology," we have seen, does not refer to simply one thing, not one person's views, one dominant consensus, or even one ideologically correct position. That a multiformed narrative theology is emerging on the scene toward the twilight of liberalism, however, is to be expected. The eclipse of biblical narrative portrayed most brilliantly by Hans Frei can be seen as itself a pathology of liberalism, by now infecting much of the American church. What Frei spotted in his diagnosis was how strongly Enlightenment assumptions shaped the ideological roots of liberal hermeneutics. In that framework those of us called to preach (1) were instructed in the need for clear statements of the sermon's theme, (2) were to look for the main idea of the biblical text, and (3) were to build a sermon with its ideational "message" buttressed by clearly outlined subpoints and supporting propositions. The biblical narrative—if indeed that text was a story—became instantly disposable once the preacher/interpreter extracted its latent thematic or moral. (Recall, for instance, that Sangster in his two-volume paean to topical preaching mentions parables only in the section of that work dealing with *illustration*.) The illustrations accompanying the propositions and points served to reintroduce stories within a rationalistic homiletic and, of course, add a large dose of "affect" to the discursive points. That liberalism's approach to preaching thereby drew on a Romantic model of inspiration, along with its Enlightment assumptions as to the real meaning of a text, remained mostly obscured until David Buttrick's article in *Interpretation* in 1981.[1] Day is dying in the West for both Enlightenment hermeneutics and Romanticism's anthropology. After the long eclipse of biblical narrative, our scriptural tradition is reasserting itself. Hence narrative theologies.

As we re-explored our home in the narrative (chapter 1), two related tasks became apparent. On one hand, the methodological distinctions between narrative theology and alternative approaches claimed attention. At a time when the theological spectrum has long been shattered (Lonnie Kliever's phrase), how shall we locate our postliberal narrative theology within a theological arena of such confusion, even chaos? Here, George Lindbeck's analysis of the cognitive, the experiential/expressive, and the cultural-linguistic models provided a way to locate ourselves and to analyze alternative approaches. (We turned up the magnification in our analysis of the experiential/expressive model of doctrine to discover three dominant means by which liberalism sought to "authorize" or "de-authorize" the biblical witness—the foundationalist approach, the illustrative approach, and the succession approach.)

On the other hand, the task of articulating our home in the narrative became that of articulating a narrative hermeneutics that avoided the Charybdis of Marc Ellingsen's rather fideistic assertions and the Scylla of Paul Ricoeur's grounding of narrative in a poetics of metaphor. Consequently, we argued (1) for the priority of narrative within Scripture, (2) for Scripture's "vested interest" in a community of faith equipped with those virtues sufficient to extend hospitality both to the stranger and to its own narrative tradition, and (3) for the claim of that communal location as normative to the hermeneutic task. There is a "scandal of particularity" with reference to the biblical narratives' claims that the *tauta* ("these things" related to Jesus Christ) are true. That scandal extends, moreover, to the claim that the "meet, right, and salutary" locus for the interpretation of Scripture is the community of faith engaged in preaching the Word, breaking bread together, and engaging in the praxis of Christian mission to the world. With Hauerwas, then, we extend the hermeneutical circle neccessarily to involve an ecclesial context of particular virtues, capacities, and convictions. (We also noted in this regard the role of reader-response criticism, along with literary criticism in completing this hermeneutical circle.)

Exploring Imagination Theory

The exploration of the house of imagination began where most homileticians have begun, with the image. Here, we noted with approval Margaret R. Miles' "lexicon of imagery" and her depiction of the image's availablity to all sorts and conditions of persons, its polyvalence (multiplicity of meanings), and its potential affective aspects (the "bodily ground" of imagery). Later, however, we called into question several other aspects of Miles' hermeneutics: her equating "texts" mostly with those at the discursive pole, identifying "language users" as almost exclusively males, and establishing a consequent hierarchy of seeing over hearing. Miles and Walter Ong (with his insistence on the preëminence of orality), then, represent two overdrawn positions regarding the respective valuation of hearing and seeing, of sound and sight, of Word and Light.

The investigations into the dynamics of imagery then expanded to include all of the senses—nothing less than the full perceptual model is sufficient, especially to the field of homiletics! Here, Mary Warnock became the pathfinder as she elaborated the perceptual model of "seeing-as" (there is that visual bias we all carry around again!). "Imagining-that" and "imagining-how" were discovered to be aligned with the perceptual model, but not necessarily dependent upon a mental imaging for their agency. With Paul Ricoeur we noted imagination's turn toward the linguistic in the poetics of metaphor, and finally Hans-Georg Gadamer's wonderful notion of imagination as play. In the former (Ricoeur), we have an expression of "text" which is precisely opposite of that depicted by Miles. In fact, the functions of metaphor discovered by Ricoeur share all of the positive qualities Miles has identified in the lexicon of imagery—social availability, polyvalence, and affective capacity. In the latter (Gadamer), a poetics of play brings imagination theory to its most expansive statement. Involving all of the senses, incorporating all sorts of imaginings-that and -how, turning to the linguistic most interestingly in the language of the game (its rules, norms, and traditions), the metaphor of imagination as play finally encompasses both player and spectator. The game involves a necessary loss of self-consciousness for all who play, and winds up with the players themselves being played by the game. In fact, we may speak of imagination theory in this respect as ranging from the play of imagery all the way to the imagery of play!

Juxtaposing Narrative and Imagination

In our juxtaposing narrative and imagination, the first issue is the quality of the relationship between a postliberal narrative hermeneutics and the dynamics of imagination theory. Is it the case that the two are *complementary*, such that a preacher should have them well-balanced in his or her preaching? With regrets, the notion of complementarity does not sufficiently express both the interplay between the two locations. Think of it this way: Every homiletic—modern and postmodern—carries with it an implied construal of the imagination. David Buttrick's approach shares elements of imagination's role with Henry Ward Beecher's and

John Broadus', while differing profoundly, for example, on the question of a "historical imagination."[2] The preaching-as-story-telling advocates emphasized the imaginative role of the preacher and encouraged an imagining-how with regard to the persons of the biblical story and the stories of the persons who are the listeners. Liberation theologians, moreover, urge preachers to a fiercely committed imagining-how with respect to the plight of the poor who suffer under the oppression of the wealthy.[3] In a bold analysis, Carol Norén focused on the performative aspects of homiletic imagination in her considerations of the nonverbal elements in the preaching of women and men.[4] For all of the above, and for other approaches as well, any proposal for preaching sufficient to be labeled a homiletic will carry with it some construal of imagination theory. One measure of any homiletic's success, then, will be the adequacy of its treatment of the dynamics of the imagination.

Like many others, a narrative homiletic begins its focus on imagination with the notion of the image. By phenomonologists, psychologists, and literary critics we have been schooled in the critical importance of point of view. Expanding on Buttrick's model of the camera in regard to homiletical imaging, we added the models of the video camera (providing preachers with options related to mobility and adding an aural to the visual component) and, finally, the simulator. The latter model retained both seeing and hearing, while adding the kinesthetic aspect of perception as well. Developing these models for homiletic imaging was driven by a prior attentiveness to the integrity of biblical narrative, along with imagery's remarkable lexicon.

One of the most important outcomes of the explorations of the activities of imaging-that and -how was in the attention devoted to the "how" of homiletic imagination. Using Wheelwright's model of poetic imagination as a foundation, and informed as well by Dykstra and Harris, we depicted the fourfold configuration of the homiletic imagination. While all four stages are essential, it is within the context of the paradigmatic imagination that homiletics and interpretation today will either falter or succeed. Images, we have insisted, are born within some narrative or other. From that ancestral "home" (images, too, have a home in the narrative!), they may gain a certain degree of independence such that they may "stand for" or come to represent the narrative home place. Also, images achieving this status vis-à-vis narrative serve as hermeneutic lenses through which their ur-narrative and others are interpreted. The images of bread and wine have precisely functioned in this regard in sacramental theology. But images, being notoriously itinerant, may in fact detach from their original context and locate in relation to other narratives, even ones that stand in contradiction to the story that gave them birth. Wine, for example, can become the interpreting image for addiction within an alcoholic family. Nevertheless, images will have some quality of relationship to the stories they inhabit. These endure, and are transformed, through living traditions within a community.

We speak of this patterned and self-interpreting entirety of a community's narrative and imagery, its nexus of relations, enduring through a story-formed tradition, as a paradigm.[5] In turn, the paradigm reveals aspects of its constitutive parts that otherwise might have remained obscure or ambiguous. This grammar of paradigms also reveals the core difficulty with liberalism's notion of pluralism related to theology and culture. To stand back and presume to pick images and stories from the various faith traditions as if they were items in a brunch buffet actually involves two problems. First, such an exercise involves the fallacy that there is some place to stand which is itself not storied, patterned, and thereby reflective of some interpretive paradigm. The second quandary involves what Garrett Green labels "the atomistic fallacy." The patterned whole is ignored, while the parts—the stories, images, and communal ritual activities—are treated as exportable *without any significant alteration or erosion in meaning.*[6] Faithful preaching of the biblical narrative, on the other hand, will entail revealing the various elements of Scripture as belonging to a patterned, paradigmatic whole.

A further insight resulting from our particular juxtaposition of narrative and imagination has been the recovery of irony as the essential sibling to metaphor in biblical hermeneutics. Though deeply indebted to Ricoeur for his analysis of the dynamics of metaphor, we are nevertheless not dependent on that "turn of indirection" for a foundational ontology. Retaining the insights regarding the generativity of metaphor, we have noticed that biblical narrative also assumes some reader competence in spotting irony. It may even be said that several biblical narratives—Mark and the Fourth Gospel in particular—not only insist on some reader skills in detecting irony, but present the gospel as in some manner inherently ironic. At a time in North American churches when sloganeering from the political left and right can stand for preaching, it is essential to reclaim this insistence on the capability of a biblically formed ironic vision. In a church caught between political correctness, reaction, and cynicism, a glimpse of the scriptural ironies may in fact help us spot our own. It may well be that this imaginative achievement in itself would be worth the risk of preaching Scripture's narratives and imagery!

Juxtaposed to a narrative hermeneutic, the insights of Hans-Georg Gadamer regarding imagination as play have led to an appreciation of the complex imaginative act that is preaching. Preaching within the liturgy, we concluded, was comprised of temporal and spatial elements along with a distinctive sense of "rhetorical stretch." The temporal and spatial aspects of this shared imaginative act quite obviously involve the issues of a homily's duration and location. Rhetorical stretch, we found, was related to John McClure's model of the "codes" of preaching and dealt with the relative tensiveness or brittleness of the rhetoric *within* rather than among McClure's four codes. Thus, we noted the range from a shared rhetoric embodying a mobile and tensive language of preaching to one hardened into stereotyped figures of speech and inflexible categories. While this notion is commended for further exploration and amendment, it seems that it represents a far more nuanced approach to the issue of preaching's rhetoric than those based on a theological spectrum model (i.e., a conclusion recently drawn that evangelicals manifest a less imaginatively expressive rhetoric of preaching than liberals). It will be interesting, indeed, to participate in this conversation as it develops.

Finally, to focus on the imaginative performance of preaching evokes questions about all the unspoken aspects of the event. Included here are the range of issues well addressed by Carol Norén in *The Woman in the Pulpit*. In our study of the formative power of preaching narrative and imagination, however, it also may be the case that a major focus of early medieval homiletics is once more of crucial concern—the character of the preacher. That is, if a central concern for narrative homiletics is that of the formation of personal and communal virtues and capacities within the congregation, then it may by extension raise the issue of the preacher and his or her character. While this extension may provoke some reflexive negativity, or even anger, let us press on with a few preliminary proposals in this regard:

1. Given the insights of applying a family therapy systems approach to congregations, the virtues and spiritual formation of the preacher are intrinsic to, rather than extrinsic of, the congregation's wellness or dysfunction. To suggest that issues of a congregation's growth in spirituality, faith, and witness are somehow assessable apart from those issues related to the pastor or preacher is both theologically docetic and indefensibly innocent of how such systems function.

2. It may well be that in the imaginatively sophisticated performance of preaching within the liturgy the issue of personal and communal character is conveyed both by verbal and nonverbal communication. The suggestion here is that clues to the preacher's character, along with her or his participation in a church's communal character, are inevitably given in preaching. The former (the preacher's character) cannot long be hidden; the latter (the preacher's role in the congregational system) cannot be exempted. In this respect, preaching may differ from the sacraments in that the preacher may not have the efficacy of the sacraments to fall back on!

3. The question must at least be raised whether this imaginative event of homiletic performance is shaped and informed as well by broader issues of clergy character outside the local parish. Is there, we ask, a sort of homiletical equivalent to the "butterfly effect" in chaos theory? By that we mean that the socially held imaginative activity that is the very prerequisite for preaching's reception may suffer harm through the destructive actions of other clergy in entirely different contexts. Put more forthrightly, have the character issues of the media preachers along with the community and character issue of clergy sexual misconduct across

the American church scene eroded the imaginative "currency" extended to even a preacher of integrity within a relatively "un-affected" parish context? If a butterfly's wings in the Amazon affect our weather in Omaha, how can most any local church remain unsullied by the violence done to us preachers because of the abuse done by some of us who preach?

If the answer to these preliminary questions is to any degree in the positive, then preaching the worlds that shape us has more at stake than even the complex issues of interpretation, method, and performance, narrowly conceived. Recall, however, the four stages of the homiletic imagination (after Wheelwright). The first and most critical step was, and remains, that those of us called to preach are ourselves conformed to the Word. Since these stages of the homiletic imagination are not woodenly sequential, the journey may begin anew whereby we are shaped by the Word. Faith does come from hearing. Our communities of faith do gather to listen, and even we who are such clay pots will soon again stand up to preach the priceless treasure.

Notes

1. David Buttrick, "Interpretation and Preaching," *Interpretation* 25 (Jan. 1981): 46–58.

2. See Appendix.

3. See, for example, Justo L. González and Catherine G. González, *The Liberating Pulpit* (Nashville: Abingdon Press, 1994).

4. See Carol M. Norén, *The Woman in the Pulpit* (Nashville: Abingdon Press, 1991).

5. See chapter 3, above.

6. Garrett Green, *Imagining God: Theology and the Religious Imagination* (San Francisco: Harper & Row, 1989), 52.

Appendix

From Beecher to Buttrick: Imagination in Modern and Postmodern Homiletics

In 1871—having hammered out the idea of a Yale lectureship in preaching, having secured a benefactor for the series, and having named it for his father—Henry Ward Beecher presented the first of three annual lectures. Over the course of about a decade and a half, from Beecher to Broadus, the place of imagination in modern preaching was fundamentally staked out and would persist with little alteration for the next hundred years. This homiletic orthodoxy was thoroughly grounded in a model of argumentation, trading in propositional "truths," and insisting as well that the preacher must possess a "lively imagination." As these early Beecher lecturers insisted, imagination was an important if not necessary capacity for the effective preacher. Although their elaboration of this vital faculty was frequently confusing if not contradictory in its presentation, an underlying pattern to their explorations remained.

From Beecher to Broadus

From Henry Ward Beecher to John Broadus, the Yale lecturers explicated their notions of imagination around one of the other (or both) of two distinct poles. The first dealt with the object, the second with the subject. The former, objective pole has its roots in the British empiricist tradition of David Hume. Here the role of imagination is to bring some object or experience that is absent into the present. The "brought near" image yields "a faded trace of perception, a weakened impression preserved and represented in memory."[1] Due to the rationalistic assumptions of these Beecher lecturers of the early, formative years, the role of objective imagination in preaching was to bring near the idea or truth not previously present to the hearers. Broadus says that the preacher "uses imagination in the production of images" while adding that frequently "the idea he wishes to present can itself be converted into an image."[2] Given the at times modest capabilities of "the audience" in grasping the great truths of which a sermon must speak, the preacher must turn to the imagination to provide images that will bring home the noble message. In R. W. Dale's lectures, this essential function of the preacher's imagination is celebrated:

> The minds of men are sometimes so sluggish that we cannot get them to listen to us unless our case is stated with a warmth and a vigour which the imagination can alone supply. There are many, again, who are not accessible to abstract argument, but who recognise truth at once when it assumes that concrete form with which the imagination may invest it. . . . Then, again, there are some truths—and these are among the greatest—which rest, not upon abstract reasoning, but upon facts. Imagination must make the facts vivid and real.[3]

For the work of the preacher, then, objective imagination brings to the hearers and translates for them the truths of Christian religion into accessible images.

The theories of imagination presented from Beecher to Broadus utilize the subjective pole as well. Here, "we find theories which explain our imaginative activity in terms of the *subject*, that is, in terms of a human consciousness that is fascinated or freed by its own images."[4] This "productive imagination" is celebrated most extensively by the German Idealists and by Samuel Coleridge et al. of the Romantic movement. Imagination presents to consciousness something that is not otherwise attainable, even through the tools of the rational mind. By way of specifically contradicting the empiricist's objective notion of imagination, Beecher calls for that faculty in the mind of the preacher that is "the power of conceiving as definite the things which are invisible to the senses,—of giving them distinct shape."[5] Beecher then adds,

"The imagination, then, is that power of the mind by which it conceives of invisible things, and is able to present them as though they were visible to others. . . . It is the quality which of necessity must belong to the ministry."[6] Notice, however, the bipolarity in Beecher's celebration of the imaginative element in preaching. On one hand, there is an objective orientation in the task of imaginatively bringing near some truth or sense of moral duty that is found to be at first at some distance from the "audience." On the other hand, that which is brought near is often sublime in its essence and is in principle beyond the grasp of human perception or rationality alone. The preacher's imagination must somehow cover both the objective and subjective polarities of imagination, according to the issue at hand.

While the subjective imagination was held in high regard by the early Beecher lecturers, it was carefully constrained due to the pervasive rationalism of their homiletical worldview. Essential to late-nineteenth-century liberalism's anthropology was the assumption that such rational formulations, presented with sufficient, vivid force, would impress themselves in such a way as to move the hearers to action. So, for example, Broadus concludes that "it is thus mainly through the imagination that we touch the feelings, and thereby bring truth powerfully to bear upon the will, which is the end and the very essence of eloquence."[7] Imagination's role in preaching is portrayed as indispensable, yet its function is consistently restrained. The primary task of the sermon is to traffic in the great ideas and moral truths of the religious sphere. Imagination's task is to make these truths more vivid and present, bringing them into subjective awareness by translating them into images. The priority is on a rationalism that trades in "main ideas," "messages," and "moral truths."

Nevertheless, the subjective focus of Romanticism persisted as a dominant strain within the formative years of modern homiletics. It was the achievement of Romanticism in the face of the new science and historiography to shift the task of theology from an articulation of objective revelation to "the imaginative *construction* of the historical experience of salvation."[8] Nowhere is this shift more clearly evidenced than in the hermeneutic understanding of these early Beecher lecturers. The notion of "historical imagination" was employed to vivify the "world" behind the biblical text, rendering it present to us in a fashion not accessible simply through the text itself. Through the historical imagination, the preacher's role becomes that of "reproducing the past" and thereby presenting what is inherently distant to the hearer.[9] It is important to note, however, that a subjective element became firmly established within the notion of the historical imagination. What is delivered to the audience by this means was never fully available through the empirical study of Scripture alone. Broadus serves us both polarities when he speaks of the historical imagination as "realizing and depicting what the Scriptures reveal."[10] This vacillation between objective and subjective expressions of imagination as well as the commitments to Rationalism and Romanticism are nicely presented by a later Yale lecturer, J. H. Jowett:

> And here I want most strongly to urge you to cultivate the power of historical imagination: I mean the power to reconstitute the dead realms of the past and to repeople them with moving life. We shall never grip an old-world message until we can re-create the old-world life.[11]

Liberal interpretation, then, took shape around a rationalist hermeneutic (the interpreter sought for a message, an idea) yet of necessity needed to achieve an inspired leap of imagination into the world behind the text.[12] Amazingly, this odd conjunction of rationalist and Romantic commitments persisted for over a century in American pulpits—perhaps in places even through last Sunday!

During the course of modern homiletical development, the functions of objective and subjective imagination persist as well, although the "content" of objective imagination's focus changes with the interest of the preacher. A social gospeler would attempt to bring near the downtrodden experience of the masses while the "therapeutic" preachers sought to make vivid the personal experience of the listener (enacting "personal counseling on a group scale").[13] So, in Fosdick, for example, the biblical analogue to the preacher's imperative to know the personal experience of the hearers is that "(the Bible's) men and women must be real people in his imagination and his affection."[14] As expected, however, such a function of the historical imagination would be firmly wedded to a persistent rationalistic model of interpretation. Armed with a notion of social Darwinism, Fosdick adds: "Not only can we believe that the Bible does represent a progressive revelation, but we can clearly and in detail watch it progress. We can know where the Scripture's major ideas started."[15] The commitment to a rationalist hermeneutic paired with a Romantic notion of historical imagination persists throughout the course of modern liberal homiletics.

. . . To Buttrick

Paul Ricoeur questions whether "the knot of aporias" within modern theories of imagination results from a fault within these systems or from "the structural feature of the imagination itself."[16] Homileticians who are working out of a self-consciously postmodern context would at least agree with the "fault" assessment of Ricoeur. Whether we encounter similar structural features of the imagination within postmodern homiletics remains to be seen. As a way into the thick of the question, the distinctly postmodern approach to the role of imagination of David Buttrick will be examined, especially with reference to any shifts from the modern notion of homiletic imagination.

Initially, Buttrick's *Homiletic* appears quite in continuity with the notion of imagination discovered within preaching's "modern" era. He speaks of the need for a sermon to "bring into view" those unseen realities conveyed by metaphor, image, and illustration.[17] However, a paradigm shift is immediately signaled which will bypass the objective-subjective split within imagination. Buttrick introduces consciousness, or more precisely "social consciousness," as the context for imagination's work and play. On one hand, such a phenomenological move obviates the need for preaching to "bring near" acts of God in history—God is discovered to be more "a 'symbol source' or 'image giver' to human consciousness" (115). On the other hand, this phenomenological approach escapes any descent into subjectivity since, "after all, 'objective' and 'subjective' are both categories of conscious-ness" (116). By virtue of the turn toward a phenomenological "bracketing" of consciousness, imagination is, with Edmund Husserl, no longer conceived as a *"thing in* consciousness" but as an *"act of* consciousness."[18] Within the phenomenological consciousness, Buttrick asserts with Husserl, "lived experience is neither objective event nor subjective affect" (123).

Imagination's role in consciousness is discovered by David Buttrick to be essential to the achievement of meaning. There is an "imaginative friskiness" to consciousness that persistently looks for analogies and entire structures of meaning. Thought is discovered not to be simply discursive mental activity; rather, the consciousness yields meanings in which imagery is tightly connected with ideas. Moreover, the human imagination extends meaning to a social level as images interconnect to form a grid-like structure of analogy and meaning. Buttrick insists on the context of consciousness as the locus of imagination, thereby liberating the preacher from prior rationalistic and romantic assumptions. Reversing the trajectory built into those modern homiletic assumptions, Buttrick proclaims that "imagination works *with* thought" (155). Then he adds that "the process involves a free associating of idea and image, a seeing of what we are saying" (155). The preacher, then, pushes toward meanings by "seeing" the imagery that interacts with thought in consciousness and by remembering personal and communal experience.

Developing his homiletic method, Buttrick projects the role of imagination in two new directions and explicitly rejects a third. The rejected function pertains to any notion of a historical imagination, as shall be seen. In its constructive roles, however, homiletic imagination ranges along two axes of sermon development: the imaging of a move and the shaping of the sermonic plot and its attendant image grid. We now turn to an explication of these two axes of imagination in Buttrick's system.

Imaging the Move

Since meanings emerge through an interplay of idea and imagery, the challenge for the preacher is to articulate each unit of meaning within a sermon (denoted a "move") within the communal consciousness of the hearers. As indicated, each move, therefore, will be presented as an "imaged thought" weaving conceptual and imaged material together in consciousness. Although the methodological considerations of move theory comprise a significant portion of *Homiletic*, the challenge for imagination is essentially that of providing an imaged analogy to the thought that is at stake in the move. Thus the language employed to form a move will be comprised both of the more rational elements of discursive speech as well as imaged ways of seeing which will interrelate with the ideas. Although Buttrick speaks of such imaging as "illustration," it precisely does not function as have conventional illustrations within modern homiletics (that is, serving to make the discursive points of the sermon more vivid and memorable or to balance rationality with subjectivity-laden anecdote).

> The patterned grid of images, examples, and illustrations is designed to function with the structural "argument" of the sermon. Older homiletics basically viewed illustrations as support for particular ideas. . . . Instead, we are suggesting that images, examples, and illustrations are woven into content and provide an underlying image grid for an entire sermon; they function similarly to the clusters of images in a poem, forming in consciousness along with a meaningful structure. (163)

Whatever the genre of the *seen* thought—image, illustration, or example—the litmus test of appropriateness within a move is whether it serves the purpose of analogy in relation to the meaning at stake in the move (see 133–35). Each move, Buttrick insists, must be imaged out of the lived experience of the hearers, both worldly and ecclesial experience. Imagination's role is to search out the most effective analogous images.[19]

One attendant consideration involving imagery for Buttrick is that of point of view. An image inevitably presents itself in consciousness with a certain point of view. And since congregational consciousness is rather sluggish these days, it will simply not do for the preacher to leave the task of supplying point of view to the hearers. Typically, such assignment will not be made by the congregation, and the imagery will become vague or, more likely, drop out of consciousness entirely. So the preacher's imagination cannot turn off once appropriate images are selected for the sermon's image grid. Point of view will be supplied with each image along the way.

Imagining the Homiletic Structure

If the first function of the homiletic imagination represents a horizontal axis—a move's conceptual content → image → single meaning—the second projects a vertical one. Here the notion of a homiletical plot comes into play. When we attend to the dynamics of thought in consciousness, we notice some sort of sequential alignment of meanings, all containing latent or explicit imagery. A phenomenological investigation of thought finds a pattern to these episodes of meaning that display some intention or other. Linked together much as frames comprising a cinema film, such meanings are inherently mobile and yet structured, are conceptual in content and yet imaged. The task of the preacher is to utilize a communal rhetoric in such a way that moves are formed in consciousness and travel in sequence much the same as thought typically occurs. There is a "connective logic" to the sermon's moves, "the logic by which one move follows another" (39). Hence, a preacher "imagines a sermon" (as Thomas Troeger nicely puts it) as he or she plots the succession of moves that will be designed to sequentially form in communal consciousness.

As a sermon's moves are stated and respectively imaged, it becomes vital that an underlying image grid emerge and interact in consciousness. "What makes a good sermon," Buttrick notes, "is not one single illustration, but a gridwork of interacting images, examples, and illustrations" (153). Such a grid system is always in the service of "the structural movement of the sermon; we are helping the sermon to do what it intends" (167). Buttrick concludes:

> Sermon craft is never intended to dazzle, but always to serve. The rhetorical systems that interrelate images must be used modestly, aiming at an all-but-subliminal action in consciousness. With images interacting we imitate human consciousness in order to serve faith-consciousness. (167)

Imagination's role is to serve the intention of the sermon!

Here we encounter point of view's second, more pervasive level of sermonic functioning since, as Buttrick notes, consciousness is inherently perspectival. Preachers must know that point of view "is always in language and, therefore, must be integral to sermon design and development" (57). The challenge, then, is to utilize this perspectual orientation as each move is formed in consciousness . . . *without fail*. Again, Buttrick's hermeneutic is determinative; consciousness is the context for all meanings as well as every meaning's perspectual orientation. Even the most dispassionate third-person address "forms the consciousness of a congregation; it shapes congregational point-of-view" (61). Homiletic imagination considers the inevitability of perspectival orientation in consciousness and shapes each move to function in ways that are remarkably variable yet controlled. "Point-of-view in language," Buttrick concludes, "is inescapable" (64).

It now becomes clear that the reasoning behind David Buttrick's rejection of the so-called historical imagination stems from his foundational phenomenological shift. Just as objective ideas or actions are only grasped as such in consciousness, so too, historical meanings occur within the mode of social consciousness. Hence, the attempt to build a first-century world behind the text—should we wish to do so—occurs within "a twentieth-century language consciousness as an act of historical imagination" (265). Modern homiletics' presumed "original meanings" are actually objects of contemporary consciousness and yield almost nothing of value for preaching.[20] What biblical texts *do* yield, rather than reconstructed original worlds, are intentions to enact meaning in consciousness. Biblical language, Buttrick suggests, "does in consciousness; . . . (it) is performative" (273). As a result, our hermeneutic interest no longer remains that of the retrieval of an original meaning behind the text, thus necessitating the use of a "historical imagination." Now the hermeneutic task becomes that of assessing the text's intention to function within personal and communal consciousness. For David Buttrick, the notion of historical imagination is rendered null and void by his phenomenological approach to language and consciousness. Imagination no longer has a task to perform, a task that was illusory after all.

But then, the preacher's imagination will have more than enough to do preaching moves and structures.

Notes

1. Richard Kearney, *Poetics of Imagining: From Husserl to Lyotard* (London: HarperCollinsAcademic, 1991), 138. Kearney is developing an analysis contained in Paul Ricoeur's essay "*L'imagination dans Le Discours et dans L'action*," in his *Du Texte à L'action* (Paris: Éditions du Seuil, 1986), 215–16.

2. Batsell Barrett Baxter, *The Heart of the Yale Lectures* (Grand Rapids: Baker, 1971), 77.

3. Ibid., 79.

4. Kearney, *Poetics*, 138.

5. Henry Ward Beecher, *Yale Lectures on Preaching*, First, Second, and Third Series (New York: Fords, Howard, & Hulbery, 1892), 1:109–10.

6. Beecher, *Yale*, 1:117.

7. Broadus, in Baxter, *Heart*, 424.

8. John E. Thiel, *Imagination and Authority: Theological Authorship in the Modern Tradition* (Minneapolis: Fortress Press, 1991), 21.

9. Broadus, in Baxter, *Heart*, 425.

10. Ibid.

11. Baxter, *Heart*, 78.

12. I am indebted to David Buttrick for this insight.

13. Robert Moats Miller, *Harry Emerson Fosdick: Preacher, Pastor, Prophet* (New York: Oxford Univ. Press, 1985), 346.

14. Harry Emerson Fosdick, *The Modern Use of the Bible* (New York: Macmillan, 1924), 21. This volume represents Fosdick's Yale Lectures of 1923–24.

15. Fosdick, *Modern*, 24.

16. Ricoeur, "*L'imagination*" in Kearney, *Poetics*, 139.

17. David Buttrick, *Homiletic: Moves and Structures* (Philadelphia: Fortress Press, 1987), 113. Hereafter cited in the text.

18. Kearney, *Poetics*, 14.

19. See my *A New Hearing: Living Options in Homiletic Method* (Nashville: Abingdon Press, 1987), 149–55.

20. Being objects of contemporary consciousness, it is no wonder that main idea parable interpretation kept finding main ideas reflective of the interpreter's own theological position! See Robert W. Funk, *Language, Hermeneutic, and Word of God: The Problem of Language in the New*

Testament and Contemporary Theology (New York: Harper & Row, 1966), 147–62. See also David Buttrick, "On Preaching a Parable: The Problem of Homiletic Method," in *Reformed Liturgy and Music* 17 (Winter 1983): 16–22, and my "Preaching the Parable and the Main Idea," *The Perkins School of Theology Journal* 36 (Fall 1983): 22–32.

Author Index

Subject Index

227